Data Modeling
A Beginner's Guide

About the Author

Andrew J. (Andy) Oppel is a proud graduate of The Boys' Latin School of Maryland and of Transylvania University (Lexington, Kentucky), where he earned a BA in computer science in 1974. Since then, he has been continuously employed in a wide variety of information technology positions, including programmer, programmer/analyst, systems architect, project manager, senior database administrator, database group manager, consultant, database designer, data modeler, and data architect. In addition, he has served as a part-time instructor with the University of California, Berkeley, Extension for more than 25 years and received the Honored Instructor Award for the year 2000. His teaching work included developing three courses for UC Extension, "Concepts of Database Management Systems," "Introduction to Relational Database Management Systems," and "Data Modeling and Database Design." He also earned his Oracle 9*i* Database Associate certification in 2003. He is currently employed as a senior data modeler for Blue Shield of California. In addition to computer systems, Andy enjoys music (guitar and vocals), amateur radio, and soccer (Referee Instructor, US Soccer).

Andy has designed and implemented hundreds of databases for a wide range of applications, including medical research, banking, insurance, apparel manufacturing, telecommunications, wireless communications, and human resources. He is the author of *Databases Demystified* (McGraw-Hill Professional, 2004), *SQL Demystified* (McGraw-Hill Professional, 2005) and *Databases: A Beginner's Guide* (McGraw-Hill Professional, 2009); and he is co-author of *SQL: A Beginner's Guide, Third Edition* (McGraw-Hill Professional, 2008), and *SQL: The Complete Reference, Third Edition* (McGraw-Hill Professional, 2009). His database product experience includes IMS, DB2, Sybase ASE, Microsoft SQL Server, Microsoft Access, MySQL, and Oracle (versions 7, 8, 8*i,* 9*i,* and 10*g*).

If you have any comments, please contact Andy at andy@andyoppel.com.

About the Technical Editor

Todd Meister has been developing using Microsoft technologies for over ten years. He has been a technical editor on over 50 titles ranging from SQL Server to the .NET Framework. Besides performing technical editing of titles, he serves as Assistant Director for Computing Services at Ball State University in Muncie, Indiana. He lives in central Indiana with his wife, Kimberly, and their four talented children.

Data Modeling
A Beginner's Guide

Andy Oppel

New York   Chicago   San Francisco
Athens   London   Madrid
Mexico City   Milan   New Delhi
Singapore   Sydney   Toronto

Library of Congress Cataloging-in-Publication Data

Oppel, Andrew J.
  Data modeling : a beginner's guide / Andy Oppel.
    p. cm.
  Includes bibliographical references and index.
  ISBN 978-0-07-162398-8 (alk. paper)
  1. Database design. 2. Data structures (Computer science) 3. Database management.
I. Title.
  QA76.9.D26O655 2010
  005.7'3—dc22

                                                                    2009048210

McGraw-Hill Education books are available at special quantity discounts to use as premiums and sales promotions or for use in corporate training programs. To contact a representative, please visit the Contact Us page at www.mhprofessional.com.

Data Modeling: A Beginner's Guide

1 2 3 4 5 6 7 8 9 0 WFR WFR 0 1 9

ISBN   978-0-07-162398-8
MHID   0-07-162398-1

Sponsoring Editor   Wendy Rinaldi

Editorial Supervisor   Janet Walden

Project Manager   Harleen Chopra, Glyph International

Acquisitions Coordinator   Joya Anthony

Technical Editor   Todd Meister

Copy Editors   Jan Jue and Bob Campbell

Proofreader   Madhu Prasher

Indexer   Claire Splan

Production Supervisor   James Kussow

Composition   Glyph International

Illustration   Glyph International

Art Director, Cover   Jeff Weeks

Cover Designer   Jeff Weeks

To the memory of my Aunt Norma, one of the strongest and kindest people I have ever known.

Contents at a Glance

PART I   Data Modeling Concepts

1 Introduction to Data Modeling 3

2 Relational Model Components 23

3 Data and Process Modeling 53

4 Organizing Database Project Work 81

PART II   Data Modeling Details

5 Conceptual Data Modeling 101

6 Logical Database Design Using Normalization 127

7 Beyond Third Normal Form 151

8 Physical Database Design 173

PART III   Design Alternatives

  9 **Alternatives for Incorporating Business Rules** 205

  10 **Alternatives for Handling Temporal Data** 219

  11 **Modeling for Analytical Databases** 237

  12 **Enterprise Data Modeling** 265

PART IV   Appendixes

  A **Answers to Self Tests** 279

  B **Solutions to Try This Exercises** 313

    Index 331

Contents

ACKNOWLEDGMENTS xvii
INTRODUCTION. xix

PART I   Data Modeling Concepts

1 Introduction to Data Modeling **3**
   Data-Centric Design   4
   Anatomy of a Data Model   6
      Layers of Data Abstraction   6
      Types of Data Models   8
   Importance of Data Modeling   12
      Documentation of Business Rules   12
      Visualization   12
      Illustration of Alternatives   13
      Foundation for Future Expansion   13
      Promotion of Common and Standard Structures   13
      Provisions for Automation   13
   Measures of a Good Data Model   14
      Enforcement of Business Rules   14
      Flexible and Adaptable   15

Easily Understood	15
Balanced Perspective	15
Promotion of Data Reusability	16
Data Integration	16
How Data Models Fit Into Application Development	16
Process-Oriented Methodologies	16
Data-Oriented Methodologies	17
Hybrid Methodologies	17
Object-Oriented Methodologies	17
Prototyping Methodologies	17
Agile Methodologies	18
Data Modeling Participants	18
Try This 1-1: Refining a Conceptual Model	19
Chapter 1 Self Test	20
2 Relational Model Components	**23**
Conceptual and Logical Model Components	24
Entities	25
Attributes	30
Relationships	32
Business Rules	39
Physical Model Components	39
Tables	39
Columns and Data Types	41
Constraints	43
Integrity Constraints	46
Views	48
Try This 2-1: Conceptual Model Modification	48
Chapter 2 Self Test	50
3 Data and Process Modeling	**53**
Data Model Diagramming Alternatives	54
ERD Formats	54
Representing Supertypes and Subtypes	60
Guidelines for Drawing ERDs	63
Process Models	63
The Flowchart	64
The Function Hierarchy Diagram	66
The Swim Lane Diagram	67
The Data Flow Diagram	68

Unified Modeling Language (UML) 70
  UML Class Diagrams 70
  Other UML Diagrams 72
Relating Entities and Processes 73
Try This 3-1: Drawing a Conceptual Model with Nested Subtypes 75
Chapter 3 Self Test 76

4 Organizing Database Project Work **81**
The Traditional Life Cycle 82
  Planning 84
  Requirements Gathering 85
  Conceptual Design 88
  Logical Design 89
  Physical Design 89
  Construction 90
  Implementation and Rollout 90
  Ongoing Support 91
Nontraditional Life Cycles 92
  Prototyping 92
  Rapid Application Development 93
The Project Triangle 93
Try This 4-1: Project Database Management Tasks 94
Chapter 4 Self Test 96

PART II   Data Modeling Details

5 Conceptual Data Modeling **101**
The Conceptual Modeling Process 102
  Preparation 102
  Solution Design 105
  What Differentiates Conceptual Modeling from Logical Modeling? 105
Creating the Model 106
  Generic Models and Patterns 106
  Roles vs. Subtypes 109
  Dealing with Hierarchies, Networks, and Linked Lists 113
  Bottom Up vs. Top Down Modeling 118
  Subject Areas 122
Evaluating the Model 123
  What Makes a Good Conceptual Model? 123
Try This 5-1: Conceptual Model for International Addresses 124
Chapter 5 Self Test 125

6 Logical Database Design Using Normalization **127**
   The Need for Normalization 130
      Insert Anomaly 130
      Delete Anomaly 130
      Update Anomaly 131
   Applying the Normalization Process 131
      Choosing a Primary Key 133
      First Normal Form: Eliminating Repeating Data 135
      Second Normal Form: Eliminating Partial Dependencies 137
      Third Normal Form: Eliminating Transitive Dependencies 139
   Denormalization 142
   Practice Problems 142
   Try This 6-1: UTLA Academic Tracking 143
      The User Views 143
   Try This 6-2: Computer Books Company 146
      The User Views 146
   Chapter 6 Self Test 148

7 Beyond Third Normal Form **151**
   Advanced Normalization 152
      Boyce-Codd Normal Form 152
      Fourth Normal Form 155
      Fifth Normal Form 157
      Domain-Key Normal Form (DKNF) 158
   Resolving Supertypes and Subtypes 158
   Generalizing Attributes 162
   Alternatives for Reference Data 166
      Common Code Structures 166
      Crosswalk Tables 167
      Language Translation Tables 168
   Try This 7-1: Complex Logical Data Model 169
   Chapter 7 Self Test 171

8 Physical Database Design **173**
   The Physical Design Process 174
   Designing Tables 176
   Try This 8-1: Drawing a Physical Data Model 182
      Implementing Supertypes and Subtypes 183
      Naming Conventions 186
   Integrating Business Rules and Data Integrity 189
      NOT NULL Constraints 191
      Primary Key Constraints 191

        Referential (Foreign Key) Constraints 191
        Unique Constraints 192
        Check Constraints 193
        Data Types, Precision, and Scale 193
        Triggers 194
    Adding Indexes for Performance 194
    Designing Views 196
    Try This 8-2: Mapping a Logical Model to a Physical Database Design 198
    Chapter 8 Self Test 199

PART III Design Alternatives

9 Alternatives for Incorporating Business Rules

9 Alternatives for Incorporating Business Rules **205**
    The Anatomy of a Business Rule 206
        The Origin of Business Rules 207
    Implementing Business Rules in Data Models 207
        Implementing Terms 207
        Implementing Facts 209
        Implementing Derivations 210
    Limitations on Implementing Business Rules in Data Models 211
        Implementing Constraints 211
        Constraints That Cannot Be Shown in Entity Relationship Models 212
    Functional Classification of Business Rules 214
        Definitional Rules 214
        Data Validation Rules 214
        Data Derivation Rules 215
        Cardinality Rules 215
        Referential Integrity Rules 215
        Process Rules 215
    Try This 9-1: Modeling Business Rules 216
    Chapter 9 Self Test 217

10 Alternatives for Handling Temporal Data

10 Alternatives for Handling Temporal Data **219**
    Temporal Data Structures 220
        When Does Time Matter? 220
        Adding History to Data Structures 221
        Processing Rules for History 228
        Handling Deletions 228
    Calendar Data Structures 230
    Business Rules for Temporal Data 231
    Try This 10-1: Adding History to Data Structures 233
    Chapter 10 Self Test 235

11 Modeling for Analytical Databases **237**
Data Warehouses 239
OLTP Systems Compared with Data Warehouse Systems 240
Data Warehouse Architecture 240
Data Marts 245
Modeling Analytical Data Structures 247
OLAP Database Requirements 247
Data Warehouse Modeling 248
Data Mart Modeling 250
Loading Data into Analytical Databases 257
The Extract Process 258
The Transform Process 258
The Load Process 259
Try This 11-1: Design Star Schema Fact and Dimension Tables 259
Chapter 11 Self Test 261

12 Enterprise Data Modeling **265**
Enterprise Data Management 266
The Case for Data Management 266
Alternatives to Centralized Data Management 267
The Enterprise Data Model 268
What Is an Enterprise Data Model? 268
The Anatomy of an Enterprise Data Model 269
Building an Enterprise Data Model 272
Try This 12-1: Enterprise Conceptual Model Development 274
Chapter 12 Self Test 274

PART IV Appendixes

A Answers to Self Tests **279**

B Solutions to Try This Exercises **313**
Try This 1-1: Refining a Conceptual Model 314
Try This 2-1: Conceptual Model Modification 315
Try This 3-1: Drawing a Conceptual Model with Nested Subtypes 316
Try This 4-1: The Database Life Cycle 317
Try This 5-1: Conceptual Model for International Addresses 318
Try This 6-1: UTLA Academic Tracking 319
Try This 6-2: Computer Books Company 322
Try This 7-1: Complex Logical Data Model 324
Try This 8-1: Drawing a Physical Data Model 325

Try This 8-2: Mapping a Logical Model to a Physical Database Design   326
Try This 9-1: Modeling Business Rules   326
Try This 10-1: Adding History to Data Structures   327
Try This 11-1: Design Star Schema Fact and Dimension Tables   328
Try This 12-1: Enterprise Conceptual Model Development   329

Index **331**

Acknowledgments

My thanks to all the people involved in the development of *Data Modeling: A Beginner's Guide.* First, the editors and staff at McGraw-Hill, many of whom I do not know by name, provided untold hours of support for this project. Thanks to editorial director Wendy Rinaldi for the inspiration to write this book and for being so supportive when so many of life's demands caught up with me at the same time. And thanks to editorial supervisor Janet Walden for all the useful comments throughout the editing process, and to acquisitions coordinator Joya Anthony for keeping the processes moving. A special thanks to technical editor Todd Meister for all his input—it really helped to make this a better book. And my hat is off to copy editors Jan Jue and Robert Campbell for their consistency and attention to detail. Thanks to project manager Harleen Chopra and all the people at Glyph International who worked on the production of the book. Finally, thanks to my family for their understanding and support, especially during those times when I had to hide away in my office to write or create art files.

Introduction

The modeling of information systems took root in the late 1950s. By the early 1960s technicians took an interest in modeling data. However, a formal technique for data modeling didn't appear until Peter Chen proposed the entity-relationship model in 1976. Data modeling emerged as a recognized specialty within the information technology (IT) industry in the 1980s. As you can see, data modeling is a relatively new discipline.

As is the case with many fast-growing technologies, industry standards and best practices have lagged behind implementations of information systems, and therefore many practitioners have learned lessons the hard way. It has become clear that one of the keys to successful IT projects is an effective database design. Some monumental project failures have proven that no amount of clever programming can save a project from a bad database design. The common thread among the most successful projects is a solid data design.

Data Modeling: A Beginner's Guide presents the latest data modeling and database design techniques in a vendor-neutral manner that works for any database management system. You'll learn how to create conceptual, logical, and physical data models as well as specialized techniques for handling temporal and analytical data such as that found in data warehouses and data marts. I've drawn on my extensive experience as an application developer, database administrator, data modeler, and instructor to provide you with this self-help guide to the complex and fascinating world of data modeling and database design.

Who Should Read This Book

Data Modeling: A Beginner's Guide is recommended for anyone trying to build a foundation in data modeling and database design, whether for personal or professional use. The book is designed specifically for those who are new or relatively new to database technology. However, those with significant experience as a developer, database administrator, or database user will also find this book beneficial and an excellent tool for expanding their skills into the realm of data modeling and database design. *Data Modeling: A Beginner's Guide* provides a strong foundation that will be useful to anyone wanting to learn more about database technology, regardless of their background and experience. Any of the following individuals will find this book helpful when trying to understand how databases are modeled and designed:

- The novice new to database technology

- The analyst or manager who wants a better understanding of how to design data structures and databases

- The database administrator who wants to learn more about database design

- The technical support professional or testing/QA engineer who will be reviewing data models and database designs

- The web designer writing applications that require databases for data persistence

- Application developers who wish to expand their design skills

- Any other individual who wants to learn how to create data models and to design databases

What the Book Covers

Data Modeling: A Beginner's Guide is divided into three parts. Part I introduces you to basic database and data modeling concepts and explains the data modeling process and how it fits with other IT project activities. Part II provides the details of creating conceptual, logical, and physical data models as well as a thorough review of the normalization process used to create logical data models that will be best for transaction processing. Part III focuses on the design alternatives you will face as you design specialized data structures for complex business rules, time-dependent data, and analytical databases (data warehouses and data marts), while also providing an overview of enterprise data modeling. In addition to the three parts, *Data Modeling: A Beginner's Guide* contains appendixes that include answers to the Self Test questions and solutions to the Try This exercises that appear throughout the book.

Content Description

The following outline describes the concepts of the book and shows how the book is broken down into task-focused chapters.

Part I: Data Modeling Concepts

Part I introduces you to basic database and data modeling concepts and explains the data modeling process and how it fits with other IT project activities.

Chapter 1: Introduction to Data Modeling   This chapter introduces fundamental concepts and definitions regarding data models, including the concept of data-centric design, the components of data models, the importance of data modeling, the criteria for measuring the quality of a data model, how data models fit into application development processes, and who should participate in the development of data models.

Chapter 2: Relational Model Components   This chapter introduces the basic components used to construct relational data models, including entities, attributes, relationships, business rules, tables, columns, constraints, and views.

Chapter 3: Data and Process Modeling   This chapter covers data and process modeling, including data model diagramming alternatives, process model diagrams, Unified Modeling Language (UML), and relating entities and processes.

Chapter 4: Organizing Database Project Work   This chapter shows you how to organize database project work, including the traditional life cycle, requirements gathering, nontraditional life cycles, the project triangle, and project database management tasks.

Part II: Data Modeling Details

Part II provides the details of creating conceptual, logical, and physical data models, as well as a thorough review of the normalization process used to create logical data models that will be best for transaction processing.

Chapter 5: Conceptual Data Modeling   This chapter explores conceptual models in detail along with the process used to create them. Topics covered include the conceptual modeling process; generic models and patterns; roles vs. subtypes; dealing with hierarchies, networks, and linked lists; bottom-up vs. top-down modeling; dividing models into subject areas; and evaluating the model.

Chapter 6: Logical Database Design Using Normalization   This chapter teaches you how to perform logical database design using a process called *normalization*. It is normalization that shows you how best to organize your data into tables. Therefore, normalization is essential to logical database design.

Chapter 7: Beyond Third Normal Form   This chapter addresses additional considerations not covered by third normal form, including Boyce-Codd normal form, fourth normal form, fifth normal form, domain key normal form, resolving supertypes and subtypes, generalizing attributes, and alternatives for reference data.

Chapter 8: Physical Database Design   This chapter focuses on the database designer's physical design work, which is transforming the logical database design into one or more physical database designs. Topics include the physical design process, designing tables, integrating business rules and data integrity, adding indexes for performance, and designing views.

Part III: Design Alternatives

Part III focuses on the design alternatives you will face as you design specialized data structures for complex business rules, temporal (time-dependent) data, and analytical databases (data warehouses and data marts); it also provides an overview of enterprise data modeling.

Chapter 9: Alternatives for Incorporating Business Rules   This chapter explores business rules, including the anatomy of a business rule, methods for implementing business rules in data models, the limitation on implementing business rules in data models, and functional classification of business rules.

Chapter 10: Alternatives for Handling Temporal Data   This chapter explores alternatives for handling temporal data, including coverage of temporal data structures, calendar data structures, and business rules for temporal data.

Chapter 11: Modeling for Analytical Databases   This chapter presents techniques and alternatives for modeling analytical databases (data warehouses and data marts). Topics include an overview of data warehouses and data marts, modeling analytical structures, and loading data into analytical databases.

Chapter 12: Enterprise Data Modeling   This chapter explores higher-level models that describe and document the data for an entire organization, including coverage of enterprise data management and the enterprise data model.

Part IV: Appendixes

The appendixes include answers to Self Test questions and solutions to the Try This exercises that appear throughout the book.

Appendix A: Answers to Self Tests   This appendix provides the answers to the Self Test questions listed at the end of each chapter.

Appendix B: Solutions to Try This Exercises   This appendix contains solutions, including diagrams, for the Try This exercises that appear in every chapter of the book.

Chapter Content

Each chapter of *Data Modeling: A Beginner's Guide* focuses on a set of key skills and concepts and contains the background information you need to understand the concepts, plus the skills required to apply these concepts. Each chapter contains additional elements to help you better understand the information covered in that chapter:

Ask the Expert

Each chapter contains one or two Ask the Expert sections that provide information on questions that might arise regarding the information presented in the chapter.

Self Test

Each chapter ends with a Self Test, a set of questions that test you on the information and skills you learned in that chapter. The answers to the Self Tests are included in Appendix A.

Try This Exercises

Most chapters contain one or two Try This exercises that allow you to apply the information that you learned in the chapter. Each exercise is broken down into steps that walk you through the process of completing a particular task. No special software is required to complete any of the Try This exercises in this book. Solutions to the Try This exercises are included in Appendix B.

Part I

Data Modeling Concepts

Chapter 1

Introduction to Data Modeling

Key Skills & Concepts

- Data-Centric Design
- Anatomy of a Data Model
- Importance of Data Modeling
- Measures of a Good Model
- How Data Models Fit Into Application Development
- Data Modeling Participants

This chapter introduces fundamental concepts and definitions regarding data models, including the concept of data-centric design, the components of data models, the importance of data modeling, the criteria for measuring the quality of a data model, how data models fit into application development processes, and who should participate in the development of data models.

Data-Centric Design

A *data model* describes how the data in an information system is represented and accessed. An information system is often thought of in terms of the processes it automates, such as order entry, insurance claims adjudication, and customer service. However, the data that the system collects, stores, and manages is equally important, or perhaps more so, because data *transcends* systems, meaning that the data exists before automated systems are developed, and survives long after the system has been retired from service. After all, one of the most important steps when migrating from an old system (whether manual or automated) to a new information system is to convert the data into a structure and format suitable to the new system.

Figure 1-1 shows a high-level diagram of a modern web-based information system. The main processing logic resides in the application server, with business users interacting with the system via web pages rendered by the web server. Note that the web interface provides users both inside and outside the enterprise the same interface to the information system. In addition to web pages, which can include various forms of reports, printed documents such as order packing slips and invoices can be produced and delivered to the business users by various methods. The application server connects with the database server, which stores and manages all the business data required by the application. Although this layer is often called the *backend* because it is the furthest from the business users, it is far from unimportant.

For example, if you access a web site such as Amazon.com to search for and purchase books and other items, your web browser connects to one of the site's web servers. The web server contains no application logic—it merely presents pages assembled by the application

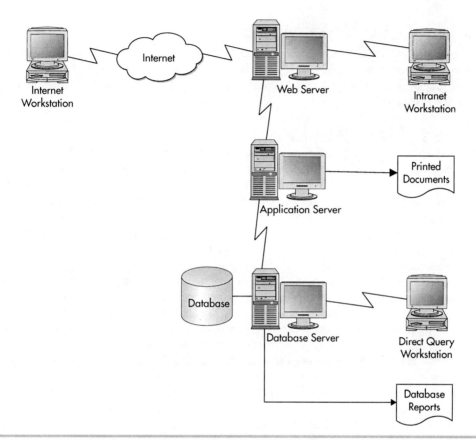

Figure 1-1   A web-based information system

server to you via your web browser. All the logic that searches available items matching your preferences runs in an application server. And all the data about the available inventory, your account, your preferences and past purchases, and so forth, resides in a database on the database server.

   If only a process-oriented design is created for an information system, the database will be designed to serve only that system. Over time this will lead to the design and implementation of redundant data structures as each new system finds the existing data structures unacceptable and implements their own customized structures. This is especially true for common classes of data such as customers, products, and employees. For example, if the inventory database at a site such as Amazon.com were designed to serve only the online shopping application used by consumers, then a separate database might be required for the application that manages inventory levels and reordering from suppliers. The proven solution is to conduct a *data-oriented* design in parallel with the process-oriented design. The main product of a data-oriented design is a data model.

Anatomy of a Data Model

Data models are abstractions of existing or proposed databases, and both databases and data models are formed using layers of abstraction. It is therefore important to understand the layers of abstraction supported by databases before we look at the parallel layers of abstraction that we find in data models.

Layers of Data Abstraction

Databases are unique in their ability to present multiple users with their own distinct views of the data while storing the underlying data only once. These are collectively called *user views*. A *user* in this context is any person or application that signs onto the database for the purpose of storing and/or retrieving data. An *application* is a set of computer programs designed to solve a particular business problem, such as an order-entry system, a payroll-processing system, or an accounting system. User views for an order-entry system would include the online shopping web page, web pages listing preferences and previous orders, printed invoices and packing slips, and so forth.

When an electronic spreadsheet application such as Microsoft Excel is used, all users must share a common view of the data, and that view must match the way the data is physically stored in the underlying data file. If a user hides some columns in a spreadsheet, reorders the rows, and saves the spreadsheet for future use, the next user who opens the spreadsheet will view the data in the manner in which the first user saved it. An alternative, of course, is for each user to save his or her copy in a separate physical file, but then as one user applies updates, the other users' data becomes out of date. Database systems present each user a view of the same data, but the views can be *tailored* to the needs of the individual users, even though they all come from one commonly stored copy of the data. Because views store no actual data, they automatically reflect any data changes made to the underlying database objects. This is all possible through *layers of abstraction,* shown in Figure 1-2.

The architecture shown in Figure 1-2 was first developed by ANSI/SPARC (American National Standards Institute/Standards Planning and Requirements Committee) in the 1970s and quickly became a foundation for much of the database research and development efforts that followed. Most modern DBMSs follow this architecture, which is composed of four primary layers: the physical layer, the logical layer, the conceptual layer, and the external layer.

The Physical Layer

The *physical layer* contains the data files that hold all the data for the database. Nearly all modern DBMSs allow the database to be stored in multiple data files, which are usually spread over multiple physical disk drives. With this arrangement, the disk drives can work in parallel for maximum performance. A notable exception among the DBMSs is Microsoft Access, which stores the entire database in a single physical file. While it simplifies database use on a single-user personal computer system, this arrangement limits the ability of the DBMS to scale to accommodate many concurrent users of the database, making it inappropriate as a solution for large enterprise systems. In all fairness, Microsoft Access was not designed to be a robust enterprise class DBMS, but some organizations make the mistake of trying to use it to support multiuser applications, which seldom turns out well.

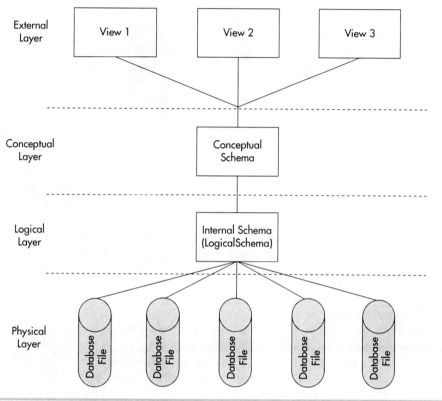

Figure 1-2   Database layers of abstraction

The database user does not need to understand how the data is actually stored within the data files or even which file contains the data item(s) of interest. In most organizations, a technician known as a *database administrator* (DBA) handles the details of installing and configuring the database software and data files and of making the database available to users. The DBMS works with the computer's operating system to manage the data files automatically, including all file opening, closing, reading, and writing operations. The database user should not be required to refer to physical data files when using a database, which is in sharp contrast to spreadsheets and word processing, where the user must consciously save the document(s) and choose filenames and storage locations. Many of the personal computer–based DBMSs are exceptions to this tenet because the user is required to locate and open a physical file as part of the process of signing onto the DBMS. Conversely, with enterprise class DBMSs (such as Oracle, Sybase, Microsoft SQL Server, DB2, and MySQL), the physical files are managed automatically, and the database user never needs to refer to them when using the database.

The Logical Layer

The *logical layer,* also known as the *internal layer* or *logical model,* comprises the first of two layers of abstraction in the database: the physical layer has a concrete existence in the operating system files, whereas the logical layer exists only as abstract data structures assembled from the physical layer as needed. The DBMS transforms the data in the data files into a common structure. This layer is sometimes called the *schema,* a term used for the collection of all the data items stored in a particular database or belonging to a particular database user. Depending on the particular DBMS, this layer can contain a set of 2-D tables, a hierarchical structure similar to a company's organization chart, or some other structure.

The Conceptual Layer

The *conceptual layer* was intended to be a layer of abstraction above the logical layer that described all the data in the database as well as the relationships among the data, but in a manner that was independent of any particular type of database system. However, none of the DBMS vendors implemented it, and thus it fell by the wayside for a time. As you will soon see, as database design disciplines matured many years later, data modelers found a need for this layer, but it evolved outside of the database itself, as a mechanism for highly abstract descriptions of the data.

The External Layer

The *external layer* or *external model* is composed of the user views discussed earlier, which are collectively called the *subschema.* In this layer, the database users (application programs as well as individuals) that access the database connect to and issue queries against the database. Ideally, only the DBA deals with the physical and logical layers. While originally specified in the ANSI/SPARC model as deriving its data from the conceptual layer, DBMS implementations skipped the conceptual layer and derived the external layer directly from the logical layer instead. The DBMS handles the transformation of selected items from one or more data structures in the logical layer to form each user view. The user views in this layer can be predefined and stored in the database for reuse, or they can be temporary items that are built by the DBMS to hold the results of a single ad hoc database query until they are no longer needed by the database user. An *ad hoc* query is a query that is not preconceived and that is not likely to be reused.

Types of Data Models

There are three primary types of data models: conceptual, logical, and physical. Furthermore, there are many variations in the way data models are created and displayed. The best way to understand the basics is to review a few simple models, starting with a conceptual model and drilling down to a physical model for the same data structure. If this material seems a little overwhelming, do not be too concerned—much more detail on these types of data models is presented to help clarify the material in subsequent chapters.

The Conceptual Model

A *conceptual data model* is a high-level model that captures data and relationship concepts in a technology-independent manner. Figure 1-3 shows a simple conceptual model for a fictitious

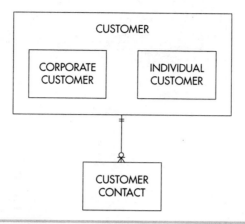

Figure 1-3   A conceptual data model

company. Each rectangle represents an *entity,* which is a person, place, thing, event, or concept about which the organization collects data. In this case, CUSTOMER represents one of the company's customers, CORPORATE CUSTOMER represents a customer that is a corporation, INDIVIDUAL CUSTOMER represents a customer who is an individual, and CUSTOMER CONTACT represents a person employed by the customer who serves as a contact with our fictitious company. For example, if you rent a car while traveling, you are an individual customer of the rental car company. However, if a movie production company rents vehicles for use by cast and crew while on location, the production company is a corporate customer. You likely noticed that the CORPORATE CUSTOMER and INDIVIDUAL CUSTOMER rectangles appear within the CUSTOMER rectangle. This denotes a *subtype,* meaning an entity that represents a subset of the things represented by the containing entity, also called a *supertype.* In this case, the two subtypes mean that a customer is either a corporate customer or an individual customer—always one or the other, and never both. You may be able to think of some other possible customer subtypes such as a partnership.

    The line between the CUSTOMER and CUSTOMER CONTACT entities is a relationship. For now, suffice it to say that this relationship line and the symbols on it indicate that one customer can have any number of customer contacts (including none at all), but that each customer contact has one and only one customer related to it. Relationships are presented in detail in Chapter 2. Conceptual data modeling is discussed in Chapter 5.

The Logical Model

A *logical data model* is a data model tailored to a particular type of database management system such as relational, object-relational, object-oriented, hierarchical, or network. Figure 1-4 shows the logical data model for the conceptual model shown in Figure 1-3. Be aware that there are many variations in the way these diagrams are drawn, so this is just one example. Each large rectangle represents an entity, with the name of the entity just above the rectangle. Note that the four entities are the same ones shown in the conceptual model in Figure 1-3.

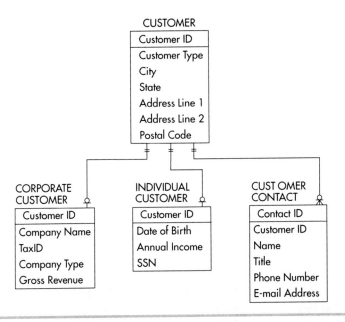

Figure 1-4 A logical data model

Within each large rectangle are two smaller rectangles formed by the horizontal line that divides the large rectangle into two. The names inside the rectangles form the list of the attributes that are included in the entity. An *attribute* is a fact that characterizes or describes the entity in some way. For example, the Date of Birth describes an Individual Customer, while Company Name describes a Corporate Customer, and all customers are described by a City and State. The attributes above the horizontal line make up the unique identifier, while the ones below the line are the non-identifying attributes. The lines between the entities indicate relationships. Relationships are explained in Chapter 2, and logical data modeling is presented in detail in Chapters 6 and 7.

The Physical Model

A *physical data model* is a data model that is tailored to the features and constraints of a particular database management system (DBMS), such as MySQL, Oracle, or Microsoft SQL Server. Figure 1-5 shows a very simple physical model in the form of four relational database tables that correspond to the four entities for our fictitious company. (Relational tables are presented in considerable detail in Chapter 2.) For the purposes of illustration, only a few columns of each table are shown. The CUSTOMER table holds information about each of the company's customers. Each customer is identified by a unique CUSTOMER_ID, and a column named CUSTOMER_TYPE indicates whether the customer is a corporate customer (C) or an individual (I). The CUSTOMER_CONTACT table holds information about people who serve as contacts within the customer's organization. Note that a customer may have any number of contacts (or no contacts at all), but each contact must belong to one and only one customer.

CUSTOMER

CUSTOMER_ID	CUSTOMER_TYPE	CITY	STATE
1001	C	Baltimore	MD
1002	I	Ajo	AZ
1003	C	New York	NY
. . .	. . .	. . .	. . .

CUSTOMER_CONTACT

CONTACT_ID	CUSTOMER_ID	NAME	TITLE
60001	1001	H.Wheels	Chairman
60002	1001	F.Leader	CEO
60003	1002	W.Coyote	Proprietor
. . .	. . .	. . .	. . .

CORPORATE_CUSTOMER

CUSTOMER_ID	COMPANY_NAME	TAX_ID
1001	Bay Hospital	00-1456439
1003	Acme Industries	00-6639652
. . .	. . .	. . .

INDIVIDUAL_CUSTOMER

CUSTOMER_ID	DATE_OF_BIRTH	ANNUAL_INCOME
1002	04/01/1958	$65,000
. . .	. . .	. . .

Figure 1-5   A physical data model

Each contact is uniquely identified by the CONTACT_ID, but note that the CUSTOMER_ID is also included to denote the customer to which the contact belongs. The CORPORATE_ CUSTOMER table contains one row for each corporate customer (CUSTOMER_TYPE = C in the CUSTOMER table). In relational database terms, this is known as an *extension table* because it logically extends the CUSTOMER table by providing more columns of information for a subset of the rows in the CUSTOMER table. Note that each corporate customer must have at most one matching row in the CORPORATE_CUSTOMER table. The CUSTOMER_ ID uniquely identifies each row. The INDIVIDUAL_CUSTOMER table is another extension of the CUSTOMER table, in this case for each individual customer (CUSTOMER_TYPE = I in the CUSTOMER table). Physical data modeling is presented in detail in Chapter 8.

Before moving on, take a moment to look back at Figures 1-2 and 1-3. Notice how conceptual models are the most abstract, physical models the most concrete, and logical models a blend of abstract and concrete elements. Also notice that conceptual models can be implemented on any type of technology, including a completely manual system, while logical models are tailored to one particular type of database system, such as relational or object-oriented, and physical models are tailored to one particular DBMS.

Ask the Expert

Q: You labeled Figure 1-5 as a physical data model, but to me it looks more like a listing of relational tables with data in them. The physical models I have seen were more like the logical model you showed in Figure 1-4.

A: While many physical models are depicted using a diagram similar to the diagram I used in Figure 1-4, relational tables are actually models. I say this because in most relational databases, the tables are not stored as tables, but rather as data in ordinary operating system files. The tables are an abstraction assembled from the operating system files. You will learn more about this in Chapter 2.

Importance of Data Modeling

With the increasing pressure to deliver information systems more quickly, why should we spend time and resources on data modeling? The simple answer is that experience has shown that the more time (within reason) that we spend in the earlier requirements gathering and design stages of a project, the more smoothly the construction and implementation phases go, yielding a higher quality information system, and perhaps at a lower overall cost. However, it's best to look at more specific reasons why data modeling is important.

Documentation of Business Rules

Constraints and assertions that define the way a business is run are called *business rules*. Good computer systems follow and enforce the business rules. Some of these rules are well suited for enforcement by the database, while others are better suited for enforcement within the application system logic; still others are best supported using both methods. Inclusion and illustration of business rules in the data models provides the database designers with the information they need to make decisions regarding implementation (enforcement) of these rules in the design of the data structures that support the organization.

For example, if there were a business rule that stated that each customer account could be owned by only one customer, we could easily indicate the relationship in the data model. However, that rule, when exposed in the data model, will lead to discussion of the definition of a customer. If a customer is a limited partnership where exactly two individuals own that business, and the organization affirms that these two individuals are really a single customer (which is the way the law recognizes limited partnerships), then the data model must show how the individuals are recognized and associated with the one customer.

Visualization

In terms of communicating complex data structures to a diverse audience, diagrams are often the very best medium. Humans absorb information most quickly through visual means, but beware that retention can suffer if the visual input is not enforced in other ways. Conducting walkthrough sessions, particularly where interaction with the audience is solicited and encouraged, is a proven method for conveying an understanding of complex models to the business sponsors and other project participants.

Illustration of Alternatives

There are almost always multiple viable alternatives for designing data structures to solve a given business problem. If data models are created showing each alternative, the result is an excellent (if not unparalleled) means by which the alternatives can be presented, analyzed, and a final design choice made. In fact, presentation of alternative models is often the best way to work through conflicts surrounding implementation of supertypes and subtypes.

Looking back at Figure 1-4, it would be easy enough to create physical models showing the alternative designs possible, depending on whether we opt for generalization or specialization. With generalization, the data elements with the Corporate Customer and Individual Customer entities would be folded into Customer, and the data model would show only the Customer and Customer Contact entities, with specific business rules about which attributes of Customer would be mandatory, optional, and not applicable depending on the customer type. On the other hand, we could opt for specialization and copy the attributes in Customer into both the Corporate Customer and Individual Customer entities, eliminating the Customer entity from the model. Finally, the third alternative is to take the middle ground, opting for neither generalization nor specialization, and implementing all the entities as tables, as shown in Figure 1-5. We will explore the trade-offs in implementing supertypes and subtypes in detail in subsequent chapters.

Foundation for Future Expansion

If models are drawn showing the data structures as currently implemented, along with the desired future state, we provide an excellent foundation for our expansion efforts. Additional models can show proposed incremental steps toward the final desired solution so that projects can be planned in an orderly fashion as the organization progresses toward its ultimate goal.

Promotion of Common and Standard Structures

Data models are an excellent vehicle for pointing out common entities and attributes across an organization. As these common items are discovered, the modelers can synchronize the diagrams, promoting a common shared structure. At the same time, if standards for naming entities and attributes are applied throughout all of the organization's models, departures from the standard become obvious. For example, if the naming standard specifies singular names for entities and attributes, it's quite easy to spot the names that are plural, and therefore not in compliance. If all models are created using common structures that follow established design and naming standards, it follows that the databases implemented from these models will comply with the same standards.

Provisions for Automation

Data models should not be throwaway design efforts. All of the leading automated data modeling tools (ERwin from Computer Associates, PowerDesigner from Sybase, and ER/Studio from Embarcadero Technologies) provide significant levels of automation that not only improve the productivity of the data modelers and database administrators, but also reduce errors. Data modeling can be extremely tedious, so the more we can use tools to automate the most repetitive and error-prone tasks, the higher the quality of the end result.

Some of the capabilities of automated modeling tools are

- Automatic generation of a first-cut logical model from a conceptual model

- Automatic generation of a first-cut physical model from a logical model

- Automatic generation of SQL scripts from the physical model, yielding the code needed to create the physical database objects

- Reverse-engineering of a physical model from an existing database, allowing for modification of the model and subsequent generation of the next-generation physical database

- Reverse-engineering of a logical model from an existing physical model, or of a conceptual model from an existing logical model, yielding models for additional study and/or modification

Measures of a Good Data Model

To be effective, a data model must be of the highest possible quality. This topic discusses some of the characteristics of good data models.

Enforcement of Business Rules

The success of a business application depends on how well it enforces the business rules that govern the organization. The database and application programs work together to achieve this goal. The selection of which business rules to enforce in the database is an important, if not essential, consideration. Some business rules can easily be enforced in the database, and these are the ones that must be specified in the data model. However, other business rules are best left up to the application to enforce, and still others can be enforced either way, or even both ways.

For example, a business rule that requires a customer's account to be in good standing in order to receive product shipments is best enforced in the shipping application to ensure that no shipments are made to customers with delinquent accounts. However, it may also be prudent to enforce the same rule in the order-entry system to prevent accepting orders from customers with insufficient credit. On the other hand, a business rule that requires an employee to be at least 18 years old can easily be handled in the database layer, where it might be easier to adjust the rule were it to change. But a rule that requires a certain level of inventory availability before an order can be shipped is best enforced by the application, because it is unlikely that inventory levels can be known until the shipping application selects it for shipping. As you can see, the design of business systems in general, and databases in particular, often involves choosing among a number of alternatives. Rules enforced within the database are more difficult to circumvent, which is great from an audit and control perspective, but not so great if exceptions to the rule must be allowed.

Flexible and Adaptable

As already mentioned, data transcends systems. Change is inevitable—even if the organization and the business it conducts are relatively stable, outside factors beyond the control of the organization such as changes in laws and regulations will force change. An important measure of a data model is how well it can survive change.

A *flexible* data model is one that can be easily adjusted to handle unexpected changes. For example, as new oversight laws come into effect, a good data model can be adjusted to handle the new requirements. An *adaptable* data model is one that has components that can be lifted and reused for other purposes. For example, a well-crafted model for a customer information system might have components that organize customer contact information (postal addresses, phone numbers, e-mail addresses, and so forth) that can be adapted for use in a human resources system.

Easily Understood

Data models have the most value to an organization when they can be understood by a wide audience. While we expect technical staff such as application developers and database administrators to understand and interpret data models, the best models can be understood by business users as well. If models can be used to communicate the similarities and differences between several alternative implementations, the business users are much better positioned to make the necessary choices.

Balanced Perspective

Data models are more useful for decision making if they present a balanced perspective with regard to a number of potential trade-offs. First, and perhaps foremost, is the balance between specialization and generalization. Models that are overly specialized prove to be less adaptable to other applications. For example, a banking model specifically built to handle checking and savings accounts may not be as easy to adapt to other lines of business such as home loans and auto loans. If the model is built to recognize checking accounts and savings accounts as subtypes of a more general entity such as Customer Account, it would likely be more adaptable when it is time to build an application to handle loans. However, models that are overly generalized are often more difficult for business users to understand, and thus are less effective for decision making between possible alternatives.

Second, when several models are developed to present different alternatives, modelers must be careful to be equally thorough and diligent with each alternative model. Stacking the deck for a technically favorable solution prevents the business users from making an informed decision.

Third, the selection of which business rules to enforce in the data model requires balance. Enforcing rules that are likely to be changed will hinder the stability and adaptability of the model. On the other hand, if we omit business rules from the data model that are best enforced in the database, then we place too large a burden on the application system and leave ourselves open to rules being bypassed when data enters the database through processes that are not part of the application system, such as bulk-loading customer data from the existing database of a company we just acquired.

Promotion of Data Reusability

A good model promotes data reusability by isolating entities and attributes that can serve many purposes. In its simplest form, reusability can be in the form of common reference tables, such as standard written-language codes and names, and standard country codes and names. For example, the ISO 639-1 standard provides standard codes and names for written languages, such as en for English, es for Spanish, de for German, and fr for French. Similarly, the ISO 3166 standard provides standard codes and names for countries. Reusability is greatly improved when the same standard codes are used by all the applications, which in turn leads to one common set of reference code tables that are shared by all.

Moreover, data reusability becomes more feasible if data structures are appropriately generalized. For example, if customer data is generalized into a more general structure to represent any organization, then the same structure can be used for suppliers. Data reusability then comes into play when an organization functions as both a customer and a supplier. For example, if a tire manufacturer supplies replacement tires to a rental car company and also rents cars from it to support business travelers, it makes more sense to store the tire manufacturer's information only once and to use the one copy for both purposes.

Data Integration

If the data to be included in the database comes from disparate sources, the data model provides an opportunity to integrate the data into common structures. This is especially true in databases designed for analysis where it is quite common to incorporate data from multiple application databases. However, application databases that support business transactions can also present opportunities for integration, particularly when data is received from multiple types of customers and/or suppliers using varying data formats, or when reference data such as lists of medical procedure codes are acquired from multiple sources.

How Data Models Fit Into Application Development

Most practitioners agree that development of a data model is an essential step in the development of a database. Since databases are the primary data storage mechanism for modern application systems, it follows that the development of data models is also essential to the development of application systems. However, there are perhaps as many application development methodologies as there are organizations undertaking such development. This section provides a brief survey of these methodologies and how data modeling fits into them.

Process-Oriented Methodologies

Traditional application development methodologies are called process-oriented because they focus on *what* the application system is to do and rely upon the processes to infer the data requirements. The typical process steps involve collecting all the screens, reports, and interface files from the process design, isolating the data elements (attributes), and creating an initial logical model by using the normalization process. Normalization is presented in detail in Chapter 6.

One of the typical criticisms of process-oriented methodologies is the so-called waterfall effect, where each step relies so heavily on the outcome of previous steps that it is difficult and expensive to go back if errors or inconsistencies are discovered. While data modeling is front-loaded in the process (data modeling being essentially complete by the time construction of the application programs begins), models must still be flexible enough to handle the seemingly inevitable changes that occur during the development process.

Data-Oriented Methodologies

Data-oriented methodologies take just the opposite tack compared with process-oriented methodologies. Data modelers study the data and use the data requirements to infer the processing requirements. While these methodologies were popular in the late 1970s, particularly the Information Engineering (IE) methodology promoted by Clive Finkelstein and James Martin, they have for the most part faded in favor of hybrid methodologies.

Hybrid Methodologies

Hybrid methodologies, also known as parallel or blended methodologies, call for development of process models and data models in parallel. Care must be taken to ensure that the models fit together properly. This requires additional effort, and it is the overhead of this on-the-fly synchronization that is the basis for much of the criticism of these methodologies. However, experience has shown that hybrid methodologies can be highly successful, particularly when management is committed to making them work.

Object-Oriented Methodologies

Object-oriented design follows principles that naturally include data design and process design because objects are composed of variables (attributes) and methods (processes) that must be designed to operate together as a single unit. However, data design for objects takes very different approaches compared with data modeling. Most object modelers prefer Unified Modeling Language (UML) diagrams over the types of data models introduced earlier in this chapter. The most prevalent methodology is the Rational Unified Process (RUP), developed by Rational Software (now an IBM company). Object-oriented development is beyond the scope of this book.

Prototyping Methodologies

Prototyping evolved from the notion that laborious and comprehensive documentation of a system's requirements and design were unnecessary. Instead, developers would quickly assemble a skeletal working model, present it to the business users, and use their feedback to build upon that model for the next round. While this method has proven highly effective in developing requirements when business users have had difficulty in expressing them with sufficient precision, care must be taken to set expectations so that business users do not assume that a prototype is a complete and robust application ready for installation and use. Prototypes can eventually be built out to be complete applications, but early versions are seldom production ready.

Another hazard is development of prototypes without any form of data modeling. When the next version of the prototype requires extensive changes to the data model, project teams learn an expensive lesson—it is far more difficult to change data structures than it is to change program logic.

Agile Methodologies

Agile methodologies evolved in response to complaints that the existing methodologies took too many resources for the results they achieved. Some believe that these agile methods evolved from prototyping. One such method is Rapid Application Development (RAD), introduced by James Martin in 1991.

Agile methods use minimal planning in favor of rapidly developing (or prototyping) the application, interleaving planning as the software is developed. One pitfall in common with prototyping is that without a data model, the development cycle can get bogged down when logic changes require extensive data structure changes. Another pitfall is the tendency in some organizations to interpret "agile" as "anything goes," with project teams haphazardly throwing together applications with virtually no discipline. In fairness, this wasn't the intent of such methodologies, but the zeal to produce better applications more quickly can lead to extremes.

Data Modeling Participants

No discussion of data modeling would be complete without mention of the people involved. In an ideal setting, all of the following roles would be represented:

- **Executive sponsor**   The individual who approves the project budget and therefore has a serious stake in its success. Typically their role is limited to reviewing completed work and settling policy questions or budget issues that surface during the modeling effort.

- **Business user**   One or more individuals who will actually use the developed application. Who better to tell the data and process modelers what the data means and how it is used in day-to-day operations?

- **Business analyst**   One or more individuals who serve as a bridge between business users and technologists. This is an optional role, but when used, they can be most valuable in running down the details of data definitions and requirements and in the translation of these into forms that the data and process modelers can easily understand.

- **Subject matter expert (SME)**   One or more individuals who are experts in the business area for which the system is being developed. They can be used to answer questions that the business users cannot, such as regulations or accounting rules that require that the system behave in a certain way.

- **Data modeler**   Usually one person, but possibly a team of people who produce the data models.

- **Process modeler**   One or more individuals who produce the process model, often in parallel with the development of the data model.

- **Database administrator (DBA)**   The person who will build the actual physical database and set up such essential functions as backup and recovery of the database. The level of involvement during modeling depends on how much the DBA is involved in the physical data model, but at the very least they need to be introduced to the application and proposed database that they will eventually be expected to support.

- **Enterprise architect**   The individual ultimately responsible for the computer systems architecture of the entire enterprise. Typically this person will assist in the selection of technologies and will ensure that the design and the standards followed dovetail with the rest of the organization's computer systems infrastructure.

- **Operations specialist**   This individual represents the computer operations department that will be responsible for getting the application installed and keeping it running. Their involvement includes capacity planning so that sufficient computer resources are available to service the application and database, and that documentation required for successful operations is developed.

Try This 1-1 Refining a Conceptual Model

In this Try This exercise, you will take an existing conceptual data model and augment it with additional entities.

Step by Step

1. Study the conceptual model shown in Figure 1-3.

2. Consider other possible subtypes of CUSTOMER and write down their names. Be sure that the subtypes you list meet the following criteria:

   - Must be exclusive, meaning that each customer must fit the definition of one and only one subtype.

   - Must not be a state the customer is in that is subject to change, such as a provisional customer (who will become a regular customer later), or a delinquent customer (who will move out of that state as soon as they settle their account).

3. Redraw the CUSTOMER entity from Figure 1-3 with the original two subtypes plus the ones you have selected for addition.

4. Redraw the CUSTOMER CONTACT entity and the relationship line connecting it with the Customer entity.

Try This Summary

In this Try This exercise, you studied an existing conceptual data model, selected some additional subtypes to add to it, and then redrew the model with the added subtypes. You no doubt discovered that the selection of subtypes can be quite challenging, while the mechanics of drawing the model once you have decided upon contents is relatively straightforward. This is a valuable lesson because most data modeling tasks involve intense thinking and visualization much more than technical or artistic skill. My solution appears in Appendix B. However, in all design work, there are multiple possible solutions, so provided the subtypes you added meet the stated criteria, yours is likely a valid solution.

Chapter 1 Self Test

1. A _____ describes how the data in an information system is represented and accessed.

2. The physical layer of the ANSI/SPARC model contains _____.

3. An entity that represents a specialization of another entity is called a _____.

4. A _____ model is a data model tailored to a particular type of database management system such as relational, object-relational, object-oriented, hierarchical, or network.

5. A _____ model is a high-level model that captures data and relationship concepts in a technology-independent manner.

6. A _____ model is a data model that is tailored to the features and constraints of a particular database management system (DBMS).

7. Data

   A. Exists before automated systems are developed

   B. Is destroyed when application systems are retired

   C. Still exists after automated systems are retired

   D. Is usually converted from old systems to the new ones that replace them

8. The logical layer of the ANSI/SPARC model

   A. Is also known as the internal layer

   B. Is sometimes called the schema

   C. Contains the data files that implement the database

   D. Always represents the data as 2-D tables

9. The external layer of the ANSI/SPARC model

   A. Is sometimes called the schema

   B. Is derived directly from the physical layer

   C. Presents data to the database users

   D. Contains user views

10. Data modeling is important because it

    A. Documents required application processes

    B. Provides a means of visualization of the data

    C. Provides standards for future development

    D. Provides a foundation for future expansion

11. Measures of good data models include
    A. Enforcement of business rules
    B. Providing a balanced perspective
    C. Meeting processing requirements
    D. Provisions for data integration
12. Participants in data modeling efforts include
    A. Application programmers
    B. Quality assurance (QA) testers
    C. Process modelers
    D. Database administrators

Chapter 2

Relational Model Components

Key Skills & Concepts

- Entities
- Attributes
- Relationships
- Business Rules
- Tables
- Columns and Data Types
- Constraints
- Views

This chapter introduces the basic components used to construct relational data models. Generally two sets of names are used for these components—one referring to abstract objects found in conceptual and logical data models, and the other referring to physical objects found in physical models and relational databases implemented from them. However, practitioners are somewhat inconsistent about which set of terms to use in logical data models. This is only natural because the logical model often represents a hybrid layer between the conceptual and physical models. On the one hand, in relational database design, the logical model needs to represent data the way all relational databases do (that is, in tables with rows and columns). On the other hand, the logical model still retains conceptual elements, and the objects found in logical models usually do not correspond directly (one for one) with objects found in the physical models derived from those logical models. I choose to use the conceptual terms in the logical layer, and I do so throughout this book. Be mindful, however, that others prefer to use the physical terms in their logical data models.

Conceptual and Logical Model Components

Figure 2-1 shows part of a conceptual data model for Online Movie Rentals (OMR), an imaginary online video rental service. The labeled items (Entity, Attribute, Relationship, Business Rule, and Intersection Data) illustrate key concepts that are presented in the topics that follow. (Chapter 5 covers conceptual data models and the process of building them.) I focus on the Information Engineering (IE) notation throughout this book because it is the most popular. However, alternative notations are presented in Chapter 3.

Figure 2-2 shows the transformation of the objects from Figure 2-1 into a corresponding logical model. You will no doubt notice many similarities, but there are differences as well.

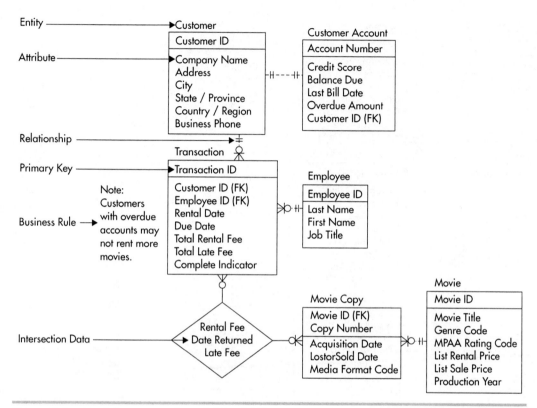

Figure 2-1 Partial conceptual model for OMR

In particular, the logical model does not contain any many-to-many relationships. There is a simple rationale for this difference—relational databases do not directly support many-to-many relationships, so they must be transformed using an intersection entity. You will learn a lot more about how this is done in Chapters 6 and 7, which cover logical models and the process used to design them.

Entities

Recall from Chapter 1 that an *entity* (or *entity class*) is a person, place, thing, event, or concept about which data is collected. In other words, entities are the real-world things in which we have sufficient interest to capture and store data about them in a database. Just about anything that can be named with a noun can be an entity. However, to avoid designing a model that includes everything on the planet, we restrict ourselves to entities of interest to the people who will use the database(s) that will be built from the model. Each entity shown in the conceptual model (Figure 2-1) represents the entire class for that entity. For example, the Customer entity

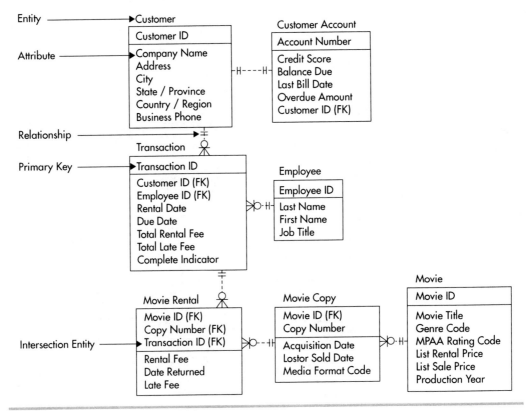

Figure 2-2 Partial logical model for OMR

represents the collection of all Online Movie Rental (OMR) customers. The individual customers are called *instances* of the entity. As you will see later in the chapter, entities in conceptual and logical models are transformed into tables in physical models and relational databases.

An *external entity* is an entity with which our database exchanges data (sending data to, receiving data from, or both) but about which we collect no data other than simple identifying information. For example, most businesses that set up credit accounts for customers purchase credit reports from one or more credit bureaus. They send a customer's identifying information to the credit bureau and receive a credit report, but all this data is about the *customer* rather than the credit bureau itself. Assuming there is no compelling reason for the database to store data about the credit bureau, such as the mailing addresses of its various offices, the credit bureau will not appear in the conceptual database design as an entity. In fact, external entities are seldom shown in database designs, but they commonly appear in process design diagrams as a source or destination of data.

Entity Notation

An entity is represented as a rectangle on the diagram. Above the rectangle is the name of the entity. Figure 2-1 shows six such entities—Customer, Customer Account, Transaction, Employee, Movie, and Movie Copy. There are many variations to the notation shown in Figure 2-1. For example, in conceptual models, it is common to place either a written description of the entity or the name of the entity inside the rectangle in place of the list of attributes shown in the figure.

Another common notation variation is to round the corners of dependent entities. A *dependent entity* (also known as a *weak entity*) is one where an instance of the entity cannot exist without a matching instance in at least one other entity. An entity that has no existence dependency on other entities is known as an *independent entity* or a *strong entity*. For example, a copy of a movie cannot exist without the movie itself, and a movie rental cannot exist without a customer to rent the movie and a movie to be rented. Therefore, Movie Copy and Transaction are dependent entities. On the other hand, a customer can exist before they rent anything, a movie can exist before it is rented, and an employee can exist before they handle a rental transaction. Therefore, Customer, Movie, and Employee are independent entities.

Entity Naming

Entity names should be drawn from the business names for the objects that the entities represent. If you expect business users to understand your data models, then the entity names must make sense to them. As you will see later, table names are based on entity names, so now is the time to get them right. Here are some guidelines for naming entities:

- **Use unique names**   Entities with duplicate names cause unnecessary confusion. The database management system (DBMS) requires unique names within a single schema or database, so it's best to solve this before you get to the physical model.

- **Avoid technical jargon**   Words like "file," "table," "record," and "entity" add no business value.

- **Use singular names**   This may seem trivial at first, but you will discover that relationships are easier to explain and understand if the entities are named in the singular. For example, Customer is better than Customers. Similarly, it is best to avoid collectives such as People or Shipping Rate Schedule in favor of singular terms such as Person and Shipping Rate.

- **Avoid attribute names**   Entities should not be given the same name as their most important attribute. For example, Genre Code is an improper entity name because we are not collecting data about genre codes; rather Genre Code is merely one data item that we are collecting that describes the movie's genre. Therefore, Genre or Movie Genre is a more appropriate name for the entity.

- **Avoid limiting terms**   With the exception of subclasses, data models are more flexible if entity names are not limited by the names of roles that subsets of the entity occurrences might serve. For example, Transaction is a more flexible name than Rental Transaction, and Rental Transaction is a more flexible name than Movie Rental Transaction. The obvious benefit is that entities need not be renamed as the business expands into other areas.

- **Avoid unnecessary abbreviations and acronyms**   Business users understand models more readily if plain language is used instead of potentially confusing shortened forms.

Entity Definition

Every entity should be accompanied by a clear written definition of its use in business terms. In fact, these definitions are essential to successfully defining the relationships between the entities. For example, consider the following two definitions for entities shown in Figure 2-1:

- **Customer**   An individual or household that rents movies from OMR

- **Customer Account**   The record of credit and debit entries for movies rented, purchased, or returned by an OMR customer

There are a couple of issues to address here. First, notice that the definition of *Customer Account* mentions purchases, while the definition of *Customer* only mentions rentals. If we ask the right question, we will discover that the video store also sells movies, particularly surplus used copies that are no longer needed for rentals. We need to adjust the definition accordingly. Second, the definition of Customer mentions an individual or a household. If we ask how the store clerks distinguish between the two, and more importantly how they know which household a person belongs to, we will likely discover that we have two entities here—individuals and households. (They cannot be subtypes of Customer because they are not independent—households are made up of individuals.) The answer should also help us sort out the relationship between customer and customer account. As you will later learn, one-to-one relationships are quite rare in business systems. It is likely in this example that *Customer* actually represents each individual and that *Customer Account* combines at least some of the individuals into households. If that turns out to be the case, then the relationship becomes one-to-many. (Relationships are formally presented later in this chapter.) All of this may seem mundane, but you cannot model what you do not understand.

Here are some guidelines for writing entity definitions:

- **Avoid technical jargon**   Just as with entity names, technical jargon such as cardinality, optionality, entity, attribute, and the like have no place in business definitions. Strive to use business terms common to the organization.

- **Distinguish the entity from all others**   Clearly stating what makes an entity different from other entities in the model helps prevent business users from misunderstanding the use of the entity. For example, the definition of the Movie Copy entity needs to clarify how it is different from the Movie entity with wording such as "a copy of a movie on a medium such as DVD or Blu-ray disc that is available for rental or sale." Note that it is perfectly acceptable to use the name of the entity in its definition.

- **Distinguish one occurrence from another**   Clearly stating what makes one occurrence of the entity different from others helps business users establish the grain of the data that will eventually be stored in the database. For example, if the definition of the Employee entity is "an individual who is employed by OMR," then the difference between an employee and a customer is clear—a customer rents or buys movies, while an employee does not. The implication is that if the employee also rents or buys from OMR, then they would also be recorded as a customer.

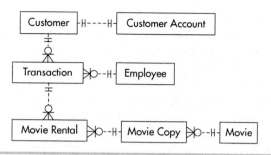

Figure 2-3   Conceptual model showing only entity names

Alternative Conceptual Model Diagram Notation

Figure 2-3 shows the conceptual data model from Figure 2-1 redrawn to show only the entity names, which are placed inside the rectangles that represent the entities. This is a very common practice, but as you can see, it leaves it up to the viewer to determine the meaning of the entities, and thus there is danger of misinterpretation and misunderstanding.

Another alternative is to include the entity definition inside the rectangle for each entity as shown in Figure 2-4. This provides the context that the viewer needs without the clutter caused

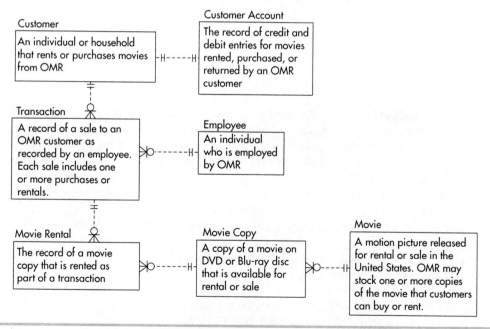

Figure 2-4   Conceptual model showing entity definitions instead of attributes

by listing all the attributes. Moreover, conceptual models done this way are less prone to changes. It is common to discover attributes as the design progresses, and it generates unnecessary work if attributes found during logical modeling mandate changes to the conceptual model.

Attributes

Recall that an *attribute* is a unit fact that characterizes or describes an entity in some way. We say attributes are *unit* facts because they should be *atomic,* meaning they cannot be broken down into smaller units in any meaningful way. An attribute is therefore the smallest named unit of data that appears in a database system. In practice, this rule is seldom followed in conceptual models where brevity is important, but it should always be followed in logical models so that attributes in the logical model correspond with table columns in the physical model. In this sense, Address should be considered a suspect attribute in a logical model such as the one shown in Figure 2-2 because it can easily be broken down into Address Line 1, Address Line 2, and perhaps Address Line 3. This change would add meaning because it makes it easier to print address labels, for example. On the other hand, database design is not an exact science, and judgment calls must be made. Although it is possible to break the Business Phone attribute into component attributes, such as Country Code, Area Code, Prefix, Suffix, and Extension, we must ask ourselves whether such a change adds meaning or value. There is no right or wrong answer here, so we must rely on the people who will be using the database, or perhaps those who are funding the database project, to help us with such decisions. Always remember that an attribute *must* describe or characterize the entity in some way (for example, size, shape, color, quantity, location).

Attribute Notation

Attributes are represented in conceptual and logical models as names inside the rectangle that represents the entity to which they belong. However, as previously noted, there is some debate among practitioners as to whether attributes should be included in conceptual data models.

Attribute Notation for Keys The attribute or attributes that appear at the top of the rectangle (above the horizontal line) form the *unique identifier* for the entity. A unique identifier, as the name suggests, provides a unique value for each instance of the entity. For example, the Customer ID attribute is the unique identifier for the Customer entity, so each customer must have a unique value for that attribute.

Keep in mind that a unique identifier can be composed of multiple attributes, but when this happens, it is still considered just *one* unique identifier. For example, in Figure 2-1, the primary key of Movie Copy is composed of the combination of Movie ID (from Movie) and Copy Number. It is the *combination* of the two that must be unique. In this case, Copy Number is a sequential number added as a tie-breaker so that each copy of the same movie has a unique key. There can be many copies of the same movie, and therefore many occurrences of Movie Copy that have the same Movie ID, but with different values for Copy Number, typically numbered 1, 2, 3, and so forth. Also, there can be many occurrences of different movies (various values of Movie ID) that have the same Copy Number.

When relationships are established between entities, the primary key attribute(s) of the parent entity is placed in the child entity and is known as a *foreign key*. We often note foreign keys in data models by placing a symbol such as "(FK)" after the attribute name. In Figure 2-1, note the *(FK)* symbols in the Transaction entity after the Customer ID (foreign key to Customer) and Employee ID (foreign key to Employee) attributes.

Attribute Naming

As you might surmise, attribute names are important in logical models because the column names in the physical model are based on the logical names. If the selected names do not effectively convey the contents of the attributes (and therefore the table columns) to business users and developers, people will find it difficult to find the data they seek, or worse yet, they will use columns for purposes other than what the designer intended.

Here are some guidelines for attribute names:

- **Avoid technical jargon**   Names such as Primary Identifier, Ordinal Number, and the like add no business value—strive for terms that businesspeople will understand.

- **Use singular names**   The normalization process (presented in Chapter 6) requires each attribute to contain only one value per row of data. Therefore, the attribute names should be singular to match.

- **Avoid unnecessary abbreviations and acronyms**   With the exception of abbreviations and acronyms that are commonly used in a particular industry, business users understand names more readily if plain language is used instead of potentially confusing shortened forms. While the DBMS may impose maximum lengths on column names, there is no reason to restrict the length of names in conceptual and logical models.

- **Use class words**   A *class word* is a term (usually a single word) added as a suffix to attribute names that describes the type of data the attribute is to contain. Most practitioners recommend using class words on all attribute names. For consistency, you should create and maintain a standard list. Class words such as "date," "time," "text," "amount," "identifier (ID)," "number," and so forth, contribute to understanding. A common exception is to allow the class word "text" to be optional.

- **Use entity name prefixes consistently**   Some practitioners insist on prefixing every attribute name in an entity with the name of the entity. For example, they would require that every attribute in the Customer entity in Figure 2-2 have a name beginning with *Customer.* The obvious problem with this approach is that some names become excessively long, especially when entity names become long. This is why many practitioners (including I) prefer to use entity name prefixes only when it adds clarity. For example, we know the Address in the Customer entity is the customer's address—after all, it is in that entity. However, it wouldn't make much sense to name the primary key using only the class word ID, so we add the entity name to form a much better name, Customer ID.

- **Use attribute names consistently**   When the same attribute is used in multiple entities, the names should be the same.

Attribute Definition

As with entities, each attribute should have a written definition that describes its data content in business terms and which distinguishes it from all other attributes.

Derivable Attributes

A derivable attribute is one that has data values that can be readily determined using other available attributes. For example, in Figure 2-2, the Total Rental Fee attribute in Transaction can be determined by summing the Rental Fee and Late Fee amounts in all the related Movie Rental rows. However, if we were to add Sales Tax to Movie Rental, it would not be easily derived over time, because tax rates not only vary from one jurisdiction to another, but they also vary over time.

It is perfectly acceptable to include derivable attributes in conceptual models. However, normalization requires readily derivable attributes to be removed, and logical models should be normalized, so in general, derivable attributes should be removed from logical models.

Relationships

Relationships are the associations among the entities. Because databases are all about storing related data, the relationships become the glue that holds the database together. Relationships are shown in data models as lines connecting one or more entities. In IE notation, each end of a relationship line shows the *maximum cardinality* of the relationship, which is the maximum number of instances of one entity that can be associated with the entity on the opposite end of the line. The maximum cardinality may be *one* (the line has no special symbol on its end) or *many* (the line has a crow's foot on the end). Just short of the end of the line is another symbol that shows the *minimum cardinality,* which is the minimum number of instances of one entity that can be associated with the entity on the opposite end of the line. The minimum cardinality may be *zero,* denoted with a circle drawn on the line, or *one,* denoted with a short perpendicular line or tick mark drawn across the relationship line. Many data modelers use two perpendicular lines to mean "one and *only* one," as I have done in Figures 2-1 through 2-4.

Learning to read relationships takes practice, and learning to define and draw them correctly takes a *lot* of practice. The trick is to think about the association between the entities in one direction, and then to reverse your perspective to think about it in the opposite direction. For the relationship between Customer and Transaction, for example, we must ask two questions: "Each customer can have how many transactions?" followed by "Each transaction can have how many customers?" Relationships may thus be classified into three types: *one-to-one, one-to-many,* and *many-to-many,* as discussed in the following sections. Some people will say many-to-one is also a relationship type, but in reality, it is only a one-to-many relationship looked at with a reverse perspective. Relationship types are best learned by example. Getting the relationships right is *essential* to a successful design.

Ask the Expert

Q: You stated that relationships in data models are between one or more entities. However, I've always been told that relationships in a relational DBMS are between only two tables. How can this be?

A: A conceptual data model is usually created at a higher level of abstraction than the corresponding logical physical models. As you will learn later in this chapter, the referential constraints placed in the relational database can support only relationships between two tables, except for a special case called *recursive relationships* that involve only one table. However, a designer can be more general in a conceptual model and can show a relationship between more than two entities. For example, the relationship between Customer and Transaction shown in Figure 2-1 might be represented in a conceptual model as one between Customer, Customer Account, and Transaction since the results of the transaction directly affect the Customer Account. Such a relationship would have to be resolved in the logical data model, just as the intersection data shown in Figure 2-1 must be (it must eventually be stored in a table). Have no fear if this seems confusing; it will all become more clear as you learn more about data modeling and database design in upcoming chapters. In reality, relationships involving more than two entities are reasonably rare, and an advanced topic, so they are not used in this book.

Relationship Types and Symbols

Let's have a closer look at the types of relationships and the symbols used to represent them in data models.

One-to-One Relationships   A *one-to-one relationship* is an association in which an instance of one entity can be associated with *at most* one instance of the other entity, and vice versa. In Figure 2-1, the relationship between the Customer and Customer Account entities is one-to-one. This means that a customer can have *at most* one associated account, and an account can have *at most* one associated customer. The relationship is also *mandatory* in both directions, meaning that a customer must have *at least* one account associated with it, and an account must have *at least* one customer associated with it. Putting this all together, we can read the relationship between the Customer and Customer Account entities as "any given customer has one and only one associated customer account, and any given customer account has one and only one associated customer." In practice, one-to-one mandatory relationships cannot be implemented in relational databases because each table requires that a matching row already exist in the other table. We therefore must look at them with a critical eye and either combine the two entities or make the relationship optional in at least one direction.

Another important concept is *transferability*. A relationship is said to be *transferable* if the parent can be changed over time—or, said another way, if the child can be reassigned to a different parent. In this case, the relationship between Customer and Customer Account is obviously not transferable because we would never take one customer's account and transfer it to another customer (it would be horribly bad accounting practice to do so). Unfortunately, no widely accepted symbol is available for showing transferability on data models, but it is an important consideration in some cases, particularly with one-to-one relationships that are mandatory in both directions.

One-to-one relationships are surprisingly rare in business systems. In practice, one-to-one relationships that are mandatory in both directions *and* not transferable represent a design flaw that should be corrected by combining the two entities. After all, isn't a customer account merely more information about the customer? We're not going to collect data *about* a customer account; instead, the information in the Customer Account entity is simply more data we want to collect *about* the customer. On the other hand, if we were to buy our financial software from an independent software vendor (a common practice), the software would almost certainly come with a predefined integrated database, so we might have to live with this situation. We won't be able to modify the vendor's database design to add customer data of interest to us, and at the same time, we won't be able to get the vendor's software to recognize anything that we store in our own database.

Figure 2-5 shows a different "flavor" of one-to-one relationship that is *optional* (some say *conditional*) in both directions. Suppose we are designing a database for an automobile dealership. The dealership issues automobiles to some employees, typically sales staff, for them to drive for a finite period. They obviously don't issue *all* the automobiles to employees (if they did, they would have none to sell). We can read the relationship between the Employee and Automobile entities as follows: "At any point in time, each employee can have zero or one automobiles issued to him or her, and each automobile can be assigned to zero or one employee." Note the clause "At any point in time." If an automobile is taken back from one employee and then reassigned to another, this would still be a one-to-one relationship, albeit a transferable one. This is because when we consider relationships, we always think in terms of a snapshot taken at an arbitrary point in time.

One-to-Many Relationships   A *one-to-many relationship* is an association between two entities in which any instance of the first entity may be associated with one or more instances of the second, and any instance of the second entity may be associated with at most one instance

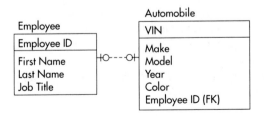

Figure 2-5   Employee-automobile relationship

of the first. Figure 2-1 shows three such relationships: between the Customer and Transaction entities, between the Employee and Transaction entities, and between the Movie and Movie Copy entities. The relationship between Customer and Transaction, which is mandatory in only one direction, is read as follows: "At any point in time, each customer can have zero to many transactions, and each transaction must have one and only one owning customer."

One-to-many relationships are quite common. In fact, they are the fundamental building block of the relational database model in that all relationships in a relational database are implemented as if they are one-to-many. It is rare for them to be optional on the "one" side and even more rare for them to be mandatory on the "many" side, but these situations do occur. Consider the examples shown in Figure 2-6. When a customer account closes, we record the reason it was closed by using an Account Closure Reason Code. Because some accounts are open at any point in time, this is an optional code. We read the relationship this way: "At any given point in time, each Account Closure Reason Code value can have zero, one, or many Customer Accounts assigned to it, and each Customer Account can have either zero or one Account Closure Reason Code values assigned to it." Let us next suppose that as a matter of company policy, no customer account can be opened without first obtaining a credit report, and that all credit reports are kept in the database, meaning that any Customer Account can have more than one credit report in the database. This makes the relationship between the Customer Account and Credit Report entities one-to-many, and mandatory in both directions. We read the relationship thus: "At any given point in time, each Customer Account can have one or many Credit Reports, and each Credit Report belongs to one and only one Customer Account."

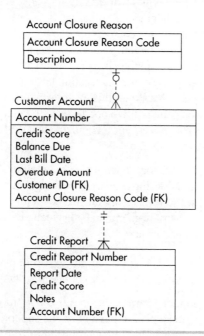

Figure 2-6   One-to-many relationships

Many-to-Many Relationships   A *many-to-many relationship* is an association between two entities in which any instance of the first entity may be associated with zero, one, or more instances of the second, and vice versa. Back in Figure 2-1, the relationship between Transaction and Movie Copy is many-to-many. We read the relationship thus: "At any given point in time, each transaction contains zero to many movie copies, and each movie copy appears on zero to many transactions." Obviously this interpretation requires the Transaction entity to have some amount of history in it, because a given Movie Copy can only be rented by one person at any given moment.

This particular relationship has data associated with it, as shown in the diamond in Figure 2-1. Data that belongs to a many-to-many relationship is called *intersection data*. The data doesn't make sense unless you associate it with both entities at the same time. For example, Rental Fee doesn't make sense unless you know *when* the rental took place (determined by the Rental Date in the Transaction entity) and which Movie Copy was rented. If you look at Figure 2-2, you will see that this data was represented as the Movie Rental entity in the corresponding logical model. So why isn't Movie Rental shown as an entity in the conceptual model? The answer is simple: It doesn't really fit the definition of an entity. We are not collecting data about the line items on the transaction; instead, the line items on the transaction are merely more data about the transaction. However, we must make a compromise in logical and physical models.

Many-to-many relationships are quite common, and most of them will have intersection data. The bad news is that the relational model does not directly support many-to-many relationships. There is no problem with having many-to-many relationships in a conceptual model because such a design is independent of any particular technology. However, if the database is going to be relational, some changes have to be made as you map the conceptual model to the corresponding logical model. The solution is to map the intersection data to a separate entity (an *intersection table* in the physical model) and the many-to-many relationship to two one-to-many relationships, with the intersection table in the middle and on the "many" side of both relationships. Figure 2-2 shows this outcome, with the Movie Rental entity holding the intersection data and participating in two one-to-many relationships that replace the original many-to-many relationship. The process for recognizing and dealing with the many-to-many problem is covered in detail in Chapter 6.

Recursive Relationships   So far, you've learned about relationships between instances of different entities. However, relationships can exist between entity instances of the same type. These are called *recursive relationships*. Any one of the relationship types already presented (one-to-one, one-to-many, or many-to-many) can be a recursive relationship. Figure 2-7 and the following list show examples of each:

- **One-to-one**   If we were to track which employees were married to other employees, we would expect each to be married to either zero or one other employee at any one point in time.

- **One-to-many**   It is common to track the employment "food chain" of who reports to whom. In most organizations, people have only one supervisor or manager. Therefore, we normally expect to see each employee reporting to zero or one other employee, and employees who are managers or supervisors to have one or more direct reports.

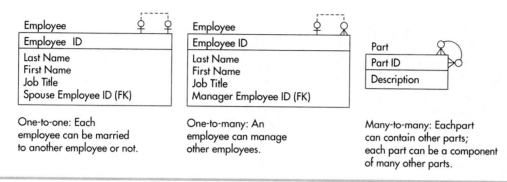

Figure 2-7   Recursive relationship examples

- **Many-to-many**   In manufacturing, a common relationship has to do with parts that make up a finished product. If you think about the CD-ROM drive in a personal computer, for example, you can imagine that it comprises multiple parts, and yet, the entire assembly shows as only one item on the parts list for your computer. So any part can be made of many other parts, and at the same time, any part can be a component of many other parts.

Relationship Naming

As with all objects in a data model, relationships need names so we can distinguish them from one another. This is particularly true when automated modeling tools are used because most of these tools list objects in a hierarchical tree. In conceptual and logical models these names can be arbitrary, and often are if default names are assigned automatically by the modeling software. However, in the physical model, names become more important.

Relationships in logical models become foreign key constraints in the physical model and physical database. When a constraint is violated, the DBMS displays the constraint name as part of the error message. To be understandable to developers and support personnel, the constraint name needs to provide some information about the tables involved. Otherwise, someone has to ask a DBA to look up the constraint and tell them how it is defined. It's always best to draft naming standards, obtain consensus among the designers, developers, and DBAs, and then to strictly follow them. A common standard for relationship names is to use a prefix such as "FK_" followed by parts of both the parent and child entity (table) names. If the data modeling tool can be set up to automatically generate names in the agreed-upon form, you can be sure that the relationships will be named consistently.

Redundant Relationships

Modelers sometimes draw redundant (unnecessary) relationships. Figure 2-8 shows three of the entities from Figure 2-2 with a redundant relationship added. Notice that Movie Copy is a child of Movie, and therefore the value of Movie ID in Movie Copy is determined by the Movie ID in Movie. Similarly, Movie Rental is a child of Movie Copy, so the value of Movie ID in Movie Rental is determined by Movie ID in Movie Copy. However, we have added an

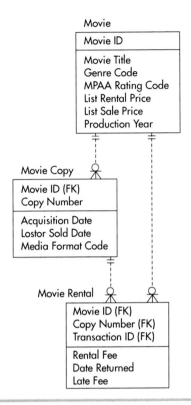

Figure 2-8 Redundant relationship

additional relationship from Movie to Movie Rental, bypassing the Movie Copy layer of the hierarchy.

Notice that there is only one Movie ID attribute in Movie Rental, and because of the two relationships, its value is determined by both the Movie ID in Movie and the one in Movie Copy. This arrangement is known as *unification*. Although most practitioners avoid redundant relationships, they are acceptable provided the common foreign key(s) are unified. While the redundant relationships do no harm in data models, and in fact may sometimes improve clarity and understanding, they should be avoided in physical models, because the DBMS has to do extra work to verify both relationships as new table rows are added.

Relationship Degrees

The number of entities participating in a relationship is known as the relationship *degree*. Recursive relationships always have a degree of 1. As already discussed, all other relationships in logical and physical models should be of degree 2. Relationships of degrees over 2 (that is, involving more than two entities) are not supported by relational DBMSs and therefore cannot be included in physical models. Most modelers also avoid relationships over degree 2 in logical models.

Business Rules

A *business rule* is a policy, procedure, or standard that an organization has adopted. Business rules are *very* important in database design because they dictate controls that must be placed upon the data. In Figure 2-1, you can see a business rule that states that customers with overdue accounts may not rent movies. Most business rules can be enforced through manual procedures that employees are directed to follow or through logic placed in the application programs. However, each of these can be circumvented—employees can forget or can choose not to follow a manual procedure, and databases can be updated directly by authorized people, bypassing the controls included in the application programs. The database can serve nicely as the last line of defense. Business rules can be implemented in the database as *constraints*, which are formally defined rules that restrict the data values in the database in some way. More information on constraints can be found in the "Constraints" section later in this chapter. Note that business rules are not normally shown on a conceptual data model diagram; the one shown in Figure 2-1 is merely for illustration. It is far more common to include them in a text document that accompanies the diagram.

Physical Model Components

The physical design is implanted in the ANSI/SPARC physical layer. We create a physical data model and use it to implement the physical layer using the DBMS. For example, when we create a table in the database, we include a clause in the *Create Table* command that tells the DBMS where we want to place it. The DBMS then automatically allocates space for the table in the requested operating system file(s). Because so much of the physical implementation is buried in the DBMS definitions of the logical structures, it can be difficult to separate them in your mind.

Ideally, the logical model should not contain any physical implementation details. As the physical model is created, physical storage properties (file or tablespace name, storage location, and sizing information) can be assigned to each database object as we map them from the logical model, or they can be omitted at first and added later. In some organizations, data modelers turn over initial physical models to DBAs, and it is the DBAs who add the physical implementation details. For time efficiency, many data modelers build the logical and physical models in parallel, and many data modeling tools support a combined logical/physical data model to assist with that alternative. Figure 2-9 shows a physical model that was built using the logical model shown in Figure 2-2.

Tables

The primary unit of storage in the relational model is the *table,* which is a 2-D structure composed of rows and columns. Each row corresponds to one occurrence of the entity that the table represents, and each column corresponds to one attribute for that entity. The process of mapping the entities in the conceptual design to tables in the logical design is called *normalization* and is covered in detail in Chapter 6. Often, an entity in the conceptual model maps to exactly one table in the logical model, but this is not always the case. For reasons you will learn with the normalization process, entities are commonly split into multiple tables, and in rare cases, multiple

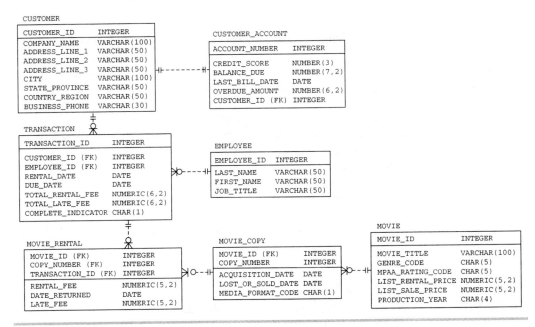

Figure 2-9 Physical data model

entities can be combined into one table. Figure 2-10 shows a listing of part of the MOVIE table from Figure 2-9.

You must remember that a relational table is a *logical* storage structure and usually does not exist in tabular form in the physical layer. When the DBA assigns a table to operating system files in the physical layer (called *tablespaces* in most DBMSs), it is common for multiple tables to be placed in a single tablespace. However, large tables can be placed in their own tablespace or split across multiple tablespaces, and this is called *partitioning*. This flexibility typically does not exist in personal computer–based DBMSs such as Microsoft Access.

MOVIE_ ID	MOVIE_TITLE	GENRE_ CODE	MPAA_ RATING_ CODE	LIST_ RENTAL_ PRICE	LIST_ SALE_ PRICE	PRODUCTION_ YEAR
1401	Crash	Drama	UR	4.50	9.95	2005
1402	The Departed	Drama	R	6.25	16.75	2006
1423	Casino Royale	ActAd	PG-13	8.25	19.98	2006
1426	Little Miss Sunshine	Cmdy	R	8.25	19.98	2006

Figure 2-10 Movie table listing

Ask the Expert

Q: You have mentioned both files and tablespaces. Are they the same thing?

A: You can think of a tablespace as a logical file that forms a layer of abstraction between the physical and logical layers, thereby providing better logical data independence. A tablespace has one or more physical files assigned to it. And instead of assigning tables to physical files, you assign them to tablespaces. This provides great flexibility in handling the physical files that make up the database. For example, when tablespaces begin to fill up, one option the DBA has is to add another file on a different device (such as a disk drive).

Each table must be given a unique name by the DBA who creates it. The maximum length for these names varies a lot among DBMS products, from as few as 18 characters to as many as 255. Table names should be descriptive and should reflect the name of the real-world entity they represent. By convention, some DBAs always name entities in the singular and tables in the plural. I prefer that both be named in the singular. The point here is that you should establish naming standards at the outset so that names are not assigned in a haphazard manner, as this leads to confusion later. As a case in point, Microsoft Access permits embedded spaces in table and column names, which is counter to industry standards. Moreover, Microsoft Access, Sybase, and Microsoft SQL Server allow mixed-case names, such as MovieCopy, whereas Oracle, DB2, MySQL on Windows, and others force all names to be uppercase letters unless they are enclosed in double quotes. Because table names such as MOVIECOPY are not very readable, the use of an underscore to separate words, per industry standards, is a much better choice. You may want to set standards that forbid the use of names with embedded spaces and names in mixed case because such names are nonstandard and make any conversion between database vendors that much more difficult.

Columns and Data Types

As mentioned, each column in a relational table represents an attribute from the conceptual model. The *column* is the smallest named unit of data that can be referenced in a relational database. Each column must be assigned a unique name (within the table) and a data type. A *data type* is a category for the format of a particular column. Data types provide several valuable benefits:

- Restricting the data in the column to characters that make sense for the data type (for example, only numeric digits or only valid calendar dates).

- Providing a set of behaviors useful to the database user. For example, if you subtract a number from another number, you get a number as a result; but if you subtract a date from another date, you get a number representing the elapsed time (usually measured in days) between the two dates as a result.

● Assisting the DBMS in efficiently storing the column data. For example, numbers can often be stored in an internal numeric format that saves space, compared with merely storing the numeric digits as a string of characters.

Following is the SQL statement that creates the MOVIE table shown in Figures 2-9 and 2-10. The data type for each column appears in the second column, and the third column specifies whether the column's data is mandatory (NOT NULL) or optional (NULL). SQL is beyond the scope of this book, but this statement is included here to help you connect the physical data model to the creation of the physical database objects. If you are using data modeling software, it should allow you to specify generic data types in the logical model, automatically translate the generic types into DBMS-specific types when you generate the physical model, and then automatically generate the SQL for creating the database objects.

```
CREATE TABLE MOVIE
( MOVIE_ID            INTEGER       NOT NULL,
  MOVIE_TITLE         VARCHAR(100)  NOT NULL,
  GENRE_CODE          CHAR(5)       NULL,
  MPAA_RATING_CODE    CHAR(5)       NULL,
  LIST_RENTAL_PRICE   NUMERIC(5,2)  NULL,
  LIST_SALE_PRICE     NUMERIC(5,2)  NULL,
  PRODUCTION_YEAR     CHAR(4)       NULL,
 PRIMARY KEY (MOVIE_ID)
);
```

It is most unfortunate that industry standards lagged behind DBMS development. Most vendors did their own thing for many years before collaborating with other vendors to develop standards, and this is clearly evident in the wide variation of data type options across the major DBMS products. Today the ANSI/ISO SQL standard covers relational data types, and the major vendors support all or most of the standard types. However, each vendor has its own "extensions" to the standards, largely in support of data types it developed before standards existed, but also to add features that differentiate its product from competitors' offerings. One could say (in jest) that the greatest thing about database standards is that there are so many from which to choose. In terms of industry standards for relational databases, Microsoft Access is probably the least compliant of the most popular products, and MySQL the most compliant. Given the many levels of standards compliance and all the vendor extensions, the DBA must have a detailed knowledge of the data types available on the particular DBMS that is in use to deploy the database successfully. And, of course, great care must be taken when converting physical designs from one vendor's product to another's.

Table 2-1 shows data types from different DBMS vendors that are roughly equivalent. As always, the devil is in the details, meaning that these are not *identical* data types, merely equivalent. For example, the VARCHAR type in Oracle can be up to 4,000 characters in length (2,000 characters in versions prior to Oracle8*i*), but the equivalent MEMO type in Microsoft Access can be up to a gigabyte of characters (roughly 1 billion characters)!

Data Type	Microsoft Access	Microsoft SQL Server	Oracle
Fixed-length character	(none)	CHAR	CHAR
Variable-length character	TEXT	VARCHAR	VARCHAR
Long text	MEMO	TEXT	CLOB or LONG (deprecated)
Integer	INTEGER or LONG INTEGER	INTEGER or SMALLINT or TINYINT	NUMBER
Decimal	NUMBER	DECIMAL or NUMERIC	NUMBER
Currency	CURRENCY	MONEY or SMALLMONEY	None, use NUMBER
Date/time	DATE/TIME	DATETIME or SMALLDATETIME	DATE or TIMESTAMP

Table 2-1   Equivalent Data Types in Major DBMS Products

Constraints

A *constraint* is a rule placed on a database object (typically a table or column) that restricts the allowable data values for that database object in some way. These are most important in relational databases in that constraints are the way we implement both the relationships and business rules specified in the logical design. Each constraint is assigned a unique name to permit it to be referenced in error messages and subsequent database commands. It is a good habit for DBAs to supply the constraint names because names generated automatically by the DBMS are never very descriptive.

Primary Key Constraints

A *primary key* is a column or a set of columns that uniquely identifies each row in a table. A unique identifier in the conceptual and logical data models is thus implemented as a primary key in the physical model and ultimately in the database. Recall that in the models shown thus far, the primary key column(s) are shown above the horizontal line within the rectangles that depict each entity. In the previous SQL example, you may have noticed the PRIMARY KEY clause used to define the primary key to the DBMS. When you define a primary key, the DBMS implements it as a *primary key constraint* to guarantee that no two rows in the table will ever have duplicate values in the primary key column(s). Note that for primary keys composed of multiple columns, each column by itself *may* have duplicate values in the table, but the *combination* of the values for all the primary key columns must be unique among all rows in the table.

Primary key constraints are nearly always implemented by the DBMS using an *index*, which is a special type of database object that permits fast searches of column values. As new rows are inserted into the table, the DBMS *automatically* searches the index to make sure the value for the primary key of the new row is not already in use in the table, rejecting the insert request if it is. Indexes can be searched much faster than tables; therefore, the index on the primary key is essential in tables of any size, so that the search for duplicate keys on every insert doesn't create a performance bottleneck.

Referential Constraints

To understand how the DBMS enforces relationships using referential constraints, you must first understand the concept of foreign keys. Recall that when one-to-many relationships are implemented in tables, the column or set of columns that is stored in the child table (the table on the "many" side of the relationship), to associate it with the parent table (the table on the "one" side), is called a foreign key. It gets its name from the column(s) copied from another (foreign) table. For example, in the TRANSACTION table shown in Figure 2-9, the EMPLOYEE_ID column is a foreign key to the EMPLOYEE table, and the CUSTOMER_ID column is a foreign key to the CUSTOMER table.

In most relational databases, the foreign key must either be the primary key of the parent table, or a column or set of columns for which a unique index is defined. This again is for efficiency. Most people prefer that the foreign key column(s) have names identical to the corresponding primary key column(s), but again there are counter opinions, especially because like-named columns are a little more difficult to use in query languages. It is best to set some standards up front and to stick with them throughout your database project.

Each relationship between entities in the conceptual design becomes a referential constraint in the logical design. A *referential constraint* (sometimes called a *referential integrity constraint*) is a constraint that enforces a relationship among tables in a relational database. *Enforces* means that the DBMS automatically checks to ensure that each foreign key value in a child table always has a corresponding primary key value in the parent table. As we update the data in the database tables, the DBMS must enforce the referential constraints we have defined on the table. The beauty of database constraints is that they are *automatic* and therefore cannot be circumvented unless the DBA removes or disables them.

Here are the particular events that the DBMS must handle when enforcing referential constraints:

- When you try to insert a new row into the child table, the insert request is rejected if the corresponding parent table row does not exist. For example, if you insert a row into the TRANSACTION table with an EMPLOYEE_ID value of 12345, the DBMS must check the EMPLOYEE table to see if a row for EMPLOYEE_ID 12345 already exists. If it doesn't exist, the insert request is rejected.

- When you try to update a foreign key value in the child table, the update request is rejected if the new value for the foreign key does not already exist in the parent table. For example, if you attempt to change the EMPLOYEE_ID for TRANSACTION 48 from 4 to 12345, the DBMS must again check the EMPLOYEE table to see if a row for EMPLOYEE_ID 12345 already exists. If it doesn't exist, the update request is rejected.

- When you try to delete a row from a parent table and that parent row has related rows in one or more child tables, either the child table rows must be deleted along with the parent row or the delete request must be rejected. Most DBMSs provide the option of automatically deleting the child rows, called a *cascading delete*. You probably wondered why anyone would ever want automatic deletion of child rows. Consider the TRANSACTION and MOVIE_RENTAL tables. If a transaction is to be deleted, why not delete the rentals that belong to it in one easy step? However, with the EMPLOYEE table, you clearly would not want that option. If you attempt to delete employee 4 from the EMPLOYEE table (perhaps because the person is no longer an employee), the DBMS must check for rows assigned to EMPLOYEE_ID 4 in the TRANSACTION table and reject the delete request if any is found. It would make no business sense to have orders automatically deleted when an employee left the company.

In most relational databases, an SQL statement is used to define a referential constraint. Many vendors also provide graphical user interface (GUI) panels for defining database objects such as referential constraints. In SQL Server, for example, these GUI panels are located within the SQL Server Management Studio tool, and in Oracle, a tool named SQL Developer has these capabilities. For Microsoft Access, the Relationships panel is used for defining referential constraints.

Intersection Tables

The discussion of many-to-many relationships earlier in this chapter pointed out that relational databases cannot implement these relationships directly and that an intersection table is formed to establish them. Looking back at the conceptual model shown in Figure 2-1, you will see a many-to-many relationship between the Transaction and Movie Copy entities that became an intersection entity in the logical model (Figure 2-2) and an intersection table in the physical model (Figure 2-9).

Using the intersection table, the relationship is then implemented as two, one-to-many relationships with the intersection table on the "many" side of each. The primary key of the MOVIE_RENTAL table can be formed using the combination of the primary keys of the MOVIE_COPY and TRANSACTION tables. The primary key thus becomes the combination of MOVIE_ID, COPY_NUMBER, and TRANSACTION_ID, forming what is known as the *natural key* of the table. It's most important to also understand that these columns are also foreign keys in the MOVIE_RENTAL table. An alternative design is to replace the natural key columns with a single column (MOVIE_RENTAL_ID, for example) that will be given an arbitrary unique value for each row of data. This arrangement is known as a *surrogate key*, because the so-called *natural key* has been replaced with another one. Figure 2-11 shows

```
MOVIE_RENTAL
┌─────────────────────────┬─────────────┐
│ MOVIE_RENTAL_ID         │ INTEGER     │
├─────────────────────────┼─────────────┤
│ MOVIE_ID (FK)           │ INTEGER     │
│ COPY_NUMBER (FK)        │ INTEGER     │
│ TRANSACTION_ID (FK)     │ INTEGER     │
│ RENTAL_FEE              │ NUMERIC(5,2)│
│ DATE_RETURNED           │ DATE        │
│ LATE_FEE                │ NUMERIC(5,2)│
└─────────────────────────┴─────────────┘
```

Figure 2-11 MOVIE_RENTAL table with surrogate key

this alternative design. Note that the foreign key columns MOVIE_ID, COPY_NUMBER, and TRANSACTION_ID are still included in the table (they must be in order to establish the relationships with the parent tables)—they are just not part of the primary key in this arrangement. Relationships where the foreign key is part of the primary key of the child table are known as *identifying relationships,* and those where the foreign key is not part of the primary key are known as *non-identifying relationships.*

Take a moment to examine the contents of the intersection table and the two referential constraints in Figure 2-9. Understanding this arrangement is fundamental to understanding how relational databases work. Here are some points to consider:

- Each row in the MOVIE_RENTAL intersection table belongs to the intersection of one MOVIE_COPY and one TRANSACTION. It would not make sense to include ACQUISITION_DATE in this table, because that date is the same every time the same movie copy appears on a transaction. Also, it would not make sense to include CUSTOMER_ID in the MOVIE_RENTAL table, because all rentals on the same transaction belong to the same customer.

- Each MOVIE_COPY table row may have many related MOVIE_RENTAL rows (one for each transaction with which the movie copy was rented), but each MOVIE_RENTAL row belongs to one and only one MOVIE_COPY table row.

- Each TRANSACTION table row may have many related MOVIE_RENTAL rows (one for each movie rented with that particular transaction), but each MOVIE_RENTAL row belongs to one and only one TRANSACTION table row.

Integrity Constraints

As mentioned, many of the business rules from the conceptual design become constraints in the logical model. An *integrity constraint* is a constraint that promotes the accuracy of the data in the database. The key benefit is that these constraints are invoked automatically by the DBMS and cannot be circumvented (unless you are a DBA) no matter how you connect to the database. The major types of integrity constraints are NOT NULL constraints, CHECK constraints, and constraints enforced with triggers.

NOT NULL Constraints

As you define columns in database tables, you have the option of specifying whether null values are permitted for the column. A *null value* in a relational database is a special code that can be placed in a column that indicates that the value for that column in that row is unknown. A null value is not the same as a blank, an empty string, or a zero—it is indeed a special code that has no other meaning in the database.

A uniform way to treat null values is specified in the ANSI/ISO SQL Standard. However, there has been much debate over the usefulness of the option because the database cannot tell you *why* the value is unknown. If you leave the value for Job Title null in the Employees table, for example, you don't know whether it is null because it is truly unknown (you know employees must have a title, but you do not know what it is), it doesn't apply (perhaps some employees do not get titles), or it is unassigned (they will get a title eventually, but the title their manager wants to use hasn't been approved yet). The other dilemma is that null values are not equal to anything, including other null values, which introduces three-valued logic into database searches. With nulls in use, a search can return the condition *true* (the column value matches), *false* (the column value does not match), or *unknown* (the column value is null). The developers who write the application programs have to handle null values as a special case.

In SQL definitions of tables, you simply include the keyword NULL or NOT NULL in the column definition. Watch out for defaults! In Oracle, if you skip the specification, the default is NULL, which means the column may contain null values. But in some implementations of DB2, Microsoft SQL Server, and Sybase, it is just the opposite: if you skip the specification, the default is NOT NULL, meaning the column *may not* contain null values.

CHECK Constraints

A CHECK constraint uses a simple logic statement to validate a column value. The outcome of the statement must be a logical *true* or *false,* with an outcome of *true* allowing the column value to be placed in the table, and a value of *false* causing the column value to be rejected with an appropriate error message. For example, we could prevent the list rental price in the MOVIE table from ever being zero or a negative number by adding a clause like this one to the SQL definition of the table:

```
CHECK (LIST_RENTAL_PRICE >=0)
```

Constraint Enforcement Using Triggers

Some constraints are too complicated to be enforced using the declarations. For example, the business rule contained in Figure 2-1 (Customers with overdue amounts may not book new orders) falls into this category because it involves more than one table. We need to prevent new rows from being added to the TRANSACTION table if the CUSTOMER_ACCOUNT row for the customer has an overdue amount that is greater than zero. As mentioned, it may be best to implement business rules such as this one in the application logic. However, if we want to add a constraint that will be enforced no matter how the database is updated, a trigger will do the job. A *trigger* is a module of programming logic that "fires" (executes) when a particular event in the database takes place. In this example, we want the trigger to fire whenever a new row is inserted into the TRANSACTION table. The trigger obtains the overdue amount for the customer from the CUSTOMER_ACCOUNT table (or wherever the column is physically stored). If this amount is greater than zero, the trigger will raise a database error that stops the insert request and causes an appropriate error message to be displayed.

As a data modeler and/or database designer, you can expect resistance to the notion of placing constraints in the database. Developers always want unfettered control over data content, arguing they need the flexibility of enforcing all constraints in application code.

However, constraints in application logic are bypassed when data enters the database via other means, such as bulk loads of data from flat files and other databases. The trick is to find the proper balance and to know which constraints are too restrictive or inflexible when enforced in the database.

Some DBMSs provide a special language for writing program modules such as triggers: PL/SQL in Oracle, Transact SQL in Microsoft SQL Server and Sybase, and Microsoft Visual Basic for Applications (VBA) in Microsoft Access. In other DBMSs, such as DB2, a generic programming language such as C may be used.

Views

A *view* is a stored database query that provides a database user with a customized subset of the data from one or more tables in the database. Said another way, a view is a *virtual table,* because it looks like a table and for the most part behaves like a table, yet it stores no data (only the defining query is stored). The user views form the external layer in the ANSI/SPARC model.

In physical databases, views serve a number of useful functions:

- Hiding columns that the user does not need to see (or should not be allowed to see)

- Hiding rows from tables that a user does not need to see (or should not be allowed to see)

- Hiding complex database operations such as table joins

- Improving query performance (in some DBMSs, such as Microsoft SQL Server)

Views play two roles in data modeling. First, requirements for views (that is, specifications of the data that business users want to get from proposed new or enhanced databases) form a primary input source for modelers during logical design. You will learn much more about using views as inputs to logical models in Chapter 6. Second, views can be included in physical models as a means of documentation. Creating these views is a good test of the quality of a data model. If the model in an automated modeling tool can be used to generate the definitions of the views required by the business users (the ones they specified when they gave us their requirements), we can be reasonably certain that our design covers all of their requirements.

Try This 2-1 Conceptual Model Modification

In this Try This exercise, you will modify the conceptual model shown in Figure 2-1 to resolve some discrepancies and to document some design decisions made by OMR management.

During a review of the preliminary conceptual model with OMR management (the one shown in Figure 2-4), the following discoveries were made:

- A Customer Account needs to be accessible to multiple individuals, and the database needs to record which of these individuals participated in each transaction.

- Management still had difficulty reaching consensus on the definition of customer, but they did agree that each customer would have one and only one account, and that the individuals who have access to a customer account should be called members.

- OMR will not sell new movies, but it will carry a sale price that members who lose a rented movie are charged.

- OMR will sell *used* movies once they are no longer needed for rental. Movie copies to be sold will no longer be listed as available for rent. In other words, there are two lists of movie copies—those available for rent and those available for sale—and each copy will be in either one list or the other.

Step by Step

Start with Figure 2-4 and draw a revised conceptual model with the following changes:

1. Change the name of Customer to Member, and adjust the definition so that it is clear that a member is an individual who rents or buys movies and who has access to a Customer Account.

2. Adjust the definition of Customer Account to note that only authorized members have access to it.

3. Change the relationship between Member and Customer Account to be many-to-one (many members to one customer account).

4. Expand Movie Copy to have two subtypes, Rental Copy and Sale Copy, with business definitions for each.

5. Change the relationship from Movie Copy to Movie Rental so it only applies to the Rental Copy subtype.

6. Add a Movie Sale entity that parallels Movie Rental. It will have a one-to-many relationship with Transaction (like Movie Rental does) and a one-to-many relationship with Sale Copy (like the one that Movie Rental has with Rental Copy).

Try This Summary

In this Try This exercise, you update a conceptual model based on emerging (newly discovered) requirements. This is typical of the iterative process that takes place as requirements are clarified and alternatives are presented and then adopted or rejected by project sponsors.

Chapter 2 Self Test

Choose the correct responses to each of the multiple-choice and fill-in-the-blank questions.
Note that there may be more than one correct response to each question.

1. Examples of an entity are

    A A customer

    B A customer order

    C An employee's paycheck

    D A customer's name

2. Examples of an attribute are

    A An employee

    B An employee's name

    C An employee's paycheck

    D An alphabetical listing of employees

3. On a relationship line, the cardinality of "one, or more" is denoted with which of the following:

    A A perpendicular tick mark near the end of the line and a crow's foot at the line end

    B A circle near the end of the line and a crow's foot at the end of the line

    C Two perpendicular tick marks near the end of the line

    D A circle and a perpendicular tick mark near the end of the line

4. Valid types of relationships in a relational database are

    A One-to-many

    B None-to-many

    C Many-to-many

    D One-to-one

5. If a product can be manufactured in many plants, and a plant can manufacture many products, this is an example of which type of relationship?

    A One-to-one

    B One-to-many

    C Many-to-many

    D Recursive

6. Which of the following are examples of recursive relationships?

A An organizational unit made up of departments

B An employee who manages other employees

C An employee who manages a department

D An employee who has many dependents

7. Examples of a business rule are

A A referential constraint must refer to the primary key of the parent table.

B An employee must be at least 18 years old.

C A database query eliminates columns an employee should not see.

D Employees below pay grade 6 are not permitted to modify orders.

8. A relational table

A Is composed of rows and columns

B Must be assigned a data type

C Must be assigned a unique name

D Is the primary unit of storage in the relational model

9. A column in a relational table

A Must be assigned a data type

B Must be assigned a unique name within the table

C Is derived from an entity in the conceptual design

D Is the smallest named unit of storage in a relational database

10. A data type

A Assists the DBMS in storing data efficiently

B Provides a set of behaviors for a column that assists the database user

C May be selected based on business rules for an attribute

D Restricts characters allowed in a database column

11. A primary key constraint

A Must reference one or more columns in a single table

B Must be defined for every database table

C Is usually implemented by using an index

D Guarantees that no two rows in a table have duplicate primary key values

12. A referential constraint

    A Must have primary key and foreign key columns that have identical names

    B Ensures that a primary key does not have duplicate values in a table

    C Defines a many-to-many relationship between two tables

    D Ensures that a foreign key value always refers to an existing primary key value in the parent table

13. A logical data model

    A May contain many-to-many relationships

    B Is used as the basis for the physical data model

    C Contains implementation details such as tablespace names

    D Usually contains view definitions

14. Major types of integrity constraints are

    A CHECK constraints

    B One-to-one relationships

    C NOT NULL constraints

    D Constraints enforced with triggers

15. _____ tables are used to resolve many-to-many relationships.

16. An entity in the conceptual model becomes a(n) _____ in the logical model.

17. An attribute in the logical model becomes a(n) _____ in the physical model.

18. Items in the external level of the ANSI/SPARC model become _____ in the physical model.

19. A relationship in the logical design becomes a(n) _____ in the physical design.

20. A unique identifier becomes a(n) _____ in the logical model.

Chapter 3

Data and Process Modeling

Key Skills & Concepts

- Data Model Diagramming Alternatives
- Process Models
- Unified Modeling Language (UML)
- Relating Entities and Processes

Data and process modeling are major undertakings that are part of the logical design stage of an application system development project. You have already seen the rudiments of data modeling in preceding chapters. In this chapter, we will look at various alternatives for drawing data models. Process modeling, on the other hand, is less important to a database designer, because application processes are designed by application designers and seldom directly involve the database designer. However, because the database designer must work closely with the application designer in gathering data requirements and in supplying a database design that will support the processes being designed, the database designer should at least be familiar with the basic concepts. For this reason, the second part of this chapter includes a high-level survey of process design concepts and diagramming techniques, followed by an introduction to basic Unified Modeling Language (UML) concepts. UML is an object modeling language that encompasses both data and process modeling. Finally, this chapter includes a technique for correlating entities and processes.

Data Model Diagramming Alternatives

Most data models are diagrammed using the *entity relationship diagram* (ERD). An ERD is a diagram that visually represents entities, attributes, and relationships. The chief advantage of ERDs is that they can be understood by nontechnical people while still providing great value to technical people. Done correctly, ERDs are platform independent and can even be used for nonrelational databases if desired.

ERD Formats

Peter Chen developed the original ERD format in 1976. Since then, vendors, computer scientists, and academics have developed many variations, all of them conceptually the same. You should understand the most commonly used variations because you are likely to encounter them actively used in IT organizations. Here are the elements common to all ERD formats:

- Entities are represented as rectangles or boxes.
- Relationships are represented as lines.

- Line ends (or symbols next to them) indicate the maximum cardinality of the relationship (that is, one or many).

- Symbols near the line ends (in most ERD formats) indicate the minimum cardinality of the relationship (that is, whether participation in the relationship is mandatory or optional).

- Attributes may be optionally included (the format for displaying attributes varies quite a bit).

Chen's Format

Figure 3-1 shows an invoice for Acme Industries, a fictitious manufacturing company. Using the entities represented on the invoice (Customer, Product, and Invoice), Figure 3-2 shows the ERD using Chen's format.

Here are the particulars of the Chen format:

- Relationship lines contain a diamond in which is written a word or short phrase that describes the relationship. For example, the relationship between Invoice and Product may be read as "An invoice *contains* many products." Some variations permit another word or phrase to be used in reading the relationship in the other direction, separated with a slash. If the diamond were to read "Contains/Appears on," then the relationship from Product to Invoice would be read as "A product *appears on* many invoices."

- For many-to-many relationships that require an intersection table in an RDBMS, such as the one between Invoice and Product, a rectangle is often drawn around the diamond.

- Maximum cardinality of each relationship is shown using the symbol *1* for "one" or *M* for "many."

Acme Industries
INVOICE

Customer Number: 1454837
Customer: W. Coyote
      General Delivery
      Falling Rocks, AZ 84211
      (599) 555-9345

Invoice Number: 09762185
Terms: Net 30
ShipVia: USPS

Order Date: 07/01/2009

Product No.	Description	Quantity	Unit Price	Extended Amount
SPR-2290	Super Strength Springs	2	24.00	$ 48.00
STR-67	Foot Straps, leather	2	2.50	$ 5.00
HLM-45	Deluxe Crash Helmet	1	67.88	$ 67.88
SFR-1	Rocket, solid fuel	1	128,200.40	$ 128,200.40
ELT-1	Emergency Location Transmitter	1	79.88	** FREE GIFT **

TOTAL ORDER AMOUNT: $ 128,321.28

Figure 3-1 Acme Industries invoice

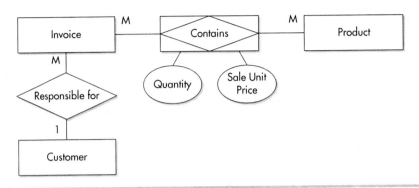

Figure 3-2 Acme Industries logical ERD format in Chen's format

- Minimum cardinality is not shown.

- Attributes, when shown, appear in ellipses (elongated circles), connected to the entity or relationship to which they belong with a line.

In practice, Chen ERDs are cumbersome for complicated data models. The diamonds take up a lot of space on the diagrams for the little added value they provide. Also, any ERD that includes many attributes becomes very difficult to read. Notwithstanding, we owe Chen a lot for his pioneering work, which laid the foundation for the techniques that followed.

The Relational Format

Over time, an ERD format known generically as the *relational format* evolved. It is available as an option in several of the better-known data modeling software tools, including PowerDesigner from Sybase, ERwin from Computer Associates, and ER/Studio from Embarcadero Technologies, and in popular general drawing tools such as Visio from Microsoft. Figure 3-3 shows the ERD from Figure 3-2 converted to the relational format. In this example, the ERD is represented at a physical level, meaning that physical table names are shown instead of logical entity names, and physical column names are shown instead of logical attribute names. Also, intersection tables are shown to resolve many-to-many relationships. As the logical data model is transformed into a physical database design, it is essential to have a physical ERD that the project team can use in developing the application system. The beginnings of the physical model are shown here to help make that point.

Here are the particulars of the relational ERD format:

- Relationship cardinality is shown with an arrowhead on the line end to signify "one" and nothing on the line end to signify "many." This will seem odd at first, but it aligns nicely with object diagrams, so this format is favored by designers and developers of object-oriented applications.

- Attributes are shown inside the rectangle that represents each entity.

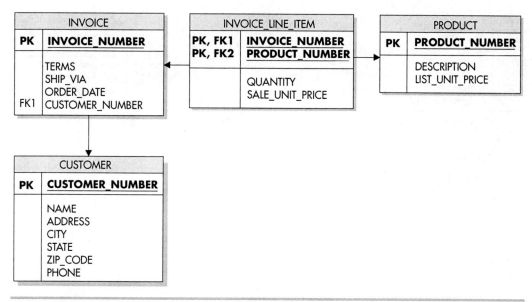

Figure 3-3   Acme Industries physical ERD, relational format

- Unique identifier attributes are shown above a horizontal line within the rectangle and are usually also shown with "**PK**" (for primary key) in bold type in the margin to the left of the attribute name.

- Attributes that are foreign keys are shown with "FK" and a number in the margin to the left of the attribute name.

The Information Engineering Format

The information engineering (IE) format was originally developed by Clive Finkelstein in Australia in the late 1970s. In the early 1980s he collaborated with James Martin to publicize it in the United States and Europe, including coauthoring the Savant Institute Report titled *Information Engineering,* published in 1981. Martin went on to be closely associated with the format and, in collaboration with Carma McClure, published a book on the subject in 1984 (*Diagramming Techniques for Analysis and Programmers,* Prentice Hall). Finkelstein published his own version in 1989 (*An Introduction to Information Engineering,* Addison-Wesley), which has some minor notation variations compared with Martin's version. Figure 3-4 shows our sample ERD converted to IE notation. You will notice that except for relationship lines, it is strikingly similar to the relational format.

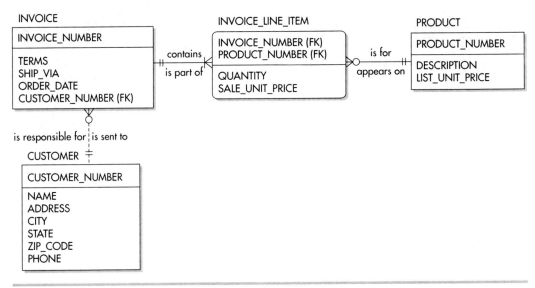

Figure 3-4   Acme Industries physical ERD, IE format

Here are some of the ways that IE notation varies from the relational format:

- **Identifying relationships**   Shown with a solid line are those for which the foreign key is part of the child entity's primary key.

- **Non-identifying relationships**   Shown with a dotted line are those for which the foreign key is a nonkey attribute in the child entity. In Figure 3-4, the relationship between PRODUCT and INVOICE_LINE_ITEM is identifying, but the one between CUSTOMER and INVOICE is non-identifying.

- **Maximum relationship cardinality**   Shown with a short perpendicular line across the relationship near its line end to signify "one" and with a "crow's foot" on the line end to signify "many." This is best understood in combination with minimum cardinality, described next.

- **Minimum relationship cardinality**   Shown with a small circle near the end of the line to signify "zero" (participation in the relationship is optional) or with a short perpendicular line across the relationship line to signify "one" (participation in the relationship is mandatory). Figure 3-4 notes a few combinations of minimum and maximum cardinality. For example:

  - **A PRODUCT**   May have zero to many associated INVOICE_LINE_ITEM occurrences (shown as a circle and a crow's foot); an INVOICE_LINE_ITEM must have one and only one associated PRODUCT (shown as two vertical bars).

● **An INVOICE**   Must have one or more associated INVOICE_LINE_ITEM occurrences (shown as a vertical bar and a crow's foot); an INVOICE_LINE_ITEM must have one and only one associated INVOICE (shown as two vertical bars).

● **Dependent entities**   Shown with the corners of the rectangle rounded, these entities have an existence dependency on one or more other entities (that is, they cannot exist without the existence of another). For example, the INVOICE_LINE_ITEM entity depends on both the PRODUCT and INVOICE entities. Therefore, you cannot delete either an invoice or a product unless you somehow deal with any related invoice line items. This is valuable information during physical database design because you must consider the options for handling situations when the application attempts to delete table rows when dependent entities exist.

The IE format is by far the most popular. Therefore, I use it for the majority of the diagrams in this book.

The IDEF1X Format

The Computer Systems Laboratory of the National Institute of Standards and Technology released the IDEF1X standard for data modeling in FIPS Publication 184, first published in December 1993. The standard covers both a method for data modeling as well as the format for the ERDs produced during the modeling effort. It is widely used and understood across the information technology industry and is the mandatory standard for many branches of the U.S. government. Thanks to its underlying standard, it has few variants. Figure 3-5 shows our sample ERD converted to the IDEF1X standard format.

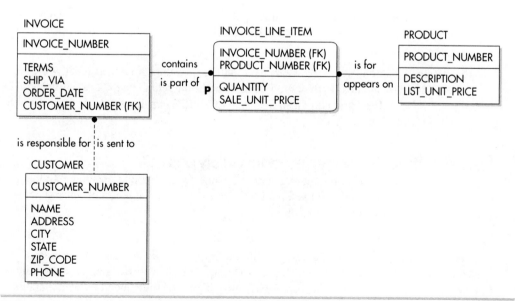

Figure 3-5   Acme Industries physical ERD, IDEF1X format

The differences between IE and IDEF1X notation are largely isolated to relationships. Unlike other formats, relationship symbols in IDEF1X are asymmetrical. Each set of symbols describes a combination of optionality and cardinality; thus, the symbols used for optionality vary depending on the cardinality of the relationship. Said another way, optionality is shown differently for the "many" and "one" sides of a relationship. Here are some key points:

- As with the IE format, a solid line indicates that the foreign key is part of the dependent entity's primary key, while a broken line indicates that the foreign key is a nonkey attribute.

- A solid circle next to an entity generally means zero, one, or more occurrences of that entity, as shown on the "many" end of the line between PRODUCT and INVOICE_LINE_ITEM. However, there are exceptions:

    - Adding the symbol *P* near the solid circle makes the relationship mandatory, signifying that the cardinality must be one or more. In Figure 3-5, the relationship from INVOICE to INVOICE_LINE_ITEM is one-to-many and mandatory, meaning that every invoice must have at least one line item.

    - Adding the symbol *1* also makes the relationship mandatory. However, this changes the cardinality of the relationship to one. Said another way, it changes the meaning of the solid circle from "may be one or more" to "must be one and only one."

- Absence of a solid circle at the end of the relationship line means that only one occurrence of the entity is involved. For example, the absence of any symbol on the end of the line next to CUSTOMER means "one and only one." It may be modified for optionality as well:

    - If no symbol appears next to the entity at that end of the line, the entity is mandatory in the relationship. Therefore an INVOICE_LINE_ITEM must be related to one and only one PRODUCT.

    - If a small diamond symbol appears next to the entity, the entity is optional. Were we to add a diamond next to the CUSTOMER end of the relationship between INVOICE and CUSTOMER, it would mean that each INVOICE *may* have zero or one related CUSTOMER occurrences.

Representing Supertypes and Subtypes

There are many variations in the representation of supertypes and subtypes in data model diagrams. In general these fall into two broad categories—those that use nested entity symbols and those that use lines with special symbols.

Using Nested Entities

Figure 3-6 shows the Customer supertype with the Corporate Customer and Individual Customer subtypes, as introduced in Chapter 1 (Figure 1-3), by using nested entity notation (rectangles within rectangles). This representation is highly recommended by data modeling experts Graeme Simsion and Len Silverston because of its simplicity and clarity. The rectangle

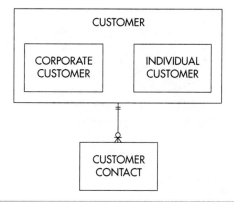

Figure 3-6   Supertype and subtypes using nested entity notation

that represents the supertype entity is simply expanded so that the rectangles representing the subtypes can be placed inside it. More layers of subtypes can be just as easily represented by expanding the subtype rectangles to place their subtypes inside. You no doubt noticed that I have chosen to use this method in most parts of this book.

Take a careful look at the Customer Contact entity and its relationship with Customer. It is important to understand that Customer Contact has a relationship with the Customer supertype, which means that the relationship is inherited by all subtypes of Customer. If the relationship line were drawn to one of the inner boxes such as Corporate Customer, then only that subtype could have related Customer Contact records.

The main advantage of this method is that there are no lines to be confused with relationship lines. The diagrams can be easily constructed in general drawing tools such as Microsoft Visio, and they are specifically supported by the Oracle Designer modeling tool. However, this diagramming technique is not supported by most other modeling tools, including ERwin from CA, PowerDesigner from Sybase, and ER/Studio from Embarcadero Technologies. Therefore, sparse support in popular modeling tools is the main disadvantage.

Using Lines and Special Symbols

Figure 3-7 shows the same supertype and subtypes from Figure 3-6 by using lines and an arc to denote subtypes. A popular alternative is to draw a smaller arc on each of the lines instead of the large one that crosses all of the subtype lines. The letter *e* next to the right end of the arc is to remind the reader that the subtypes are exclusive, meaning that any given occurrence of the supertype (any given customer, in this example) can only be one subtype (either a corporate customer or an individual customer, in this example). You may have noticed that I moved the Customer Contact entity and its relationship to Customer off to the side so it wouldn't clutter the representation of the supertype and subtypes. Keep in mind that relationships are determined by the symbols on the relationship lines rather than the position on the diagram, so this entity and relationship are the same as shown in Figure 3-6, even though the symbols were moved.

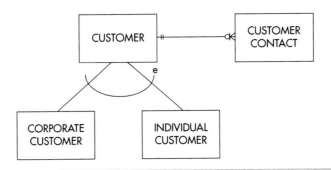

Figure 3-7 Supertype and subtypes using lines and an arc

While this notation can be found in many academic texts on data modeling and database design, support among modeling tools is quite sparse. General drawing tools can be used to draw diagrams using this notation, but the arcs can be tricky to draw so they fit correctly into the diagram. These are obvious disadvantages.

Figure 3-8 shows the same model drawn using a special symbol connected to the supertype and subtypes by lines, serving as a visual junction box for the lines that connect the supertype to the subtypes. The particular symbol shown is the one used by ERwin. PowerDesigner and ER/Studio use similar symbols.

In modeling tools that support this notation, drawing the diagram is quick and easy. Usually it is as simple as clicking on the subtype symbol on a toolbar, followed by clicking on the supertype and then one of the subtypes. However, using a general drawing tool to create diagrams using these symbols is a lot more work, and thus the nested rectangle diagrams are likely the easiest to draw using general drawing tools.

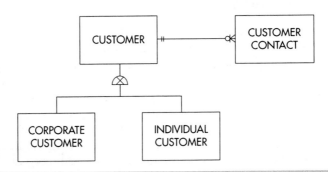

Figure 3-8 Supertype and subtypes using lines and a special symbol

Guidelines for Drawing ERDs

Here are some general guidelines to follow when constructing ERDs:

- Do not try to relate every entity to every other entity. Entities should be related only when the *entire* primary key in one entity appears as a foreign key in another.

- Except for subtypes, avoid relationships involving more than two entities. Although drawing fewer lines might seem simpler, it is far too easy to misinterpret relationships drawn from one parent entity to multiple child entities by using a single line.

- Be consistent with entity and attribute names. Develop a naming convention and stick with it.

- Use abbreviations in names only when absolutely necessary, and in those cases, use a standard list of abbreviations.

- Name primary keys and foreign keys consistently. Most experts prefer that the foreign key have exactly the same name as the primary key.

- When relationships are named, strive for action words, avoiding nondescriptive terms such as "has," "belongs to," "is associated with," and so on.

Process Models

As mentioned, process design is seldom the responsibility of the database designer or DBA, but understanding the basics helps the DBA communicate with the process designers and ensure that the database design supports the process design. Therefore, this section presents a brief survey of common process model diagram techniques. If you want more detail about these or other process model techniques, find a good book on systems analysis and design.

Throughout this section, the Acme Industries order-fulfillment process, a very simple business process, is used as an example. This process has the following steps:

1. Find all unshipped orders in the database.

2. For each order, do the following:

   - Check for available inventory. If sufficient inventory for the order is not available, skip to the next order.

   - Check the customer's credit to make sure they are not over their credit limit and do not have some other credit problem, such as overdue payments. This would typically occur at the time the order is entered, but it needs to occur again here because a customer's credit status with Acme Industries can change at any time. If a credit problem is found, skip to the next order.

   - Generate the documents required to pack and ship the order (packing slip, shipping labels, and so on) and route them to the shipping department.

   - When the shipping department has finished with the order, create the invoice for the order and bill the customer accordingly.

Obviously, this process could be a lot more complicated in a large company, but here it has been reduced to the basics so that it is easier to use to illustrate process models.

The Flowchart

The flowchart (or structure chart) is probably the oldest form of computer systems documentation. Flowcharts are often considered outmoded, but they have much to offer in certain circumstances and are still widely used. Figure 3-9 shows the flowchart for our sample order-fulfillment process.

Here are the basic components of the flowchart:

● Process steps are shown with rectangles.

● Decision points are shown with diamonds. At each decision point, the logic branches are based on the outcome of the decision. For example, a decision might be "Is today Friday?" with a "Yes" outcome going in one direction and a "No" outcome going in another.

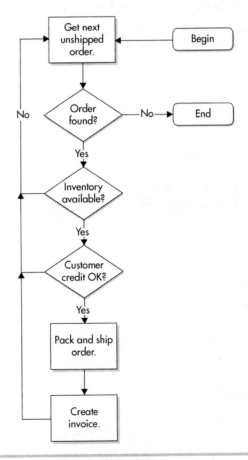

Figure 3-9 Flowchart of Acme Industries order-fulfillment process

- Lines with arrows show the flow of control through the diagram. When one process completes, it hands over control to the next process or decision point.

- Start and end points are shown with either ellipses or rounded rectangles. Flowcharts can be used to show perpetual processes that have no start and no end, but more often they are used to show finite processes with specific beginning and ending points.

- Connector symbols that look like home plates on a baseball diamond (not shown in Figure 3-9) can be used to connect lines to processes or decision points, on the same or another page. Usually these are given a reference letter with a control flow line assumed between any two connectors that have the same reference letter.

Figure 3-9 shows a very straightforward loop process flow. It begins with a process step that gets the next unshipped order from the database. A decision is added after it to stop the loop (end the flow) if we don't find an unshipped order. If we do find the order, the process continues with decision points that check for available inventory and acceptable customer credit; a "No" outcome goes back to the top of the loop (the "Get next unshipped order" process), which essentially skips the order and moves on to find the next one. If we get a "Yes" outcome from all the decision points, the "Pack and ship order" process is invoked next, followed by "Create invoice." After the "Create invoice" process completes, control goes back to "Get next unshipped order," at the top of the loop. The loop continues until no more unshipped orders are found.

Flowcharts have the following strengths:

- Procedural language programmers find them naturally easy to learn and use. A *procedural language* is a programming language by which the programmer must describe the process steps required to do something, as opposed to a *nonprocedural language,* such as SQL, with which the programmer merely describes the desired results. The most commonly used procedural language today is probably C and its variants (C++, C#, and so on), but others, such as FORTRAN and COBOL, still see some use. Also, specialized procedural languages for relational databases, including PL/SQL for Oracle and Transact SQL for Sybase and Microsoft SQL Server, are heavily used.

- Flowcharts are applicable to procedures outside of a programming context. For example, flowcharts are often used to walk repair technicians through troubleshooting procedures for the equipment they service.

- Flowcharts are useful for spotting reusable (common) components. The designer can easily find any process that appears multiple times in the flowcharts for a particular application system.

- Flowcharts may be easily modified and can evolve as requirements change.

On the other hand, flowcharts present these weaknesses:

- They are not applicable to nonprocedural or object-oriented languages.

- They cannot easily model some situations, such as *recursive* processes (processes that invoke themselves).

The Function Hierarchy Diagram

The *function hierarchy diagram,* as the name suggests, shows all the functions of a particular application system or business process, organized into a hierarchical tree. Figure 3-10 shows this type of process model diagram from our sample order-fulfillment process.

Because the function hierarchy for a single process makes little sense out of context, two other processes have been added to the hierarchy: Order Entry and History Management. To be effective, a function hierarchy must contain *all* the processes required to carry out the function it describes. Figure 3-10 attempts to show all the processes required for the Order Management function at Acme Industries. Order Entry is intended to cover all the process steps involved in a customer placing an order and having it recorded in Acme's database. History Management is intended to cover all the steps required to archive and purge old (historical) orders and any required reporting on order history. Both of these processes need to be expanded by adding process steps below them (as was done with Order Fulfillment) to make this a complete diagram. Under Order Fulfillment, the four main process steps involved in fulfilling orders have been added.

The strengths of function hierarchy diagrams are as follows:

- They are quick and easy to learn and use.

- They can quickly document the bulk of the function (they get to 80 percent of the processes quickly).

- They provide a good overview at high and medium levels of detail.

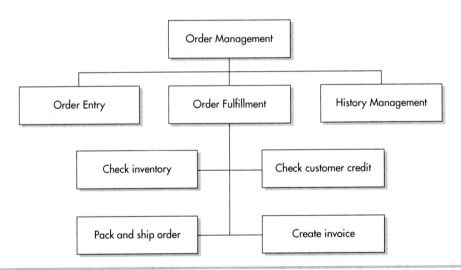

Figure 3-10   Function hierarchy of the Acme order-fulfillment process

And here are the weaknesses of function hierarchy diagrams:

- Checking quality is difficult and subjective.

- They cannot handle complex interactions between functions.

- They do not clearly show the sequence of process steps or dependencies between steps.

- They are not an effective presentation tool for large hierarchies or at very detailed levels.

The Swim Lane Diagram

The *swim lane diagram* gets its name from the vertical lanes in the diagram, which resemble the lanes in a swimming pool. Each lane represents an organizational unit such as a department, with ellipse-enclosed process steps placed in the lane for the unit that is responsible for the step. Lines with arrows show the sequence or the control flow of the process steps. Figure 3-11 shows the swim lane diagram for our sample order-fulfillment process.

Strengths of the swim lane diagram include

- It has the unmatched ability to show who does what in the organization.

- It's excellent for identifying inefficiencies in existing processes and lends itself well to business process re-engineering efforts.

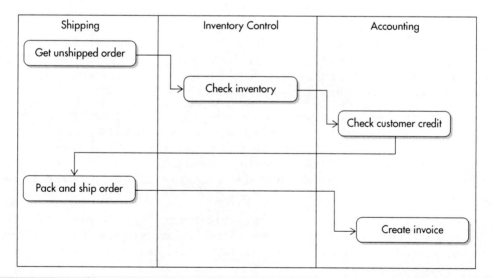

Figure 3-11 Swim lane diagram for the Acme Industries order-fulfillment process

Its weaknesses include

- It does not represent complicated processes (those with many steps or with complex step dependencies) well.

- It does not show error and exception handling.

The Data Flow Diagram

The *data flow diagram* (DFD) is the most data-centric of all the process diagrams. Instead of showing a control flow through a series of process steps, it focuses on the data that flows through the process steps. By combining diagrams hierarchically, the DFD combines the best of the flowchart and the function diagram. DFDs became immensely popular in the late 1970s and early 1980s, largely due to the work of Chris Gane and Trish Sarson. Each process on a DFD can be broken down using another complete page until the desired level of detail is reached. Figure 3-12 shows one page of the DFD for the Acme Industries order-fulfillment process.

The components of a DFD are simple:

- Processes are represented with rounded rectangles. Processes are typically numbered hierarchically. The first page of a DFD might have processes numbered 1, 2, 3, and 4. The next page might break down process number 1 and would have processes numbered 1.1, 1.2, and so forth. If process 1.2 were broken down on yet another page, the processes on that page would be numbered 1.2.1, 1.2.2, and so forth.

- Data stores are represented with an open-ended rectangle. A *data store* is a generic representation of data that is made persistent through being stored somewhere, such as a file, database, or even a written document. The term was chosen so that no particular type of storage is implied. Because we already have an ERD for our example, we should closely align the data stores with the entities we have already identified.

- Sources and destinations of data ("external entities" in relational terminology) are shown using squares. Figure 3-12 shows the Customer as the destination of the invoice data flow (in addition to a local data store that will hold the invoice data). Try not to confuse data flows with material flows. Yes, the invoice is printed and mailed to the customer, but the data flow is attempting to show that the *data* is sent to the customer with no regard for the medium used to send it.

- Flows of data are shown using lines with arrowheads indicating the direction of flow. Above each flow, words are used to describe the content of the data being sent. Bidirectional flows are permissible, but are usually shown as separate flows because the data is seldom exactly the same in both directions.

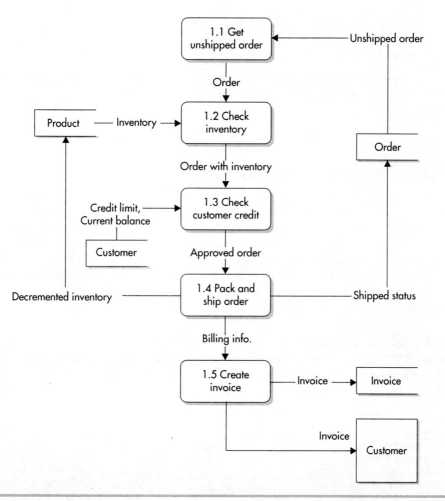

Figure 3-12 Data flow diagram page for the Acme Industries order-fulfillment process

The strengths of the data flow diagram are as follows:

- It easily shows the overall structure of the system without sacrificing detail (details are shown on subsequent pages that expand on the higher-level processes).

- It's good for top-down design work.

- It's good for presentation of systems designs to management and business users.

Here are the weaknesses of the data flow diagram:

- It's time-consuming and labor-intensive to develop for complex systems.

- Top-down design has proved to be ineffective for situations in which requirements are sketchy and continuously evolving during the life of the project.

- It's poor at showing complex logic, but the lowest-level diagrams can easily be supplemented with other documents, such as narratives or decision tables.

Unified Modeling Language (UML)

With the rising popularity of object programming languages, the *Unified Modeling Language (UML)* has also become more popular. UML is a standardized visual specification language for object modeling that includes a graphical notation used to create an abstract model of a system, which is known as a UML model. The Rational Unified Process (RUP), which is an iterative software development process framework originally developed by the Rational Software Corporation (which became a division of IBM in 2003), uses UML exclusively. UML has 13 types of diagrams that can be used to model the behavior and structure of the system. However, the one of interest to data modelers is the class diagram.

UML Class Diagrams

Figure 3-13 shows the Acme Industries invoice model converted to a UML class diagram.

While the differences in notation are strikingly obvious, an individual skilled in reading ER diagrams can easily adapt. I have used so-called "camelcase" names in the diagram,

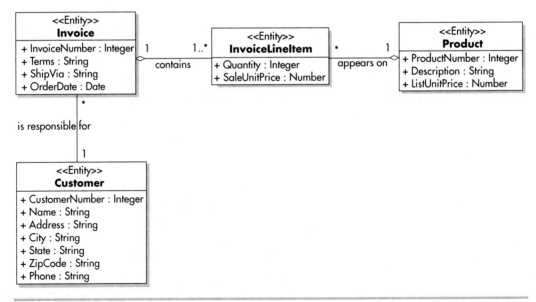

Figure 3-13 UML class diagram for Acme Industries

meaning names with the first letter of each word capitalized and no delimiters between words, because nearly all UML modelers do so. Here are some key points regarding modeling entities using UML class diagrams:

- Each entity is shown as an object class in a rectangle. The symbol <<Entity>> is included with the class name to denote the type of class.

- Unique identifiers (primary keys) are not shown in class diagrams; they are specified elsewhere within the UML model.

- Foreign keys are not shown because they are not used in object-oriented systems.

- Attributes are shown with a name and a type (separated with a colon). The type is very much like a relational data type. Attributes in entities are preceded by the symbol +, which means they are public (visible throughout the entire model).

- Relationships are shown with lines.

- Cardinality and optionality are shown with a combined symbol near the end of the line. Available symbols include those shown in the following table:

Symbol	Meaning
1	One and only one.
*	Zero, one, or more.
1..*	One or more.
x..y	Between x and y occurrences. Also, x can be 0 or any positive integer. y can be any positive integer or * to denote "or more." y must be greater than x (if y and x are the same, then y is simply omitted).

- The diamond symbol on the end of a relationship line, as shown in Figure 3-13 on the "one" end of the two relationships connected to InvoiceLineItem, denotes what UML calls an aggregation. An *aggregation* is a dependency between two entity types that is required for the existence of the dependent entity. In this case, a line item cannot exist without both the product and the invoice. If the dependency is always a single entity, the diamond is shown as a solid diamond instead of a hollow one.

- Generalization and specialization (supertypes and subtypes) are denoted using a line between the two entities with a hollow arrow pointing toward the general class (the supertype).

Ask the Expert

Q: In the discussion of UML in the chapter, you mentioned that generalization is shown using lines and arrows. How would you convert the supertype and subtypes in Figures 3-6 through 3-8 to UML notation?

A: First, you remove the existing symbols (the lines, type symbol, and discriminator attribute name). Then you draw a line between each subtype and its supertype, placing a hollow arrowhead on the supertype end of the line, pointing toward the supertype entity. Figure 3-14 shows the same model as Figures 3-6 through 3-8, but in UML notation.

Other UML Diagrams

As mentioned, UML 2.x offers 13 different diagrams, 6 of which are *structure diagrams* that emphasize what things must be in the system being modeled (including the class diagram previously presented), and 7 of which are *behavior diagrams* that emphasize what must happen in the system being modeled. There's not enough space in this book to cover them all,

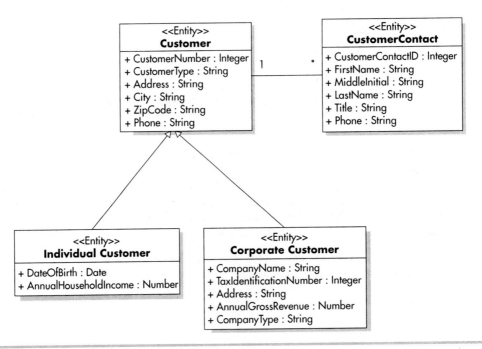

Figure 3-14 Customer subtypes converted to UML

but you'll find lots of information on the Internet and in books on the subject. The following table provides a summary description of each UML diagram:

Type	Name	Description
Structure	Class diagram	Shows a collection of static model elements such as classes and types, their contents, and their relationships
Structure	Component diagram	Depicts the components that make up an application, system, or enterprise
Structure	Composite Structure diagram	Depicts that internal structure of a classifier (such as a class, component, or use case), including the classifier's interaction points to other parts of the system (added in UML 2.x)
Structure	Deployment diagram	Shows the execution architecture of systems, including nodes, hardware/software environments, and the middleware that connects them
Structure	Object diagram	Depicts objects and their relationships at a point in time
Structure	Package diagram	Shows how model elements are assembled into packages as well as the dependencies between packages
Behavior	Activity diagram	Depicts high-level business processes, including data flow
Behavior	State Machine diagram	Describes the states an object or interaction may be in, and the transitions between states
Behavior	Use Case diagram	Shows actors, use cases, and their interactions
Behavior	Communication diagram	Shows instances of classes, their interrelationships, and the message flow between them
Behavior	Interaction Overview diagram	A variant of an activity diagram that depicts an overview of the control flow within a system or business process (added in UML 2.x)
Behavior	Sequence diagram	Depicts the time ordering of messages between classifiers, essentially showing the sequential logic of the system
Behavior	Timing diagram	Depicts the change in state or condition of a classifier instance or role over time (added in UML 2.x)

Note that some references show a subtype of Interaction diagram under Behavior diagram, containing the Sequence, Interaction Overview, Communication, and Timing diagrams.

Relating Entities and Processes

Once the database designer has completed logical database design and an ERD for the proposed database and, in parallel, the process designers have completed their process model, how can we have any confidence that the two will be able to work together in solving the business problem the new project is supposed to address? Part of the answer lies in a charting technique intended to show how the entities and processes interact, known as the CRUD matrix.

Fortunately, CRUD is not slang for a lousy design, but rather is an acronym formed from the first letters for the words "Create," "Read," "Update," and "Delete," which are the letters used in the body of the diagram. The concept of the CRUD matrix is very simple:

- One axis of the matrix represents the major processes of the application system.
- The other axis represents the major entities used by the application system.
- In each cell of the matrix, the appropriate combination of letters is written:
  - C, if the process creates new occurrences of the entity
  - R, if the process reads information about the entity from a data source
  - U, if the process updates one or more attributes for the entity
  - D, if the process deletes occurrences of the entity

Here is a sample CRUD matrix for the order management function at Acme Industries, following the major processes shown in the function hierarchy diagram (refer to Figure 3-10). To be effective, only high-level processes and supertype entities should be shown in the matrix. Too much detail clouds the effect of the diagram.

	ENTITY: Product	Order	Customer	Invoice
PROCESS: Order Entry	R	CRU	RU	
Order Fulfillment	RU	RU	R	C
History Management		RD	R	

The CRUD matrix is valuable for verifying the consistency of the process and data (entity) designs. At a glance, you can find the following potential problems:

- Entities that have no Create process
- Entities that have no Delete process
- Entities that are never updated
- Entities that are never read
- Processes that delete or update entities without reading them
- Processes that only read (no Create, Delete, or Update actions)

Our example has multiple problems, which only proves that our process design is incomplete (that is, we are probably missing some key processes for the application system). At the conclusion of the logical design phase of a project, the CRUD matrix is an excellent vehicle for a final review of the work completed.

Try This 3-1 Drawing a Conceptual Model with Nested Subtypes

In this Try This exercise, you will draw a new conceptual model for a shipping and logistics company that owns various types of motor vehicles and aircraft. The company wants to create a single database to track all of its vehicles, and thus the data model must include nested subtypes (subtypes of subtypes).

Step by Step

1. Here is a list of the kinds of vehicles owned by the company, broken down into subtypes that were agreed upon in a requirements-gathering session:

   Vehicle
       Motor Vehicle
           Automobile
           Truck
           Motorcycle
       Aircraft
           Fixed Wing Airplane
           Rotary Wing Aircraft

2. Draw a conceptual data model using nested rectangles notation to show all the types and subtypes listed in step 1. It's usually easier to draw the lowest level of subtypes first so you can avoid resizing boxes to fit more subtypes into them. In this case, the lowest level consists of Automobile, Truck, Motorcycle, Fixed Wing Airplane, and Rotary Wing Aircraft.

3. Each vehicle has a single maintenance schedule, but a given maintenance schedule can be used by multiple vehicles (usually ones of the same type, make, and model). Draw an entity named Maintenance Schedule and the appropriate one-to-many relationship between the schedule and the Vehicle supertype.

4. All aircraft must undergo periodic airworthiness inspections as specified by various regulatory agencies. A given inspection schedule can be used by multiple aircraft, but each aircraft has only one such schedule. Draw an entity named Inspection Schedule and the appropriate one-to-many relationship between the schedule and the Aircraft subtype.

(continued)

Try This Summary

In this Try This exercise, you drew a new conceptual model to represent a supertype, subtypes, and nested subtypes along with two other entities and their relationships. My solution appears in Appendix B. You will create the logical model for this same vehicle database in a Try This exercise later in the book. In the meantime, you will gain a better understanding of supertypes and subtypes if you develop an idea of the attributes that you might assign to each. For example, motor vehicles have vehicle identification numbers (VINs), and maintenance is triggered by the odometer mileage reading and the number of months of operation. On the other hand, aircraft have registration numbers (tail numbers), and maintenance is triggered by the number of engine hours and in many cases the number of takeoffs and landings. Understanding that subtypes exist because they have different relationships and/or attributes than other subtypes is essential to understanding data modeling.

Chapter 3 Self Test

Choose the correct responses to each of the multiple-choice and fill-in-the-blank questions. Note that there may be more than one correct response to each question.

1. Why is it important for a database designer to understand process modeling?

   A Process design is a primary responsibility of the DBA

   B The process model must be completed before the data model

   C The data model must be completed before the process model

   D The database designer must work closely with the process designer

   E The database design must support the intended process model

2. The IDEF1X ERD format

   A Was first released in 1983

   B Follows a standard developed by the National Institute of Standards and Technology

   C Has many variants

   D Has been adopted as a standard by many U.S. government agencies

   E Covers both data and process models

3. The IDEF1X ERD format shows

   A Identifying relationships with a solid line

   B Minimal cardinality using a combination of small circles and vertical lines shown on the relationship line

    C Maximum cardinality using a combination of small vertical lines and crow's feet drawn on the relationship line

    D Dependent entities with squared corners on the rectangle

    E Independent entities with rounded corners on the rectangle

4. A subtype

    A Is a subset of the supertype

    B Has a one-to-many relationship with the supertype

    C Has a conditional one-to-one relationship with the supertype

    D Shows various states of the supertype

    E Is a superset of the supertype

5. Examples of possible subtypes for an Order entity supertype include

    A Order line items

    B Shipped order, unshipped order, invoiced order

    C Office supplies order, professional services order

    D Approved order, pending order, canceled order

    E Auto parts order, aircraft parts order, truck parts order

6. In IE notation, subtypes

    A May be shown with a type discriminator attribute name

    B May be connected to the supertype via a symbol composed of a circle with a line under it

    C Have the primary key of the subtype shown as a foreign key in the supertype

    D Usually have the same primary key as the supertype

    E May be shown using a crow's foot

7. The strengths of flowcharts are

    A They are natural and easy to use for procedural language programmers

    B They are useful for spotting reusable components

    C They are specific to application programming only

    D They are equally useful for nonprocedural and object-oriented languages

    E They can be easily modified as requirements change

8. The basic components of a function hierarchy diagram are

    A Ellipses to show attributes

    B Rectangles to show process functions

    C Lines connecting the processes in order of execution

    D A hierarchy to show which functions are subordinate to others

    E Diamonds to show decision points

9. The strengths of the function hierarchy diagram are

    A Checking quality is easy and straightforward

    B Complex interactions between functions are easily modeled

    C It is quick and easy to learn and use

    D It clearly shows the sequence of process steps

    E It provides a good overview at high and medium levels of detail

10. The basic components of a swim lane diagram are

    A Lines with arrows to show the sequence of process steps

    B Diamonds to show decision points

    C Vertical lanes to show the organization units that carry out process steps

    D Ellipses to show process steps

    E Open-ended rectangles to show data stores

11. The data flow diagram (DFD)

    A Is the most data-centric of all process models

    B Was first developed in the 1980s

    C Combines diagram pages together hierarchically

    D Was first developed by E. F. Codd

    E Combines the best of the flowchart and the function diagram

12. The strengths of the DFD are

    A It's good for top-down design work

    B It's quick and easy to develop, even for complex systems

    C It shows overall structure without sacrificing detail

    D It shows complex logic easily

    E It's great for presentation to management

13. The components of the CRUD matrix are

    A Ellipses to show attributes

    B Major processes shown on one axis

    C Major entities shown on the other axis

    D Reference numbers to show the hierarchy of processes

    E Letters to show the operations that processes carry out on entities

14. The CRUD matrix helps find the following problems:

    A Entities that are never read

    B Processes that are never deleted

    C Processes that only read

    D Entities that are never updated

    E Processes that have no create entity

15. Peter Chen's ERD format represents "many" with _____.

16. The diamond in Chen's ERD format represents a(n) _____.

17. The relational ERD format represents "many" with _____.

18. When subtypes are being considered in a database design, a trade-off exists between _____ and _____.

19. In a flowchart, process steps are shown as _____, and decision points are shown as _____.

20. In a DFD, data stores are shown as _____, and processes are shown as _____.

Chapter 4

Organizing Database Project Work

Key Skills & Concepts

- The Traditional Life Cycle

- Requirements Gathering

- Nontraditional Life Cycles

- The Project Triangle

- Project Database Management Tasks

Data modeling is usually conducted relatively early in a systems development project. This is necessary because the physical database must be available to application developers when they are ready to begin testing the application code they write, which means physical data modeling has to be complete when the application design is complete and construction of the application begins. However, you'll find it useful to understand the framework in which the entire project takes place. The *life cycle* of a database (or computer system) encompasses all the events that occur from the time you first recognize the need for a database, through its development and deployment, and finally ending with the day the database is retired from service.

Most businesses that develop computer systems follow a formal process that ensures that development runs smoothly, that it is cost-effective, and that the outcome is a complete computer system that meets expectations. However, some people strongly feel that formal processes are a waste of time and effort, and that a conceptual data model should be all that is needed in terms of formal requirements for the database to be built. In any case, databases are never designed and implemented in a vacuum—other components of the complete system are always developed along with the database, such as the user interface, application programs, web pages, and reports. All the work to be accomplished over the long term is typically divided into *projects,* with each project having its own finite list of goals (sometimes called *deliverables*), an expected timeframe for completion, and a project manager or leader who will be held accountable for delivery of the project. To understand the database life cycle, you must also understand the life cycle of the entire systems-development effort and the way projects are organized and managed. This chapter takes a look at both traditional and nontraditional systems-development processes, with an emphasis on requirements gathering.

Not all databases are built by businesses using formal projects and funding. However, the disciplines outlined in this chapter can assist you in thinking through your database project and asking the tough questions before you embark on an extended effort.

The Traditional Life Cycle

The traditional method for developing computer systems follows a process called the *system development life cycle* (SDLC), which divides the work into the phases shown in Figure 4-1. There are perhaps as many variations of the SDLC as there are authors, project management

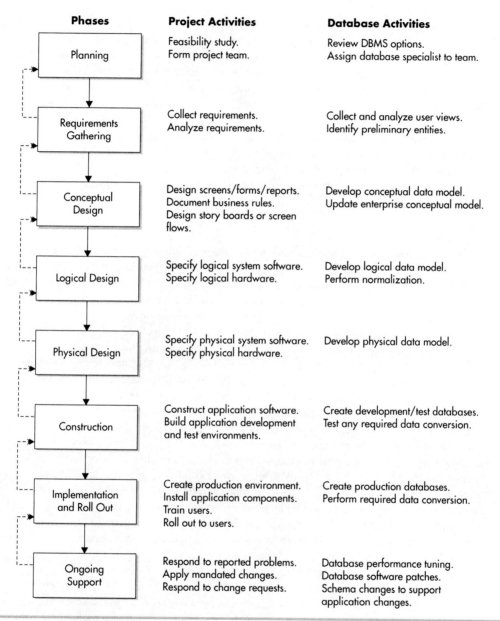

Phases	Project Activities	Database Activities
Planning	Feasibility study. Form project team.	Review DBMS options. Assign database specialist to team.
Requirements Gathering	Collect requirements. Analyze requirements.	Collect and analyze user views. Identify preliminary entities.
Conceptual Design	Design screens/forms/reports. Document business rules. Design story boards or screen flows.	Develop conceptual data model. Update enterprise conceptual model.
Logical Design	Specify logical system software. Specify logical hardware.	Develop logical data model. Perform normalization.
Physical Design	Specify physical system software. Specify physical hardware.	Develop physical data model.
Construction	Construct application software. Build application development and test environments.	Create development/test databases. Test any required data conversion.
Implementation and Roll Out	Create production environment. Install application components. Train users. Roll out to users.	Create production databases. Perform required data conversion.
Ongoing Support	Respond to reported problems. Apply mandated changes. Respond to change requests.	Database performance tuning. Database software patches. Schema changes to support application changes.

Figure 4-1 Traditional system development life cycle (SDLC)

software vendors, and companies that have elected to create their own methodologies. However, they all have the basic components, and in that sense, are all cut from the same cloth. I could argue the merits of one variation versus another, but that would merely confuse matters when all you need is a basic overview. A good textbook on systems analysis can provide greater detail should you need it. Figure 4-1 shows the traditional SDLC steps in the left column, the basic project activities in the middle column, and the database steps that support the project activities in the right column. Each step is explored further in the sections that follow. Note that the process is not always unidirectional—at times, missing or incomplete information is discovered and requires that you go back one phase and adjust the work done there. The dotted lines pointing back to prior phases in Figure 4-1 serve as reminders that a certain amount of rework is normal and expected during a project following the SDLC methodology.

Planning

During the planning phase, the organization must reach a high-level understanding of where they are, where they want to be, and a reasonable approach or plan for getting from one place to the other. Planning often occurs over a longer period than any single project, and the overall information systems plan for the organization forms the basis from which projects should be launched to achieve the overall objectives. For example, a long-range objective in the plan might be "Increase profits by 15 percent." In support of that objective, a project to develop an application system and database to track customer profitability might be proposed.

Once a particular project is proposed, a *feasibility study* is usually launched to determine whether the project can be reasonably expected to achieve (or help achieve) the objective and whether preliminary estimates of time, staff, and materials required for the project fit within the required timeframe and available budget. Often a return on investment (ROI) or similar calculation is used to measure the expected value of the proposed project to the organization. If the feasibility study meets management approval, the project is placed on the overall schedule for the organization, and the project team is formed. The composition of the project team will change over the life of the project, with people added and released as particular skill and staffing levels are needed. The one consistent member of the project team will be the *project manager* (or project leader), who is responsible for the overall management and execution of the project.

Many organizations assign a *database specialist* (database administrator or data modeler) to projects at their inception, as shown in Figure 4-1. In a *data-driven* approach, where the emphasis is on studying the data in order to discover the processing that must take place to transform the data as required by the project, early assignment of someone skilled at analyzing the data is essential. In a *process-driven* approach, where the emphasis is on studying the processes required to discover what the data should be, a database specialist is less essential during the earliest phases of the project. Industry experience suggests that the very best results are obtained by applying *both* a process-driven and a data-driven approach. However, there is seldom time and staff to do so, so the next-best results for a project involving databases come from the data-driven approach. Processes still need to be designed, but if we study the data first, the required processes become apparent. For example, in designing our customer profitability system, if we have customer sales data and know that customers who place fewer, larger orders are more profitable, then we can conclude that we need a process to rank customers by order volume and size. On the other hand, if all we know is that we need a process that ranks customers, it may take considerably more work to arrive at the criteria we should use to rank them.

The database activities in this phase involve reviewing DBMS options and determining whether the technologies currently in use meet the overall needs of the project. Most organizations settle on one, or perhaps two, standard DBMS products that they use for all projects. At this point, the goals of the project should be compared with the current technology to ensure that the project can be reasonably expected to be successful using that technology. If a newer version of the DBMS is required, or if a completely different DBMS is required, the planning phase is the time to find out, so the acquisition and installation of the DBMS can be started.

Requirements Gathering

Complete and accurate requirements are of the utmost importance to a successful database project. Research clearly shows that poor requirements are a leading cause of project failures. My experience is that the more time you spend in the earlier phases of a project (within reason), the higher the chances that the project will be successful.

During the requirements-gathering phase, the project team must gather and document a high-level, yet precise, description of what the project is to accomplish. The focus must be on *what* rather than *how*; the how is developed during the subsequent design phases. It is important for the requirements to include as much as can be known about the existing and expected business processes, business rules, and entities. The more work that is done in the early stages of a project, the more smoothly the subsequent stages will proceed. On the other hand, without some tolerance for the unknown (that is, those gray areas that have no solid answers), *analysis paralysis* can occur, wherein the entire project stalls while analysts spin their wheels looking for answers and clarifications that are not forthcoming.

From a database design perspective, the items of most interest during requirements gathering are user views. A *user view* is the method employed for presenting a set of data to the database user in a manner tailored to the needs of that person or application. At this phase of development, user views take the form of existing or proposed reports, forms, screens, web pages, and the like.

Many techniques can be used in gathering requirements. The more commonly used techniques are compared and contrasted here: conducting interviews, conducting surveys, observing business operations, and reviewing documentation. No particular technique is clearly superior to another, and it is best to find a blend of techniques that works well for the particular organization rather than rely on one over the others. For example, whether it is better to conduct a survey and follow up with interviews with key people, or to start with interviews and use the interview findings to formulate a survey, is often a question of what works best given the organization's culture and operating methods. With each technique detailed in the following subsections, some advantages and disadvantages are listed to assist in decision making.

Conducting Interviews

Interviewing key individuals who have information about what the project is expected to accomplish is a popular approach. One of the common errors, however, is to interview only management. While you clearly need management's input, perspective, and approval, if you do not include those who are actually going to use the new application(s) and database(s), the project may end up delivering something that is not practical, because management may not fully understand all the details of the requirements necessary to run the business of the organization. In particular, you need to start a dialogue with one or more *subject matter experts* (SMEs)—professionals who have expertise in the field of the application but who usually do not have technical computer system knowledge. However, you should also make an effort to include individuals who may be offended if you leave them out—they will be far more supportive of your project if you include them, even if you don't believe they have new information to offer.

The advantages of requirements gathering using interviews include the following:

- The interviewer can get answers to questions that were not asked. Side topics often come up that provide additional useful information.

- The interviewer can learn a lot from the body language of the interviewee. It is far easier to detect uncertainty and attempts at deception in person rather than in written responses to questions.

The disadvantages include the following:

- Interviews take considerably more time than other methods.

- Poorly skilled interviewers can "telegraph" the answers they are expecting by the way they ask the questions or by their reactions to the answers received.

Be aware that data models are not a good communication medium for most business users. Therefore, data models should not be used in interviews. However, you may find other types of diagrams such as UML Use Cases, UML Activity Diagrams, data flow diagrams, flowcharts, and function hierarchies useful for illustrating points and documenting your understanding during the interview, particularly in a group interview situation.

Conducting Surveys

Another popular approach is to write a survey seeking responses to key questions regarding the requirements for a project. The survey is sent to all the decision makers and potential users of the application(s) and database(s) the project is expected to deliver, and responses are analyzed for items to be included in the requirements.

The advantages of requirements gathering using surveys include the following:

- A lot of ground can be covered in a short time. Once the survey is written, it takes little additional effort to distribute it to a wider audience if necessary.

- Questions are presented in the same manner to every participant.

The disadvantages include the following:

- Surveys typically have very poor response rates. Consider yourself fortunate if 10 percent respond without having to be prodded or threatened with consequences.

- Unbiased survey questions are much more difficult to compose than you might imagine.

- The project team does not get the benefit of the nonverbal clues that an interview provides.

Observing Business Operations

Observing the business operation and the people who will be using the new application(s) and database(s) is another popular technique for gathering requirements.

The advantages of requirements gathering using observation include the following:

- Assuming you watch in an unobtrusive manner, you get to see people following normal processes in everyday use. Note that these may not be the processes that management believes are being followed, or even those in existing documentation. Instead, you may observe adaptations that were made so that the processes actually work or so they are more efficient.

- You may observe events that people would not think (or dare) to mention in response to questionnaires or interview questions.

- You may observe local variations in the interpretation of policies, the use of codes, terminology, or the use of particular data fields.

The disadvantages include the following:

- If the people know they are being watched, their behaviors change, and you may not get an accurate picture of their business processes. This is often termed the *Hawthorne effect* after a phenomenon first noticed in the Hawthorne Plant of Western Electric, where production improved not because of improvements in working conditions but rather because management demonstrated interest in such improvements by sending observers to the plant.

- Unless enormous periods are dedicated to observation, you may never see the exceptions that subvert existing business processes. To bend an old analogy, you may end up paving the cow path while cows are wandering on the highway on the other side of the pasture due to a hole in the fence.

- Travel to various business locations can add considerably to project expense.

Reviewing Documentation

This technique involves locating and reviewing all available documents for the existing business units and processes that will be affected by the new program(s) and database(s).

The advantages of requirements gathering using document review include the following:

- Document review is typically less time-consuming than any of the other methods.
- Documents often provide an overview of the system that is better thought out compared with the introductory information you receive in an interview.
- Pictures and diagrams really are worth a thousand words each.
- You can quickly assemble a list of current system capabilities to ensure that these features and functions are included in the new system where applicable.

The disadvantages are the following:

- The documents may not reflect actual practices. Documents often deal with what *should* happen rather than what *really* happens.
- Documentation is often out of date.

Conceptual Design

The conceptual design phase involves designing the externals of the application(s) and database(s). In fact, many methodologies use the term *external design* for this project phase. The layout of reports, screens, forms, web pages, and other data entry and presentation vehicles are finalized during this phase. In addition, the flow of the external application is documented in the form of a flowchart, storyboard, or screen flow diagram. This helps the project team understand the logical flow of the system. Process diagramming techniques are presented in Chapter 3.

During this phase, the database specialist (DBA or data modeler) assigned to the project develops the conceptual model for the project and, if applicable, updates the enterprise conceptual data model, which is usually maintained in the form of an entity relationship diagram (ERD). New or changed entities discovered are added to the ERD, and any additional or changed business rules are also noted. The user views, entities, and business rules are essential for the successful logical database design that follows in the next phase. Conceptual data modeling, which was introduced in Chapter 1, is covered in detail in Chapter 5.

In practice, it's not uncommon during the requirements-gathering phase for designers to begin sketching out ideas as a way of documenting their understanding of the requirements. Therefore, the conceptual data model is often started during the requirements-gathering phase. Also, some organizations and methodologies combine the requirements-gathering and conceptual design phases. This has proven to be a viable alternative provided that the rigor of gathering requirements isn't lost in the rush to complete the design and move on. However, creating a conceptual model based on a formally written requirements document has the following advantages:

- Written requirements can include a reference to their source, making them traceable.
- The combination of the requirements document and a conceptual data model is effective for requirements that cannot be adequately expressed using only a conceptual data model. For example, if the conceptual model does not include attributes, business rules involving how an attribute relates to other attributes cannot be easily expressed in the conceptual model.

- It is easier to develop and present alternative designs using conceptual models when there is a requirements document to show how each alternative model meets the stated requirements.

Logical Design

During logical design, the bulk of the technical design of the application(s) and database(s) included in the project is carried out. Many methodologies call this phase *internal design,* because it involves the design of the internals of the project that the business users will never see.

The work to be accomplished by the application(s) is segmented into *modules* (individual units of application programming that will be written and tested together), and a detailed specification is written for each unit. The specification should be complete enough that any programmer with the proper programming skills can write the module and test it with little or no additional information. Diagrams such as data flow diagrams or flowcharts (an older technique) are often used to document the logic flow between modules. Process modeling is covered in more detail in Chapter 3.

From the database perspective, the major effort in this phase is development of the logical data model using *normalization,* a technique developed by E. F. (Ted) Codd for designing relational database tables that are best for transaction-based systems (that is, those that insert, update, and delete data in the relational database tables). Logical database design using normalization is covered in great detail in Chapters 6 and 7. Once normalization and the logical model for the project database(s) are completed, the overall logical data model for the enterprise (assuming one exists) is updated to reflect any newly discovered entities.

Physical Design

During the physical design phase, the logical design is mapped or converted to the actual hardware and systems software that will be used to implement the application(s) and database(s). From the process side, little or nothing needs to be done if the application specifications were written in a manner that can be directly implemented. However, much work is required to specify the hardware on which the application(s) and database(s) will be installed, including capacity estimates for the processors, disk devices, and network bandwidth on which the system will run.

On the database side, the normalized relations that were designed in the logical model are mapped to a physical model tailored to the relational DBMS(s) to be used. In particular, data definition language (DDL) is coded, or generated from the physical data model, to define the database objects, including the SQL clauses that define the physical storage of the tables and indexes. Preliminary analyses of required database queries are conducted to identify any additional indexes that may be necessary to achieve acceptable database performance. An essential outcome of this phase is the DDL for creation of the development database objects that the developers will need for testing the application programs during the construction phase that follows. Physical database design is covered in more detail in Chapter 8, including the roles of the data modeler and the DBA and the handoffs between them.

Construction

During the construction phase, the application developers code and test the individual programming units. Tested program units are promoted to a system test environment, where the entire application and database system is assembled and tested from end to end. Figure 4-2 shows the environments that are typically used as an application system is developed, tested, and implemented. Each environment is a complete hardware and software environment that includes all the components necessary to run the application system. Once system testing is completed, the system is promoted to a quality assurance (QA) environment. Most medium and large organizations have a separate QA department that tests the application system to ensure that it conforms to the stated requirements. Some organizations also have business users test the system to make sure it also meets their needs. The sooner errors are found in a computer system, the less expensive they are to repair. After QA has passed the application system, it is promoted to a staging environment. The staging environment must be as near a duplicate of the production environment as possible. In this environment, stress testing is conducted to ensure that the application and database will perform reasonably when deployed into live production use. Often final user training is conducted here as well, because it will be most like the live environment users will soon use.

The major work of the data modeler and the DBA is already complete by the time construction begins. However, as each part of the application system is migrated from one environment to the next, the database components needed by the application must also be migrated. Hopefully, a script is written that deploys the database components to the development environment, and that script is reused in each subsequent environment. However, complications can occur when an existing database is being enhanced or an older data storage system is being replaced, because data must be converted from the old storage structures to the new. Data transcends systems. Therefore, data conversion between old and new versions of systems is quite commonplace, ranging from simply adding new tables and columns to complex conversions that require extensive programming efforts in and of themselves.

Implementation and Rollout

Implementation is the process of installing the new application system's components (application programs, forms or web pages, reports, database objects, and so on) into the live system and carrying out any required data conversions. *Rollout* is the process of introducing groups of business users to the new application. Sometimes a new project is implemented *cold turkey*,

Figure 4-2 Development hardware/software environments

Ask the Expert

Q: I've been hearing about the Rational Unified Process (RUP) lately. How does that fit in with SDLC?

A: The Rational Unified Process (RUP) is an iterative software development process framework originally developed by the Rational Software Corporation, which became a division of IBM in 2003. Organizations that use the RUP toolset for application development usually also use the companion process framework. RUP is intended to be tailored by the organization using it, so no two implementations are the same. Unlike an SDLC, RUP has iterations designed into the framework. While the phases in RUP (Inception, Elaboration, Construction, and Transition) have somewhat different names than SDLC phases, the tasks are categorized into six engineering disciplines that align nicely with the classic SDLC (Business Modeling, Requirements, Analysis and Design, Implementation, Test, and Deployment).

meaning every user starts on the new version at the same time. However, with more complicated applications or those involving large numbers of users, a *phased* implementation is often used to reduce risk. The old and new versions of the application must run in parallel for a time while groups of users—often partitioned by physical work location or by department—are trained and migrated over to the new application. This method is often humorously referred to as the *chicken method* (in contrast to the cold turkey method).

Ongoing Support

Once a new application system and database have been implemented in a production environment, support of the application is often turned over to a production support team. This team must be prepared to isolate and respond to any issues that may arise, which could include performance issues, abnormal or unexpected results, complete failures, or the inevitable requests for enhancements. With enhancements, it is best to categorize and prioritize them and then fold them into future projects. However, genuine errors found in the existing application or database (called *bugs* in IT parlance) must be fixed more immediately. Each bug fix becomes a mini-project, where all the SDLC phases must be revisited. If attributes or entities must be added or revised, then a data modeler is usually involved to update the data models. At the very least, documentation must be updated as changes are made. As noted in Figure 4-2, the staging environment provides an ideal place for the validation of errors and their fixes and makes it possible to fix errors in parallel with the next major enhancement to the application system, which may have already been started in the development environment.

Assuming no gross errors were made during database design, the database support required during this phase is usually minor. Here are some of the tasks that may be required:

- Patches must be applied when the problems turn out to be bugs in the vendor's RDBMS software.

- Performance tuning, such as moving data files or adding indexes, may be necessary to circumvent performance problems.

- Space must be monitored and storage added as the database grows.

- Some application bug fixes may require new table columns or alterations to existing columns. If testing was done well, gross errors that require extensive database changes simply do not occur. Some application changes are required by statutory or regulatory changes beyond the control of the organization, and those changes can lead to extensive modifications to application(s) and database(s).

Nontraditional Life Cycles

In response to the belief that SDLC projects take too much time and consume too many resources, some nontraditional methods have come into routine use in some organizations. The two most prevalent of these are *prototyping* and *Rapid Application Development* (RAD).

Prototyping

Prototyping involves rapid development of the application by using iterative sets of design, development, and implementation steps as a method of determining user requirements. Extensive business user involvement is required throughout the development process. In its extreme form, the prototyping process starts with a meeting conducted during the business day to review the latest iteration of the application, followed by the development team working through the evening and often late into the night. The next iteration is then reviewed during the following workday.

Some prototyping techniques carry all the way through to a production version of the application and database. In this variation, iterations have increasing levels of detail added to them until they become completely functional applications. If you choose this path, keep in mind that prototyping never ends, and even after implementation and rollout, any future enhancements fall right back into more prototyping. The most common downside to this implementation technique is development team burnout.

Another variation of prototyping restricts the effort to the definition of requirements. Once requirements and the user-facing parts of the conceptual design (that is, user views) are determined, a traditional SDLC methodology is used to complete the project. IBM introduced a version of this methodology called *Joint Application Design* (JAD), which was highly successful in situations where user requirements could not be determined using more traditional techniques. The biggest exposure for this variant of prototyping is in not setting and maintaining expectations with the business sponsors of the project. The prototype is more or less a façade, much like a movie set where the buildings look real from the front but have no substance beyond that. Nontechnical audiences have no understanding of what it takes to develop the logic and data storage structures that form the inner workings of the application, and they become most disappointed when they realize that what looked like a complete, functional application system was really just an empty shell. However, when done correctly, this technique can be remarkably successful in determining user requirements that describe precisely the application system the business users want and need.

Rapid Application Development

Rapid Application Development (RAD) is a software development process that allows functioning application systems to be built using very short development cycles. Compromises are often made by using the *80/20 rule,* which assumes that 80 percent of the required work can be completed in 20 percent of the time. Complicated exception handling, for example, can be omitted in the interest of delivering a working system sooner. If the process is repeated on the same set of requirements, the system is ultimately built out to meet 100 percent of the requirements in a manner similar to prototyping.

RAD is not useful in controlling project schedules or budgets, and in fact it requires a project manager who is highly skilled at managing schedules and controlling costs. It is most useful in situations for which a rapid schedule is more important than product quality (measured in terms of conforming to all known requirements).

The Project Triangle

The motivation behind the growth of nontraditional development processes is pressure from business management to develop better business applications more quickly and at less expense. Said simply, they want fast delivery of high quality and inexpensive application software systems. However, despite the claims of some of the vendors selling development tools and methodologies, all three objectives simply cannot be maximized.

Figure 4-3 shows a graphical representation of the dilemma using the *project triangle.* The three points of the triangle represent the three objectives: quality, delivery time, and cost (often known as good, fast, and cheap). The lines between the points remind us that the objectives are interrelated. In fact, most experts agree only two of the objectives can be optimized, and when they are, the third objective always suffers. The commonly understood rule is that you must pick two and optimize your project accordingly. It has also been generally proven that the rule applies to human endeavors and not to matters of pure technology. For example, you can create a new video format that renders higher quality images faster and less expensively. However, if you launched a project to design such a new format, the project tasks could not be optimized for all three objectives.

Figure 4-3   The project triangle

This rule didn't start with the software industry. In fact, some claim that it is an old Hollywood maxim about filmmaking. While every producer wants a high-quality film, made quickly, and finished on a modest budget, it simply cannot be done. A good movie made quickly isn't cheap. A movie made quickly and cheaply won't be good. And a movie that is good and cheaply made can't be made quickly. Applying the analogy to application development projects, three choices emerge:

- Design and develop the system quickly and to a high standard, but expect higher costs.

- Design and develop the system quickly while minimizing costs, but expect lower quality.

- Design and develop the system to a high standard while minimizing costs, but expect the project to take much longer.

Try This 4-1 Project Database Management Tasks

In this Try This exercise, you will assign typical project management database management tasks to SDLC project phases. You may have to do a little research on your own to understand the particulars of one or more tasks, but that will only enhance your learning experience.

Step by Step

1. Make a list of the SDLC project phases:

   - Planning

   - Requirements Gathering

   - Conceptual Design

   - Logical Design

   - Physical Design

   - Construction

   - Implementation and Rollout

   - Ongoing Support

2. Using what you learned in this chapter along with what you are able to find out using other sources, assign each of the following tasks to one of the project phases. Note that some may apply to more than one phase. Also, methodologies are usually tailored to fit the organization in which they are used, so there are no absolute correct or incorrect answers for some of the tasks.

   a Normalization.

   b Add foreign keys to the database.

   c Specify the physical placement of database objects on storage media.

d Specify the unique identifier for each relation.

e Specify the primary key for each table.

f Determine the views required by the business users.

g Remove data that is easily derived.

h Resolve many-to-many relationships.

i Define views in the database.

j Modify the database to meet business requirements.

k Denormalize the database for performance.

l Specify a logical name for each entity and attribute.

m Specify a physical name for each table and column.

n Add redundant data to improve performance.

o Specify database indexes.

p Translate the conceptual data model into a logical model.

q Document business rules that cannot be represented in the data model.

r Identify the attributes required by the business users.

s Identify the relationships between the entities.

t Identify and document business data requirements.

u Ensure that user data requirements are met.

v Tune the database to improve performance.

w Evaluate available DBMS options.

Try This Summary

In this Try This exercise, you assigned project tasks to SDLC phases using information in
this chapter as well as independent research. My solution can be found in Appendix B, but as
already stated, there is no single correct solution to this exercise.

Chapter 4 Self Test

Choose the correct responses to each of the multiple-choice and fill-in-the-blank questions.
Note that there may be more than one correct response to each question.

1. The phases of a systems development life cycle (SDLC) methodology include which of the following?

   A Physical design

   B Logical design

   C Prototyping

   D Requirements gathering

   E Ongoing support

2. During the requirements phase of an SDLC project,

   A User views are discovered

   B The quality assurance (QA) environment is used

   C Surveys may be conducted

   D Interviews are often conducted

   E Observation may be used

3. The advantages of conducting interviews are

   A Interviews take less time than other methods

   B Answers may be obtained for unasked questions

   C A lot can be learned from nonverbal responses

   D Questions are presented more objectively than with survey techniques

   E Entities are more easily discovered

4. The advantages of conducting surveys include

   A A lot of ground can be covered quickly

   B Nonverbal responses are not included

   C Most survey recipients respond

   D Surveys are simple to develop

   E Prototyping of requirements is unnecessary

5. The advantages of observation are

    A You always see people acting normally

    B You are likely to see lots of situations in which exceptions are handled

    C You may see the way things really are instead of the way management and/or documentation presents them

    D The Hawthorne effect enhances your results

    E You may observe events that would not be described to you by anyone

6. The advantages of document reviews are

    A Pictures and diagrams are valuable tools for understanding systems

    B Document reviews can be done relatively quickly

    C Documents will always be up to date

    D Documents will always reflect current practices

    E Documents often present overviews better than other techniques can

7. During implementation and rollout,

    A Users are placed on the live system

    B Enhancements are designed

    C The old and new applications may be run in parallel

    D Quality assurance testing takes place

    E User training takes place

8. During ongoing support,

    A Enhancements are immediately implemented

    B Storage for the database may require expansion

    C The staging environment is no longer required

    D Bug fixes may take place

    E Patches may be applied if needed

9. Application program modules are specified during the SDLC _____ phase.

10. A feasibility study is often conducted during the _____ phase of an SDLC project.

11. Normalization takes place during the _____ phase of an SDLC project.

12. DDL is written to define database objects during the _____ phase of an SDLC project.

13. Program specifications are written during the _____ phase of an SDLC project.

14. When requirements are sketchy, _____ can work well.

15. Rapid Application Development develops systems rapidly by skipping _____.

16. The three objectives depicted in the application triangle are _____, _____, and _____.

17. The database is initially constructed in the _____ environment.

18. Database conversion is tested during the _____ phase of an SDLC project.

19. User views are analyzed during the _____ phase of an SDLC project.

20. The relational database was invented by _____.

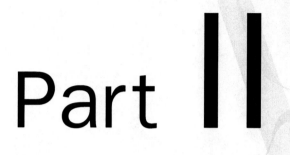

Part II

Data Modeling Details

Chapter 5

Conceptual Data Modeling

Key Skills & Concepts

- The Conceptual Modeling Process
- Generic Models and Patterns
- Roles vs. Subtypes
- Dealing with Hierarchies, Networks, and Linked Lists
- Bottom Up vs. Top Down Modeling
- Subject Areas
- Evaluating the Model

Recall from Chapter 1 that a conceptual data model is a high-level model that captures data and relationship concepts in a technology-independent manner. This chapter explores conceptual models in detail along with the process used to create them.

The Conceptual Modeling Process

Conceptual modeling is important because it establishes scope for the subsequent logical and physical modeling phases. However, it is the most difficult among all the data modeling phases because there are no set rules to follow, and thus it does not involve mechanical transformation from one type of model to another. In many ways conceptual modeling involves raw design work.

Figure 5-1 shows the essential steps that must take place during the conceptual data modeling phase: Preparation, Solution Design, and Evaluation of Solutions. Figure 5-1 also shows the most essential inputs and outputs, which are requirements from the Requirements Gathering phase and the promotion of the selected conceptual data model to the Logical Database Design (Logical Data Modeling) phase.

Preparation

As the name suggests, the Preparation step includes all the planning and organization tasks necessary to get started with the conceptual data model. The topics that follow cover the most important tasks. You will no doubt need to adapt these topics to fit the culture and systems development methodology of the organization for which the model is being produced.

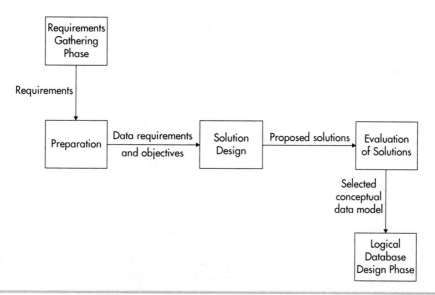

Figure 5-1   Conceptual modeling process flow

Establish Objectives

This may seem obvious, but the objectives of the conceptual modeling effort must be established so you will be able to determine when the model is complete and so you can plan the work required to meet the objectives. Of particular import is the intended audience for the model and what you expect the model to convey to them.

A more technical or detail-oriented audience will expect a more detailed conceptual model. The needs of the audience will drive many of the decisions regarding the modeling effort, including the decision as to whether to include attributes in the model as well as the subject matter.

Collect and Evaluate Inputs

The most essential input is the set of requirements from the Requirements Gathering phase of the project. The requirements need to be carefully evaluated to make sure they are both clear and complete. Existing data models for the same application (or a similar one) form another important input. The use of generic pattern models is discussed later in this chapter, but the preparation step is a good place to search for ones you might wish to use.

Establish Conceptual Modeling Guidelines

Based on the objectives of the project and the intended audience for the completed conceptual data model, the planning step is the best place for the modeler, working with the project team and project sponsor, to establish guidelines that will shape the development of the data model. Considerations include the following:

- **Inclusion of attributes** There is a clear division among expert data modelers as to whether attributes should be included in conceptual data models. Many prefer to keep conceptual models at a high level of abstraction, showing entity definitions instead of lists of attributes on the entity relationship diagrams. Many others strongly believe that detail is essential for business user understanding of the contents of the model. Still others are somewhere between those two positions, picking and choosing attributes for inclusion based on what they believe is necessary to convey understanding to the intended audience. If your organization has prevailing standards or practices, your choice may have already been made for you. In practice, I seldom include attributes in conceptual models, which has the benefit of streamlining the effort and focusing the conceptual modeling effort on getting high-level entities and relationships right. However, to enhance your understanding of the material, I have included attributes in a number of the models in this chapter. In less familiar subject areas, you might do the same to enhance your own understanding of the model and the way you expect the business to use it.

- **Naming conventions** Entities and attributes (if included) must be named clearly and consistently. It's best to establish naming conventions early and to stick to them throughout the project. In particular, logical object names chosen during conceptual modeling should be carried forward to the logical model and later used as the basis for physical table and column names in the physical data model.

- **Generalization vs. specialization** As discussed in Chapter 1, the choice between generalization and specialization leads to some of the most significant disagreements among professional data modelers. Some believe that you should generalize whenever possible. Taken to the extreme, you end up with a single entity named "Thing," and a relationship that shows that things are related to many other things, which of course no one does because it is useless in terms of conveying useful information about the intended database. (The "Thing" model is a running joke among data modelers, but I have seen real models that come mighty close to it.) Other experienced modelers believe that you should only generalize when the requirements dictate it, a notion that can yield models that are overly specialized. Often a middle position based on which data structures offer the highest probability of reuse works best. However, this approach takes a lot of experience and forethought in order to achieve the proper balance. If you are going to err on the side of generalization, the conceptual model is the best place to do so. You can always opt to specialize in subsequent logical models when more is known about the intended use of the database. For example, generalizations that work nicely for transaction-based applications databases can get in the way in an analysis database. (Modeling for analytical databases is covered in Chapter 11.) If your organization uses UML, the Object Class Diagram is a good vehicle for sorting out the best use of supertypes and subtypes.

● **Subject area selection**   Large or complex models should be divided into subject areas. A *subject area* is a functional area of an enterprise, such as Sales, Marketing, and Order Management. Dividing models into subject areas not only makes it easier to organize the modeling effort into parallel tasks, assigning different areas to different modelers, but it also makes it easier to present models tailored to the particular audience based on their interest in the various business functions.

Solution Design

Solution design is where the work of actually creating one or more conceptual models takes place. Much of the remainder of this chapter addresses the tasks that must take place during this step.

The conceptual modeling phase presents a unique opportunity for sorting out various design alternatives. Models can be created quickly and presented to the project team and business users to determine which ones best match their understanding of the requirements. The earlier the errors are found in a software development project, the less time and money it takes to correct them. In terms of data modeling, the conceptual model is the very first opportunity to review a model and to adjust/correct it as needed. There is no more compelling reason for creating a conceptual model than validating the requirements and your understanding of them as early in the systems development process as possible. As shown in Figure 5-1, the selected conceptual model is promoted to the logical design phase for further elaboration. See the "Evaluating the Model" topic later in this chapter for more details on evaluating models and selecting the model to be promoted.

What Differentiates Conceptual Modeling from Logical Modeling?

Generally speaking, a conceptual model is at a higher level of abstraction compared with the corresponding logical model(s). In many cases, the conceptual model also contains less detail. The following table highlights these differences.

Criteria	Conceptual Model	Logical Model
Attributes included?	Attributes may be optionally included, but are not required.	Every attribute should be included, and they should correspond directly with the columns to be created in the physical database tables.
Generalized or specialized?	Generalized data structures as described later in this chapter are common in conceptual models.	Logical models are only generalized to the extent that the desired physical database is to be generalized.

(continued)

Criteria	Conceptual Model	Logical Model
Model normalized? (Normalization is presented in Chapters 6 and 7.)	Conceptual models are seldom normalized, so conceptual models can contain objects such as many-to-many relationships.	Logical models are always normalized to at least third normal form. (Normalization is a process that removes certain anomalies from the data model. Third normal form adheres to rules that require every non-key attribute to be dependent on the entire primary key and nothing else. It is discussed at length in Chapter 6.) The objects in the model will correspond closely with the desired physical database.
Multiple alternatives shown?	If there are multiple design alternatives to explore, the conceptual model is the place to do so.	The logical model should only show the alternative deemed best when the conceptual model was evaluated.
Layers of detail shown?	It is a common practice to develop multiple diagrams of varying detail when there are diverse audiences that must review the model.	While logical models may also contain multiple diagrams of varying detail, most practitioners attempt to show a consistent level of detail throughout the model whenever possible.

Creating the Model

It should be no surprise that the bulk of the time and energy you devote to conceptual modeling is spent creating the model. However, skipping over the planning step is not a shortcut in most cases, and poor planning (or no planning) will actually cost you more time in the long run. Once you have adequately planned, the creation step should go smoothly.

Modelers often deliberately construct multiple alternative models. The evaluation step (described later in this chapter) is then used to select the alternative that best fits the requirements for promotion to the logical modeling phase. It is important to involve subject matter experts (SMEs), project team members, the project sponsor, and others in order to consider as many perspectives as possible.

Generic Models and Patterns

Very few data modeling projects require you to start with the proverbial blank slate. Seek out a conceptual model for a similar application or database that has worked either for you or for the organization. If none is found, look for common data structures and patterns that you or the organization have used before. Over time, you will develop your own library of models and common structures available for reuse. Most modelers start with some sort of generic model or pattern even if they don't consciously realize it.

A number of publications and web pages can provide useful generic models and patterns. One of the very best sources is the three-volume set *The Data Model Resource Book*, Volumes 1 and 2 by Len Silverston (Wiley Publishing, 2001), and Volume 3 by Len Silverston and

Paul Agnew (Wiley Publishing, 2009). Silverston has long touted the concept of a universal data model. Even if you cannot adapt generic models directly, they provide a very attractive starting point. The key is to *adapt* rather than to force a model fit.

The following topics present the Party and Communication Channel data structures as examples of commonly used pattern data structures.

The Party Data Structure

Figure 5-2 shows a pattern model for the supertype commonly called Party. A *party* is a person or organization of interest to the database application. The advantage of using the supertype in data models is the ability to hide the party's implementation details in cases where it doesn't matter. For example, in a workflow application some tasks are assigned to individual specialists, while others are assigned to workgroups. If we were to use separate entities for an individual and a workgroup, we'd have to have two relationships, one between tasks and individuals and another between tasks and workgroups. And if that weren't complicated enough, we'd have to know the type of task in order to write a database query that links a task to the person or workgroup to which it was assigned. On the other hand, using the Party supertype, we need only a single relationship and can assign tasks to parties without regard for whether the party is an individual or organization.

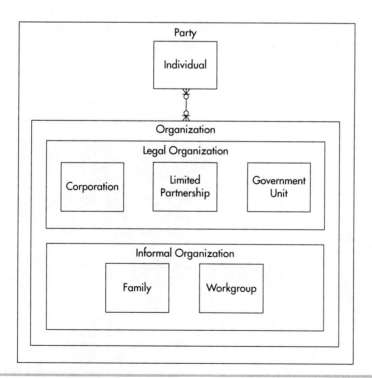

Figure 5-2 Party data structure

Note that supertypes do not have to be uniformly broken into subtypes. For example, in Figure 5-2, Party is broken down into Individual and Organization, and while Individual isn't broken down further, Organization is broken down into Legal Organization and Informal Organization, and each of those is also broken into subtypes. Obviously, the subtypes need to be adjusted to fit the organization and the particular requirements of the project. Said another way, you should never generalize or specialize data structures merely for the sake of doing so—your design decisions should *always* be driven by your *requirements*.

The Party structure shown in Figure 5-2 has an unusual element: the subtype Individual has a many-to-many relationship with the subtype Organization. An individual can be a member of a family and a workgroup, for example. Later in this chapter, I introduce roles as another option for implementing relationships such as this one.

The Communication Channel Data Structure

Another commonly used data structure is the Communication Channel (also known as the Contact Method structure), which is used to organize all the methods that can be used to communicate with (or contact) a Party. Figure 5-3 shows the basic structure, including some of the commonly used attributes.

The Communication Channel supertype, shown on the right side of Figure 5-3, has subtypes of Telephonic Device (to handle telephones, cell phones, fax machines, pagers, and the like), E-mail Address, and Postal Address. You may notice that Postal Address is tailored to U.S. addresses. We'll look at what it takes to accommodate international addresses in the Try This exercise toward the end of this chapter.

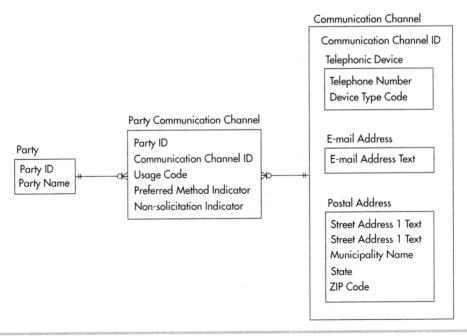

Figure 5-3 The Communication Channel data structure

On the left of Figure 5-3 is a scaled-back representation of the Party data structure. This being a conceptual model, I could have gotten away with drawing a many-to-many relationship between Party and Communication Channel, showing graphically that a party can have many communication channels and that each communication channel can be used by many parties. However, to better illustrate how such an abstract structure could be used in a real-world database, I elected to include the intersection entity Party Communication Channel. (Intersection entities were introduced in Chapter 2.) Notice that Party Communication Channel contains not only the keys of the party and the communication channel used by it, but also attributes that help define the use of the channel by that particular party, such as the Usage Code that defines how the party uses the channel (work versus home, or perhaps primary versus secondary), the Preferred Method Indicator to denote whether the channel is preferred by the party, and the Non-solicitation Indicator to denote a request by the party to not be solicited via the channel. The decision to include the intersection entity is a great example of tailoring the model to the intended audience to enhance understanding.

First Cut Diagrams

First cut diagrams should be produced with the understanding that they will most likely be adjusted during the review process. Few models (even high-level conceptual ones) are drawn in final form at the outset. During all of the conceptual modeling process, it's most important not to get bogged down in details. The details can be added during logical modeling. Most first cut conceptual diagrams meet the following criteria:

- The most important entities are included.

- Relationships are included with maximum cardinalities, but the relationships are not named.

- Attributes are included only when necessary for clarity.

- A high-level of generalization is maintained, with details such as transaction logs, audit data, exception handling, and the handling of history omitted.

- When specialization is included, the subclasses shown are areas where the data is markedly different or where the business handles the data in a significantly different manner.

Roles vs. Subtypes

When we break entities down into subtypes, there are two guiding principles. First, the subtypes must not overlap, meaning any given occurrence of the entity must be exactly one subtype. For example, you won't often see customer and supplier as subtypes of organization because there will likely be cases where the same organization is both a customer and supplier such as the electrical contractor that buys a truck from the vehicle dealer for which they perform electrical work. Second, subtypes must cover all the possible cases, meaning that when an entity is broken into subtypes, every occurrence must fit one of the subtypes. If, for example, an organization deals with regulatory agencies, the agencies are neither customers nor suppliers, so we would have to make a Regulatory Agency subtype in the previous example. Putting the two principles together, if we break an entity into subtypes, then every occurrence of the entity must map to one and only one subtype. (Note that not all practitioners agree with these two principles.)

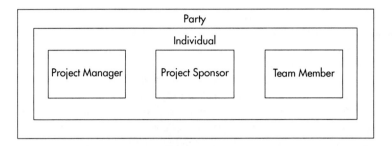

Figure 5-4 Party entity with subtypes for Individual

Figure 5-4 shows a different version of the Party entity from Figure 5-2, with the Individual subtype broken down into Project Manager, Project Sponsor, and Team Member subtypes. Even if an individual would never serve in more than one of these functions at the same time, imagine how awkward it would be every time a person changed from one to the other—if each subtype were implemented as a separate table, we would be forever moving rows from one table to another as individuals changed job functions within the organization.

In situations where it is impossible or impractical to design subtypes that conform to the guiding principles previously described, the solution is to use roles. In data modeling, a *role* represents the part that a particular entity class might play in the organization, much like a role played by an actor on stage or screen. Figure 5-5 shows a conceptual model where Project Manager, Project Sponsor, and Team Member are treated as subtypes of Individual Role,

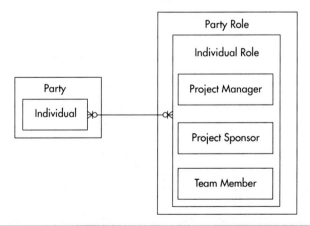

Figure 5-5 Conceptual model showing Party and Party Role

which in turn is a subtype of Party Role. The assignment of an Individual to a role is now done with a relationship between the Individual entity and the Individual Role entity, which allows the assignment of more than one role at a given point in time if needed.

In reality, we would never implement such a complicated supertype/subtype structure as shown in the Party Role entity in Figure 5-5, but as a conceptual model, it has the benefit of graphically showing that an Individual can be assigned only roles defined as Individual Roles, which are Project Manager, Project Sponsor, or Team Member. Perhaps the most significant reason we would not actually implement this structure in a logical or physical model is that we would have to modify the data model (and perhaps the database) every time a new role type became necessary, which is obviously too inflexible for most organizations.

Figure 5-6 shows the most likely logical model derived from the conceptual model in Figure 5-5. Note that I have flattened the Party Role structure into a single table that contains all possible roles a party can play and have placed an intersection entity between Party and Party Role to show the assignment of parties to party roles. (The intersection entity also resolves the many-to-many relationship between Party and Party Role to comply with normalization rules that are presented in Chapter 6. However, normalization is not necessary in conceptual models.) I added begin and end effective dates to the intersection entity (Party Role Assignment) to allow past and future role assignments to exist along with current assignments. Options for handling history and other forms of time-dependent data are presented in Chapter 10.

Note in Figure 5-6 that a Party can have zero to many related Party Role Assignment instances, and similarly, a Party Role can have zero to many related Party Role Assignment instances. To help you visualize how this model works, Figure 5-7 shows three physical tables (a rather rudimentary form of physical data model) with sample data. The three possible individual roles from Figure 5-5 (Project Manager, Project Sponsor, and Team Member) now appear as rows in the Party Role table. Three parties are shown in the Party table, and the Party Role Assignment table shows various past and present role assignments. In particular, note that Tiana C. Steger (Party 101) served as both a Project Sponsor and a Project Manager between January 5, 2009, and June 30, 2009. Such a dual assignment would be against the rules had we used subtypes instead of roles.

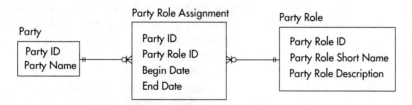

Figure 5-6 Logical model using the Party Role concept

Party

Party ID	Party Name
101	Tiana C. Steger
102	Andrew T. Guay
103	Sherry L. Johnson

Party Role Assignment

Party ID	Party Role ID	Begin Date	End Date
101	PS	01/05/2009	12/31/2010
101	PM	01/05/2009	06/30/2009
102	TM	01/05/2009	12/31/2010
103	PM	07/01/2009	12/31/2010
103	TM	07/01/2009	12/31/2010

Party Role

Party Role ID	Party Role Short Name	Party Role Description
PS	Prj Spnsr	Project Sponsor
PM	Prj Mgr	Project Manager
TM	Mbr	Project Team Member

Figure 5-7 Table structure to illustrate the Party Role concept

Ask the Expert

Q: The model in Figure 5-5 shows that only individuals can be assigned the Project Manager, Project Sponsor, and Team Member roles. However, the model in Figure 5-6 implies that any party (regardless of subtype) can be assigned those roles. Can the model in Figure 5-6 be modified to impose this restriction?

A: Enforcement of data restrictions (constraints) such as this one can be done in several ways, ranging from leaving it entirely up to application logic, to full enforcement within the database without the need for any application logic. In cases like this, most designers opt for a hybrid approach and add data structures to show which party types are permitted to use which party roles, leaving the actual checking for valid assignment of roles up to the application. To do this, we first need to add a Party Type entity and make it a parent of Party—this gives us a Party Type Code attribute in Party, so we can know the subtype to which each occurrence of Party belongs. Second, we need to add an intersection entity between Party Type and Party Role to hold the valid combinations (that is, which party roles are permitted for each party type).

Dealing with Hierarchies, Networks, and Linked Lists

As you deal with common structures in data models, you will inevitably encounter structures containing recursive relationships (relationships where the parent and child are the same entity class). The three major types of structures that use recursive relationships are hierarchies, networks, and linked lists, which are covered in this section.

Hierarchies

Hierarchies are structures where entities are organized into layers in which each entity can have any number of children (subordinate entities) at lower layers, but can have only one parent (superior entity) at the next higher layer. And, of course, there is a single entity in the top layer that has no parents with respect to the hierarchy, and entities at the bottom of the hierarchy have no children. Hierarchies are sometimes called tree structures because they look like an upside-down tree, with the topmost entity called the root and the bottommost entities called leaves.

Figure 5-8 shows a familiar three-layer hierarchy for an enterprise organization chart containing the entities Company, Division, and Department. A conceptual model with attributes is shown at the top of the figure, and a physical representation with sample data values is shown at the bottom of the figure. The model is constructed using familiar one-to-many relationships, which yields a very straightforward representation. In fact, I know of several commercial payroll applications that use this same basic structure. However, the structure is quite rigid, leading to the following issues:

- If we need another layer, for example, we must add an entity and a new relationship to the model, which, of course, cascades all the way through to adding a table to the physical database.

- If some companies in the database have departments but no divisions, we will have to add a dummy division in their hierarchy to link their departments to the company layer.

- Even for companies with three-layer hierarchies, the structure can be confusing to use if they use different names for the layers. For example, a company that had departments at the second layer and workgroups under departments does not fit the structure well.

Figure 5-9 shows a generalized structure that can accommodate an organizational hierarchy of any number of layers. The top of Figure 5-9 shows a conceptual model with attributes, and the physical representation at the bottom of the figure shows the same data that appeared in Figure 5-8.

The Organizational Unit Type entity contains all the valid unit types such as Company, Division, and Department as used in Figure 5-8. New types, which can be used to form new layers in the hierarchy, can be added by simply adding a new occurrence of the entity (in the database, this amounts to inserting a new row into a table).

The Organizational Unit entity contains all the organization units, regardless of their position in the hierarchy. The recursive one-to-many relationship (Parent Org Unit Key is a foreign key for Org Unit Key) links the occurrences of Organizational Unit together into the desired hierarchy. You can see how this works by comparing the physical representation at the bottom of Figure 5-9 with the one at the bottom of Figure 5-8.

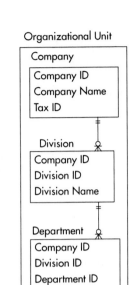

Organizational Unit

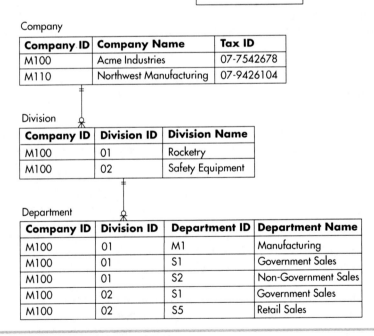

Company

Company ID	Company Name	Tax ID
M100	Acme Industries	07-7542678
M110	Northwest Manufacturing	07-9426104

Division

Company ID	Division ID	Division Name
M100	01	Rocketry
M100	02	Safety Equipment

Department

Company ID	Division ID	Department ID	Department Name
M100	01	M1	Manufacturing
M100	01	S1	Government Sales
M100	01	S2	Non-Government Sales
M100	02	S1	Government Sales
M100	02	S5	Retail Sales

Figure 5-8   Rigid (specialized) hierarchical structure

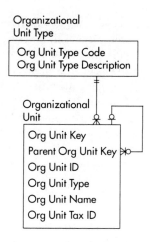

Organizational
Unit Type

Org Unit Type Code	Org Unit Type Description
CO	Company
DIV	Division
DEPT	Department

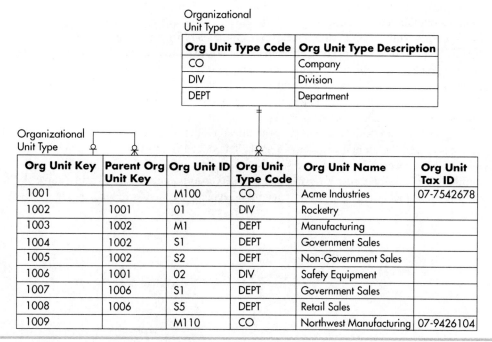

Org Unit Key	Parent Org Unit Key	Org Unit ID	Org Unit Type Code	Org Unit Name	Org Unit Tax ID
1001		M100	CO	Acme Industries	07-7542678
1002	1001	01	DIV	Rocketry	
1003	1002	M1	DEPT	Manufacturing	
1004	1002	S1	DEPT	Government Sales	
1005	1002	S2	DEPT	Non-Government Sales	
1006	1001	02	DIV	Safety Equipment	
1007	1006	S1	DEPT	Government Sales	
1008	1006	S5	DEPT	Retail Sales	
1009		M110	CO	Northwest Manufacturing	07-9426104

Figure 5-9   Flexible (generalized) hierarchical structures

The generalized version has the distinct advantage of flexibility—it can handle any number of layers and any type of organizational unit. Moreover, the layers do not have to be uniform. For example, some departments could report directly to the company, while others report to the company through a division. On the downside, it is more difficult for concrete thinkers to understand, and we are forced into using a generic identifier (Org Unit Key) instead of more familiar attributes such as Company ID, Division ID, and Department ID. Most experienced modelers immediately opt for the generalized structure, but if the organizational structure is expected to remain stable, a lot can be said for the simplicity of the specialized structure. The best guideline I can offer is to avoid generalizing for the sake of generalizing, but don't hesitate to generalize when there is a reasonable possibility that flexibility will be needed to handle future changes in the structure.

Networks

Networks are structures in which entities are organized into layers where each entity can have any number of children (subordinate entities) at lower layers, and can have any number of parents (superior entities) at the next higher layer. Said another way, networks are like hierarchies, except they do not have the single-parent restriction.

In manufacturing, parts can be made of parts (sometimes called subassemblies), which can be made of still more parts. Also, any part can be a subassembly for many assemblies. Manufacturers often call these network structures a *bill of materials* because they are used to track parts required for each product. For example, a refrigerator might have a ½-inch #10 sheet metal screw as one part of an electrical box assembly, and that assembly might be mounted on a motor with more of the same screws to form a motor assembly, and elsewhere in the refrigerator, still more of the same screws might be used in the door handle assembly. The manufacturer needs to know not only how many of the screws are needed for the entire product, but also where each one belongs.

Figure 5-10 shows specialized and generalized models of a network structure side-by-side. The specialized representation is shown on the left side of Figure 5-10 with a many-to-many relationship between assemblies and subassemblies. However, this model does not handle multiple layers well because if a particular part serves as both an assembly and a subassembly, information about it must appear in both entities, which of course is redundant. On the right

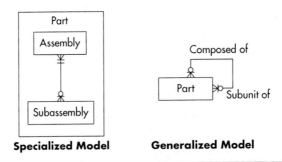

Specialized Model   **Generalized Model**

Figure 5-10   Specialized and generalized network structures

side of Figure 5-10 is a generalized version of the same network structure that shows parts related to other parts with a many-to-many relationship.

Linked Lists

Linked lists, also called chains, are structures where each entity instance has only one related instance in each direction. One of the most common uses for linked lists is to show versions of something, such as releases of software products or editions of a book. Figure 5-11 shows three possible models that can be used to implement a linked list for editions of a book.

On the left side of Figure 5-11 is a conventional structure that separates basic information about a book that will not change across editions into a Book entity, with the information that varies by edition into a Book Edition entity. The familiar one-to-many relationship is used to connect books to their editions. The main benefit of this model over the others shown is that it is easier to understand. A sequence number such as the edition number must be placed in the Book Edition entity to allow users to sort the editions into chronological sequence when necessary. However, there are some drawbacks. First, very little information remains constant across book editions. In fact, just about anything can change, including the title, the authors, and even the publisher. Second, the model doesn't convey the concept of editions being a sequential series of published versions of the book—it only tells you that a book can have multiple editions.

In the middle of Figure 5-11 is a different model that is more typical of linked lists. Book and Book Edition have been collapsed into a single entity called Book. (This isn't a huge leap since nearly anything that describes the book can vary from one edition to the next.) A one-to-one recursive relationship ties each book to the next edition, or alternatively to the preceding edition. Generally, the chain should be constructed in only one direction. To build a forward chain, each instance of Book would have a foreign key that contains the primary key value of the *next* edition of the book. The latest edition would have a null foreign key. To build a reverse chain, each instance of Book would have a foreign key that contains the primary key value of the *previous* edition of the book. Of course, both chains can be built (known as a *bi-directional* linked list), but that takes two foreign keys in each instance (establishing two recursive one-to-one relationships, one pointing to the previous edition and the other to the next edition). However, with this arrangement developers must be careful to make changes to *two* foreign key values every time an

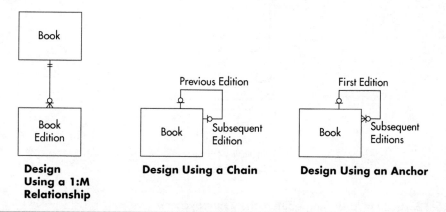

Figure 5-11   Chain structure design alternatives

edition is added to or removed from the bi-directional list, so that both the forward and backward chains yield consistent results.

One of the drawbacks of the chain model shown in the middle of Figure 5-11 is that it is not easy to write a query that finds all the editions of a particular book because there isn't a consistent attribute value across all editions of the book. The model on the right side of Figure 5-11 is a modified model that solves this problem. Instead of storing the key of the previous or subsequent edition in the foreign key, each edition contains the key of the first edition. This is sometimes called an *anchor* because each edition is tied to a common point, and technically it is a bit of a departure from the traditional definition of a linked list. Note that we are placing the primary key value from the first edition in the foreign key of every subsequent edition, which ties the first edition to many subsequent editions instead of just the next edition. Therefore, the relationship must be changed from one-to-one to one-to-many.

Bottom Up vs. Top Down Modeling

Another consideration when creating new data models is whether to work from the bottom up or from the top down.

Bottom Up Modeling

With bottom up modeling, you start with a literal implementation that is often very close to a basic physical table structure and work up to more generalized structures. If you need to present early versions of your models to the rank and file workers who will directly use the new database application, this approach may help by bringing literal thinkers on board quickly. The bottom up approach also works well in a workshop-style design session where you are building a prototype model interactively during the workshop sessions. By starting with concrete structures, you avoid having to be too creative while you establish credibility with the workshop participants.

Let's have a look at bottom up modeling for a payroll application. Figure 5-12 shows a typical starting point for a payroll application, which is the actual paycheck that is delivered

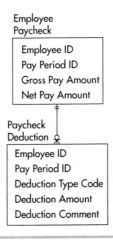

Figure 5-12 Bottom up starting point model (the paycheck)

to the employee. I have added attributes to make the example easier to follow, and in doing so, I came across a group of attributes representing payroll deductions that can (and usually do) have multiple occurrences per paycheck. Rather than write the attributes many times within the Employee Paycheck entity, I chose to move them to a child entity called Paycheck Deduction. All of this makes the model look more like a logical model than a conceptual one, but that actually matches reality, because bottom up modeling is seldom used in the development of conceptual data models.

Figure 5-13 shows the next version of the model, where I added some of the hierarchy that exists above the paycheck, including Employee and Pay Period. In the next version, I would

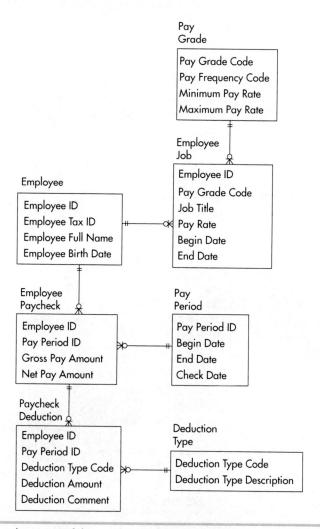

Figure 5-13 Second version of the model developed bottom up

likely add an organization structure to show the enterprise hierarchy (such as division and department) above either Employee or Employee Job, depending on whether the enterprise views an employee as an individual assigned to an organizational unit or as an individual who holds a job that belongs to an organizational unit. Note how seemingly subtle differences in how an enterprise operates can have a significant effect on the outcome of a data model. The Organization structure shown in Figure 5-2 might provide a good starting pattern.

Another choice to be made is how to fit Employee into more generalized structures. Making Employee a subclass of Individual will likely seem attractive at first. However, business users with real-world experience with human resources (HR) systems will point out that there are complications such as departures and reinstatements along with leaves of absence that make the use of a role much more attractive.

Top Down Modeling

With top down modeling, you start with a general concept and expand downward to fill in the details. If you must present early models to an audience or you find yourself using the top down approach in a workshop setting (which is not a good idea in my opinion), the abstract thinkers will be able to follow along much more readily than the literal thinkers, so expect to work harder, using examples to illustrate concepts.

Figure 5-14 shows an initial model for a new human resources (HR) application system. I used two patterns to form this initial model. First, I lifted the generalized Organization structure from Figure 5-9. Second, I lifted Employee, Employee Job, and Pay Grade from Figure 5-13. This is often the way modeling works in practice—we start by adapting patterns we know, combining them in different (sometimes unique) ways to form an initial model.

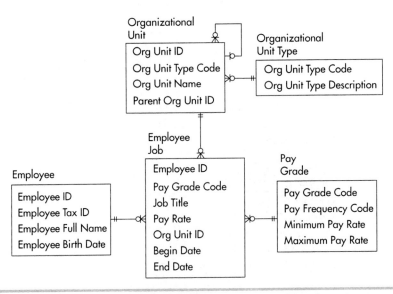

Figure 5-14 Top down starting point model (Organization and Employee)

For the next version of the model, I looked at the requirements for the application system and found that employee training needs to be tracked along with union membership and performance reviews. I noticed that an employee could have multiple jobs and asked whether it was possible for an employee to hold multiple jobs at the same time and how reviews would be handled in that situation. The HR manager had not considered this possibility, but on checking the employment rules, found that nothing prohibited one person from taking two part-time jobs at the same time, and since performance reviews included pay recommendations, the reviews would thus have to be associated with the employee's job instead of directly with the employee. This illustrates the power and benefits of data modeling. In constructing a model of what the database should be, we are able to design solutions for circumstances that we had not previously considered, as a side benefit of the rigor we apply to getting the entities and relationships right. Figure 5-15 shows the second version of the model from Figure 5-14.

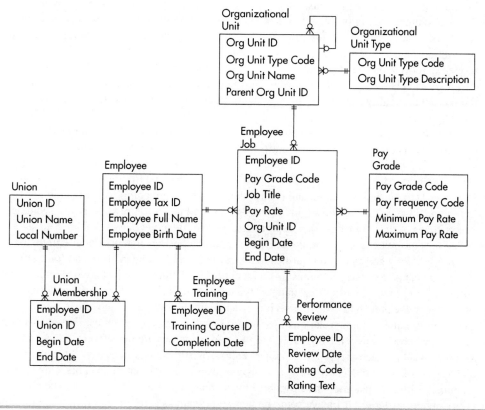

Figure 5-15 Second version of the model developed top down

Which Is Best, Bottom Up or Top Down?

Conceptual models are abstract by nature, so in most cases the top down approach works best. Conversely, logical models are more concrete in nature, and the normalization process (introduced in Chapter 6) is a bottom up design approach, so a bottom up approach is usually more appropriate for logical models (and the physical models that are often developed in parallel with them).

However, what you have available to use in the starting point has a huge effect. If the patterns and generic models you have for starters are more generalized and/or abstract, the top down approach becomes the obvious one. On the other hand, if the starting material is highly detailed and specialized, such as a logical or physical model for an existing database, the bottom up approach is a more natural choice. Most experienced modelers shift freely between the two approaches, often without consciously doing so.

Subject Areas

For large and/or complex models, one of the best ways to cope with seemingly overwhelming detail is to break the big problem into smaller ones. Not only do subject areas permit you to focus your attention on a meaningful subset of the objects, but they also permit parallel work by multiple data modelers with less risk of them getting in each other's way. Most popular data modeling tools support subsets within the model, which are most often called subject areas. A *subject area* is simply a grouping of objects that have similar business use or meaning. Often there is a major entity that shares its name with the subject area such as Customer, Product, and Supplier.

Avoid selecting subject areas based on processes (for example, Order Entry) and organizational components of your enterprise (for example, Legal Department). However, you may find it useful to conduct modeling workshop sessions with one department at a time, focusing only on the data that they care about. Just be sure to synthesize your results into models organized by subject areas after the workshops are complete, but avoid the urge to begin synthesizing too soon—doing so may lead to a lot of rework as you see other perspectives of the data from other departments. Strive for subject areas that are logical collections of entities along with the attributes and relationships that go along with them.

It is perfectly acceptable for entities to appear in multiple subject areas and for entities in one subject area to have relationships with entities in different subject areas. Ideally your data modeling tool provides direct support for subject areas such that an entity is defined only once in the metadata even though it may show up in multiple subject areas, and that it is easy to create and maintain relationships that cross subject area boundaries. For intersection entities that cross subject areas (that is, the two parent entities are in different subject areas), you may want to place them in both subject areas. Also, it is sometimes useful for clarity and a sense of completeness to show a few significant entities in multiple subject areas. For example, if I have Customer and Product subject areas, it might be best to place the Order entity in both. After all, if I leave something as significant as a customer's orders out of either of those, someone from the business unit closest to that subject area's data is going to ask where it is. Assuming the modeling tool stores the entity only one time internally, it is easier to include the entity than to drag out another model (that could lead to more confusion and even more probing questions from audience members) merely to demonstrate that you have not overlooked an important entity.

As a final note, establishing standard colors for each subject area and filling in the background color of each entity with its subject area color can greatly enhance your ability to present complex models. When you have included an entity from another subject area for clarity, you will know at a glance that it belongs to a different subject area by its color (and soon your audience will know also).

Evaluating the Model

As with all *deliverables* (work products), conceptual models must be reviewed before they are used in subsequent project phases. Moreover, if multiple conceptual models have been created to illustrate different design options, then we must go through an evaluation to determine which one is the best fit for the requirements and the organization.

We test software that we write for defects before unleashing it on unsuspecting business users, so it only makes sense to test data models before promoting them to the next project phase. To ensure that reviewers properly interpret the model, a walkthrough in a workshop setting typically achieves better results than distributing documents and diagrams for review. For highly complex models (or subsets thereof), consider walking through tables with sample data or even constructing a prototype database with sample data.

What Makes a Good Conceptual Model?

In addition to the criteria described in the section on measures of a good data model in Chapter 1, here are some measures of a good conceptual model:

- **Completeness** The best way to judge the completeness of the model is to review the project's data requirements one by one and to verify that the model supports them.

- **Conciseness** There should be no unnecessary entities or relationships. The same applies to attributes if they are included.

- **Precision** Every entity and attribute (when attributes are included in the model) must have a complete and accurate definition.

- **Balance** The model should have achieved a good balance between generalization and specialization.

- **Process support** A comparison with processes called out in the requirements and preliminary process designs should show that the model provides the proper support for the processes. This doesn't mean that every exception and every possible entity is accounted for, but rather that the major entities align well with the processes. A CRUD matrix as introduced in Chapter 3 is an excellent tool to use for this comparison.

Try This 5-1   Conceptual Model for International Addresses

In the description of Figure 5-3, I noted that the postal address shown was specialized for U.S. addresses. In this Try This exercise, you will build a conceptual model for a generalized postal address structure usable for all countries.

Step by Step

During Requirements Gathering, the following requirements were developed for the postal address structure:

- Each address must include one and only one country.

- Each address may include any number of regions, including no regions at all. A *region* in this case means any geographic or political subdivision of a country that is recognized by that country's postal service as part of a postal address. In Japan, for example, there can be up to seven regions associated with an address, starting with prefectures and working all the way down to neighborhoods within major cities.

- While the list of regions in an international address is usually written on a single address line, the business wants to be able to search the database for individual regions. This means that the database must include a structure for the hierarchy of regions within a country.

- In addition to the region line(s) and country name line, addresses can have any number of freeform address lines. In remote areas of some countries, the address line may contain directions to the location.

Try This Summary

In this Try This exercise, you created a conceptual model for a generalized postal address structure. My solution is in Appendix B. I included some basic attributes in my solution to better illustrate how the entities in the structure work together. However, remember that attributes are never required in conceptual models. Note the following in my solution:

- Region is classified using the Region Type entity, which contains the name of the region type (state, province, canton, prefecture, city, county, neighborhood, and so on).

- Region has a one-to-many recursive relationship to establish the hierarchy of regions.

- The relationship between Country and Postal Address may look redundant, but we must assign a country to an address that has no regions. Creating a dummy region for addresses that have no regions is not nearly as good a solution.

Chapter 5 Self Test

1. The essential steps that must take place during conceptual data modeling are

   A Evaluation of solutions

   B Normalization

   C Preparation

   D Solution design

   E Bottom up modeling

2. Inputs to the conceptual modeling phase may include

   A Existing physical models

   B Programming specifications

   C Requirements from the Requirements Gathering phase

   D Existing logical models

   E A CRUD matrix

3. Guidelines for conceptual modeling should include

   A Normalization rules

   B Naming conventions

   C Inclusion of attributes

   D Subject area selection

   E Generalization versus specialization

4. Individuals who should have input to conceptual modeling include

   A Subject matter experts (SMEs)

   B Project team members

   C The project sponsor

   D Other data modelers

   E Others who may offer useful perspectives

5. Criteria for first cut models are

   A Attributes are always included

   B The most important entities are included

   C The more specialized, the better

    D Relationships are included with maximum cardinalities

    E Details such as transaction logs and audit data are included

6. The modeling approach most commonly used in conceptual modeling is

    A Normalization

    B Bottom up

    C Structured design

    D Top down

    E Specialization

7. Measures of a good conceptual model include

    A Balance between generalization and specialization

    B Completeness

    C Independence from processes

    D Conciseness

    E Precision

8. An advantage of using supertypes is that they _____ unimportant implementation details.

9. Application program modules are specified during the SDLC _____ phase.

10. Attributes are _____ in conceptual models.

11. Generalized data structures are _____ in conceptual models.

12. Conceptual models are _____ normalized.

13. The guiding principles for subtypes are that they do not _____, and every occurrence of the supertype must fit into _____ subtype.

14. In hierarchies, each entity has _____ parent entity/entities.

15. Generalized structures can be _____ for literal thinkers to understand.

16. In network structures, each entity has _____ parent entity/entities.

17. In linked lists, each entity instance has _____ related instance in each direction.

18. Large and/or complex models can be broken up using _____.

Chapter 6

Logical Database Design Using Normalization

Key Skills & Concepts

- The Need for Normalization

- Applying the Normalization Process

- Denormalization

I n this chapter, you will learn how to perform logical database design using a process called *normalization.* It is normalization that teaches you how best to organize your data into tables. Therefore, normalization is essential to logical database design. The design is most often documented using a logical data model. The main inputs to the logical database design phase are the requirements from the Requirements Gathering phase, the conceptual data model, and user views (the collection of all the web pages, screens, reports, printed reports, and other presentations of the data that the database application system is expected to produce).

Normalization is a technique for producing a set of *relations* (data represented logically in a two-dimensional format using rows and columns) that possesses a certain set of properties. E.F. (Ted) Codd, an IBM researcher (later an IBM fellow), became known as the father of the relational database after he published a research paper in June 1970 titled "A Relational Model of Data for Large Shared Data Banks" in *Communications of the ACM,* the Journal of the Association for Computing Machinery. Codd developed the normalization process in 1972, using three normal forms. The name was a bit of a political gag at the time. President Nixon was "normalizing" relations with China, so Codd figured if you could normalize relations with a country, you should be able to "normalize" data relations as well. Additional normal forms were added later, as discussed in Chapter 7.

The normalization process is shown in Figure 6-1. On the surface, it is quite simple and straightforward, but it takes considerable practice to execute the process consistently and correctly. Briefly, we take any relation and choose a unique identifier for the entity that the relation represents. Then, through a series of steps that apply various rules, we reorganize the relation into continuously more progressive normal forms. The definitions of each of these normal forms and the process required to arrive at each one are covered in the sections that follow.

Throughout the normalization process, I consistently use the *logical terms* whenever possible. The only exception is the term *primary key,* which I use in lieu of *unique identifier* for consistency with current industry practice. Beginners may find it easier to think in terms of the physical objects that will eventually be created from the logical design. This is because learning to think of databases at the conceptual and logical levels of abstraction instead of the physical level is, in fact, a very difficult discipline for your mind to master. If you find yourself thinking of tables instead of relations, and columns instead of attributes, you need

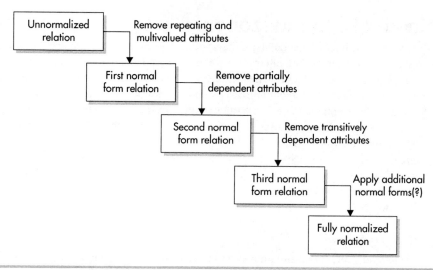

Figure 6-1   The normalization process

to break the habit as soon as possible. Those who think only physically while attempting to normalize tables run into difficulties later, because a one-to-one correspondence does not necessarily exist between normalized relations and tables. In fact, it is physical database design that transforms the normalized relations into relational tables, and there is some latitude in mapping normalized relations to physical tables. The following table may help you remember the correspondence between the logical and physical terms:

Logical Term	Physical Term
Relation or Entity	Table
Unique identifier	Primary key
Attribute	Column
Tuple	Row

NOTE

Relation was Codd's original name for a data structure made of rows and columns, and it is the basis for the name *relational database*. However, over time the term *entity* became more popular, even though the definitions of the two are not exactly the same. Be careful not to confuse *relation* (a data structure) with *relationship* (how one structure is related to another). If fact, it may be this confusion that has driven people away from using the term *relation*.

The Need for Normalization

In his early work with relational database theory, Codd discovered that unnormalized relations presented certain problems when attempts were made to update the data in them. He used the term *anomalies* for these problems. The reason we normalize the relations is to *remove* these anomalies from the data. It is essential that you understand these anomalies, because they also tell you when it is acceptable to bend the rules during physical design by "denormalizing" the relations (covered later in this chapter). It makes sense that in order to bend the rules, you need to understand why the rules exist in the first place.

Figure 6-2 shows an invoice from Acme Industries, a fictitious company. The invoice contains attributes that are typical for a printed invoice from a supply company. Conceptually, the invoice is a user view. We will use this invoice example throughout our exploration of the normalization process.

Insert Anomaly

The *insert anomaly* refers to a situation in which you cannot insert a new tuple into a relation because of an artificial dependency on another relation. (A *tuple* is a collection of data values that form one occurrence of an entity. In a physical database, a tuple is called a row of data.) The error that has caused the anomaly is that attributes of two different entities are mixed into the same relation. Referring to Figure 6-2, we see that the ID, name, and address of the customer are included in the invoice view. Were you merely to make a relation from this view as it is, and eventually a table from the relation, you would soon discover that you could not insert a new customer into the database unless the customer had bought something. This is because all the customer data is embedded in the invoice.

Delete Anomaly

The *delete anomaly* is the opposite of the insert anomaly. It refers to a situation wherein a deletion of data about one particular entity causes unintended loss of data that characterizes

Acme Industries
INVOICE

Customer Number: 1454837
Customer: W. Coyote
General Delivery
Falling Rocks, AZ 84211
(599) 555-9345

Terms: Net 30
Ship Via: USPS

Order Date: 07/31/2009

Product No.	Description	Quantity	Unit Price	Extended Amount
SPR-2290	Super Strength Springs	2	24.00	$48.00
STR-67	Foot Straps, Leather	2	2.50	$5.00
HLM-45	Deluxe Crash Helmet	1	67.88	$67.88
SFR-1	Rocket, Solid Fuel	1	128,200.40	$128,200.40
ELT-1	Emergency Location Transmitter	1	79.88	** FREE GIFT **
ORDER TOTAL:		7		$128,321.28

Figure 6-2 Invoice from Acme Industries

another entity. In the case of the Acme Industries invoice, if we delete the last invoice that belongs to a particular customer, we lose all the data related to that customer. Again, this is because data from two entities (customers and invoices) would be incorrectly mixed into a single relation if we merely implemented the invoice as a table without applying the normalization process to the relation.

Update Anomaly

The *update anomaly* refers to a situation in which an update of a single data value requires multiple tuples (rows) of data to be updated. In our invoice example, if we wanted to change the customer's address, we would have to change it on every single invoice for the customer. This is because the customer address would be redundantly stored in every invoice for the customer. To make matters worse, redundant data provides a golden opportunity to update many copies of the data but miss a few of them, resulting in inconsistent data. The mantra of the skilled database designer and data modeler is this: For each attribute, capture it once, store it once, and use that one copy everywhere.

Applying the Normalization Process

The normalization process is applied to each user view collected during earlier design stages. In this context, the entities identified in the conceptual data model, particularly those containing attributes, can be treated as user views. Some people find it easier to apply the first step (choosing a primary key) to each user view, and then to apply the next step (converting to first normal form), and so forth. Other people prefer to take the first user view and apply all the normalization steps to it, and then the next user view, and so forth. With practice, you'll know which process works best for you, but whichever you choose, you must be *very* systematic in your approach, lest you overlook something. Our example has only one user view (the Acme Industries invoice), so this may seem a moot point, but two practice problems toward the end of the chapter contain several user views each, so you will be able to try this out soon enough. Using dry-erase markers or chalk on a wall-mounted board is most helpful because you can easily erase and rewrite relations as you go.

Start with each user view being a relation, which means you represent it as if it were a two-dimensional table. As you work through the normalization process, you will be rewriting existing relations and creating new ones. Some find it useful to draw the relations with sample tuples (rows) of data in them to assist in visualizing the work. If you take this approach, be certain that your data represents real-world situations. For example, you might not realize that two customers can have exactly the same name in the invoice example—as a result, your normalization results might be incorrect. Therefore, you should *always* think of as many possibilities as you can when using this approach. Figure 6-3 shows the information from the invoice example (Figure 6-2) represented in tabular form. Only one invoice is shown here, but many more could be filled in to show examples of multiple invoices per customer, multiple customers, the same product on multiple invoices, and so on.

You probably noticed that each invoice has many line items. This will be essential information when we get to first normal form. In Figure 6-3, multiple values are placed in the cells for the columns that hold data from the line items. These are called *multivalued attributes* because they

Customer Number	Customer Name	Customer Address	Cust. City	Cust. State	Cust. ZIP	Customer Phone	Terms	Ship Via	Order Date	Product Number	Description	Quantity	Unit Price	Extended Amount
										SPR-2290	Super Strength Springs	2	24.00	$48.00
										STR-67	Foot Straps, Leather	2	2.50	$5.00
										HLM-45	Deluxe Crash Helmet	1	67.88	$67.88
										SFR-1	Rocket, Solid Fuel	1	128,200.40	$128,200.40
145837	W. Coyote	General Delivery	Falling Rocks	AZ	84211	599-555-9345	Net 30	USPS	07/31/2009	ELT-1	Emergency Location Transmitter	1	79.88	$0.00
											ORDER TOTAL	7		$128,321.28

Figure 6-3 Acme Industries invoice represented in tabular form

have multiple values for at least some tuples (rows) in the relation. If you were to construct an actual database table in this manner, your ability to use a language such as SQL to query those columns would be limited. For example, finding all orders that contain a particular product would require you to parse the column data with a LIKE operator. Updates would be equally awkward because SQL was not designed to handle multivalued columns. Worst of all, a delete of one product from an invoice would require an SQL UPDATE instead of a DELETE because you would not want to delete the entire invoice. As you consider the first normal form later in this chapter, you will see how to mitigate this problem.

Figure 6-4 shows another way a relation could be organized using the invoice shown in Figure 6-2. Here, the multivalued column data has been placed in separate rows and the other columns' data has been repeated to match. The obvious problem here is all the repeated data. For example, the customer's name and address are repeated for each line item on the invoice, which is not only wasteful of resources but also exposes you to inconsistencies whenever the data is not maintained uniformly (for example, if you update the city for one line item but not all the others).

Rewriting user views into tables with representative data is a tedious and time-consuming process. For this reason, you can simply write the attributes as a list and visualize them in your mind as the two-dimensional tables they will eventually become. This takes some practice and some training of the mind, but once you master it, you'll find it considerably faster to visualize the data rather than writing out exhaustive examples. Here is the list for the invoice example from Figure 6-2:

```
INVOICE: Customer Number, Customer Name, Customer Address,
         Customer City, Customer State, Customer Zip Code,
         Customer Phone, Terms, Ship Via, Order Date,
         Product Number, Product Description, Quantity,
         Unit Price, Extended Amount, Total Order Quantity,
         Total Order Amount
```

Customer Number	Customer Name	Customer Address	Cust. City	Cust. State	Cust. ZIP	Customer Phone	Terms	Ship Via	Order Date	Product Number	Description	Quantity	Unit Price	Extended Amount
145837	W. Coyote	General Delivery	Falling Rocks	AZ	84211	599-555-9345	Net 30	USPS	07/31/2009	SPR-2290	Super Strength Springs	2	24.00	$48.00
145837	W. Coyote	General Delivery	Falling Rocks	AZ	84211	599-555-9345	Net 30	USPS	07/31/2009	STR-67	Foot Straps, Leather	2	2.50	$5.00
145837	W. Coyote	General Delivery	Falling Rocks	AZ	84211	599-555-9345	Net 30	USPS	07/31/2009	HLM-45	Deluxe Crash Helmet	1	67.88	$67.88
145837	W. Coyote	General Delivery	Falling Rocks	AZ	84211	599-555-9345	Net 30	USPS	07/31/2009	SFR-1	Rocket, Solid Fuel	1	128,200.40	$128,200.40
145837	W. Coyote	General Delivery	Falling Rocks	AZ	84211	599-555-9345	Net 30	USPS	07/31/2009	ELT-1	Emergency Location Transmitter	1	79.88	$0.00
											ORDER TOTAL	7		$128,321.28

Figure 6-4 Acme Industries invoice represented without multivalued attributes

For clarity, a name for the relation has been added, with the relation name in uppercase letters and separated from the attributes with a colon. This is the convention I will use for the remainder of this chapter. However, if another technique works better for you, by all means use it. The best news of all is that no matter which representation you use (Figure 6-3, Figure 6-4, or the preceding list), if you properly apply the normalization process and its rules, you will create a comparable database design.

Choosing a Primary Key

As you normalize, you consider each user view as a relation. In other words, you conceptualize each user view as if it is already implemented in a two-dimensional table. The first step in normalization is to choose a primary key from among the unique identifiers you find in the relation.

Recall that a *unique identifier* is a collection of one or more attributes that uniquely identifies each occurrence of a relation. In many cases, a single attribute can be found. In our example, the customer number on the invoice uniquely identifies the customer data within the invoice, but because a customer may have multiple invoices, it is inadequate as an identifier for the entire invoice.

When no single attribute can be found to use for a unique identifier, you can concatenate several attributes to form the unique identifier. You will see this happen with our invoice example when we split the line items from the invoice as we normalize it. It is very important to understand that when a unique identifier is composed of multiple attributes, the attributes themselves are not combined—they still exist as independent attributes and will become individual columns in the table(s) created from our normalized relations.

In a few cases, no set of attributes in a relation can reasonably be used as the unique identifier. (You will find that many practitioners use the terms *identifier* and *key* interchangeably.) When this occurs, you must invent a unique identifier, often with values assigned sequentially or randomly as you add entity occurrences to the database. This technique (some might say "act of desperation") is the source of such unique identifiers as Social Security numbers, employee IDs, and driver's license numbers. Unique identifiers that have real-world meaning are called *natural* identifiers, and those that do not (which of course includes those we must invent), *surrogate* or *artificial* identifiers. In our invoice example, there appears to be no natural unique identifier for the relation. You could try using the customer number combined with the order date, but if a customer has two invoices on the same date, this would not be unique. Therefore, it would be much better to invent an identifier, such as an invoice number.

Whenever you choose a unique identifier for a relation, you must be *certain* that the identifier's data values will not change over time and that the identifier will be unique under *all* circumstances. If even *one* case exists to render the identifier not unique, you cannot use it. People's names, for example, make lousy unique identifiers. You may have never met someone with exactly your name, but there are people out there with completely identical names. As an example of the harm poorly chosen unique identifiers cause, consider the case of the Brazilian government when it started registering voters in 1994 to reduce election fraud. Father's name, mother's name, and date of birth were chosen as the unique identifier. Unfortunately, this combination is unique only for siblings born on *different* dates, so as a result, when siblings born on the same date (twins, triplets, and so on) tried to register to vote, the first one that showed up was allowed to register and the rest were turned away. Sound impossible? It's not—this really happened. And to make matters worse, citizens are *required* to vote in Brazil and sometimes have to prove they voted in order to get a job. Someone should have spent more time thinking about the uniqueness of the chosen "unique" identifier.

Social Security Numbers as Identifiers

Since I mentioned Social Security numbers in the text, let me add that I strongly recommend against using them as unique identifiers for individuals for several reasons. First, various state and federal privacy laws either forbid or severely restrict such use. Second, there have been cases where the Social Security Administration has issued duplicate numbers. Third, anyone with payroll system experience can tell you that some workers illegally use someone else's number because they don't have one of their own. Finally, anyone who has become a victim of identity theft must get a new Social Security number, which means the values are not always stable.

Sometimes a relation will have more than one possible unique identifier. When this occurs, each possibility is called a *candidate key*. Once you have identified all the possible candidate keys for a relation, you must choose one of them to be the primary key for the relation. Choosing a primary key is *essential* to the normalization process because all the normalization rules reference the primary key. The criteria for choosing the primary key from among the candidates are as follows (in order of precedence, most important first):

- *If only one candidate is available, choose it.*

- *Choose the candidate least likely to have its value change.* Changing primary key values once you store the data in tables is a complicated matter because the primary key can appear as a foreign key in many other tables. Incidentally, surrogate keys are almost always less likely to change compared with natural keys.

- *Choose the simplest candidate.* The one that comprises the fewest number of attributes is considered the simplest.

- *Choose the shortest candidate.* This is purely an efficiency consideration. However, when a primary key can appear in many tables as a foreign key, it is often worth it to save some space with each one.

For our invoice example, I have elected to add a surrogate primary identifier called Invoice Number. This yields a simple primary key for the Acme Industries invoices that is guaranteed unique, because we can have the DBMS automatically assign sequential numbers to new invoices as they are generated. This will likely make Acme's accountants happy at the same time, because it gives them a simple tracking number for the invoices.

Many conventions can be used for signifying the primary key as you write the contents of relations. Using capitalized names causes confusion because most of us tend to write acronyms such as DOB (date of birth) that way, and those attributes are not always the primary key. Likewise, underlining and bolding the attribute names can be troublesome because these may not always display in the same way. Therefore, I use the letters *PK* enclosed in parentheses following the attribute name(s) of the primary key. Rewriting the invoice relation in list form with the primary key added provides the following:

```
INVOICE: Invoice Number (PK), Customer Number, Customer Name,
         Customer Address, Customer City, Customer State,
         Customer Zip Code, Customer Phone, Terms,
         Ship Via, Order Date, Product Number,
         Product Description, Quantity, Unit Price,
         Extended Amount, Total Order Quantity,
         Total Order Amount
```

First Normal Form: Eliminating Repeating Data

A relation is said to be in *first normal form* when it contains no multivalued attributes—that is, every intersection of a row and column in the relation must contain *at most* one data value (saying "at most" allows for missing or null values). Sometimes, you will find a group of attributes that repeat together, as with the line items on the invoice. Each attribute in the group is multivalued, but several attributes are so closely related that their values repeat together. This is called a *repeating group,* but in reality, it is just a special case of the multivalued attribute problem.

By convention, I enclose repeating groups and multivalued attributes in pairs of parentheses. Rewriting our invoice in this way to show the line item data as a repeating group, we get this:

```
INVOICE: Invoice Number (PK), Customer Number, Customer Name,
         Customer Address, Customer City, Customer State,
         Customer Zip Code, Customer Phone, Terms,
         Ship Via, Order Date, (Product Number,
         Product Description, Quantity, Unit Price,
         Extended Amount), Total Order Quantity,
         Total Order Amount
```

It is essential that you understand that although you know that Acme Industries has many customers, only one customer exists for any given invoice, so the customer data on the invoice is *not* a repeating group. A quick look back at the original invoice document as shown in Figure 6-2 will confirm that each invoice has only one value for Customer Name, Customer Address, Customer City, and so on. You may have noticed that the customer data for a given customer is repeated on every invoice for that customer, but this problem will be addressed when we get to third normal form. Because there is only one customer per invoice, the problem is not addressed when we transform the relation to first normal form.

To transform unnormalized relations into first normal form, you must move multivalued attributes and repeating groups to new relations. Because a repeating group is a set of attributes that repeat *together,* all attributes in a repeating group should be moved to the same new relation. However, a multivalued attribute (individual attributes that have multiple values) should be moved to its own new relation rather than combined with other multivalued attributes in the new relation. As you will see later, this technique avoids fourth normal form problems.

The procedure for moving a multivalued attribute or repeating group to a new relation is as follows:

1. Create a new relation with a meaningful name. Often, it makes sense to include all or part of the original relation's name in the new relation's name.

2. Copy the primary key from the original relation to the new one. The data depends on this primary key in the original relation, so it must still depend on this key in the new relation. This copied primary key now becomes a *foreign key* to the original relation. As you apply normalization to a database design, always keep in mind that eventually you will have to write SQL to reproduce the original user view from which you started. So the foreign keys used to join things back together are nothing less than essential.

3. Move the repeating group or multivalued attribute to the new relation. (The word *move* is used because these attributes are *removed* from the original relation.)

4. Make the primary key (as copied from the original relation) unique by adding attributes from the repeating group to it. If you move a multivalued attribute, which is basically a repeating group of only one attribute, that attribute is added to the primary key. This will seem odd at first, but the primary key attribute(s) that you copied from the original table is a *foreign key* in the new relation. It is quite normal for part of a primary key also to be a foreign key. One additional point: It is perfectly acceptable to have a relation in which all the attributes are part of the primary key (that is, where there are no "nonkey" attributes). This is relatively common in intersection tables.

5. Optionally, you can choose to replace the primary key with a single surrogate key attribute. If you do so, you must keep the attributes that make up the natural primary key formed in steps 2 and 4.

For our Acme Industries invoice example, here is the result of converting the original relation to first normal form:

```
INVOICE: Invoice Number (PK), Customer Number, Customer Name,
         Customer Address, Customer City, Customer State,
         Customer Zip Code, Customer Phone, Terms,
         Ship Via, Order Date, Total Order Quantity,
         Total Order Amount

INVOICE LINE ITEM: Invoice Number (PK, FK), Product Number (PK),
         Product Description, Quantity, Unit Price,
         Extended Amount
```

Note the following:

- The Invoice Number attribute was copied from INVOICE to INVOICE LINE ITEM and Product Number was added to it to form the primary key of the INVOICE LINE ITEM relation.

- The entire repeating group (Product Number, Product Description, Quantity, Unit Price, and Extended Amount) was removed from the INVOICE relation.

- Invoice Number is still the primary key in INVOICE, and it now also serves as a foreign key in INVOICE LINE ITEM as well as being *part* of the primary key of INVOICE LINE ITEM.

- There are no repeating groups or multivalued attributes in the relations, so they are therefore in first normal form.

Note an interesting consequence of composing a natural primary key for the INVOICE LINE ITEM relation: You cannot put the same product on a given invoice more than one time. This might be desirable, but it could also restrict Acme Industries. You have to understand their business rules to know. If Acme Industries wants the option of putting multiple line items on the same invoice for the same product (perhaps with different prices), you should make up a surrogate key instead. Moreover, there are those who believe that primary keys composed of multiple attributes are undesirable, along with software products that simply do not support them. The alternative is to make up a surrogate primary key for the INVOICE LINE ITEM relation. If you choose to do so, the relation can be rewritten this way:

```
INVOICE LINE ITEM: Invoice Line Item ID (PK),
                   Invoice Number, Product Number,
                   Product Description, Quantity,
                   Unit Price, Extended Amount
```

I am going to use the previous form (the one with the compound primary key made up of Invoice Number and Product Number, often called the *natural key*) as we continue with normalization, primarily because experience has taught me that normalization is easier to understand when natural keys are used. Know that there are lots of IT professionals who believe that surrogate keys should always be used, arguing that natural key values tend to change over time and that table joins are easier to write when all the foreign keys consist of only a single column. However, properly selected natural keys (that is, those that won't tend to change over time) are easier for business users who will be validating your model to understand, and on the physical side, you don't have to worry about multiple unique indexes (one on the primary key and another on the natural key).

Second Normal Form: Eliminating Partial Dependencies

Before you explore second normal form, you must understand the concept of *functional dependence.* For this definition, we'll use two arbitrary attributes, cleverly named "A" and "B." Attribute B is *functionally dependent* on attribute A if at any moment in time no more than one value of attribute B is associated with a given value of attribute A. Lest you wonder what planet I lived on before this one, I'll try to make the definition more understandable. First, suppose that attribute B is functionally dependent on attribute A; this is also saying that attribute A *determines* attribute B, or that A is a *determinant* (unique identifier) of attribute B. Second, let's look again at the first normal form relations in our Acme Industries example:

```
INVOICE: Invoice Number (PK), Customer Number, Customer Name,
         Customer Address, Customer City, Customer State,
         Customer Zip Code, Customer Phone, Terms,
         Ship Via, Order Date, Total Order Quantity,
         Total Order Amount

INVOICE LINE ITEM: Invoice Number (PK), Product Number (PK),
         Product Description, Quantity, Unit Price,
         Extended Amount
```

In the INVOICE relation, you can easily see that Customer Number is functionally dependent on Invoice Number because at any point in time, there can be only one value of Customer Number associated with a given value of Invoice Number. The very fact that the Invoice Number uniquely identifies the Customer Number in this relation means that, in return, the Customer Number is *functionally dependent* on the Invoice Number.

In the INVOICE LINE ITEM relation, you can also say that Product Description is functionally dependent on Product Number because, at any point in time, there is only one value of Product Description associated with the Product Number. However, the fact that the Product Number is only part of the key of the INVOICE LINE ITEM is the very issue addressed by second normal form.

A relation is said to be in *second normal form* if it meets both the following criteria:

- The relation is in first normal form.

- All nonkey attributes are functionally dependent on the *entire* primary key.

Look again at Product Description, and it should be easy to see that Product Number *alone* determines the value. Said another way, if the same product appears as a line item on many different invoices, the Product Description is the same *regardless* of the Invoice Number. Or you can say that Product Description is functionally dependent on only *part of* the primary key, meaning it depends only on Product Number and not on the *combination* of Invoice Number *and* Product Number.

It should also be clear by now that second normal form applies only to relations where we have concatenated primary keys (that is, those made up of multiple attributes). If a primary key is composed of only a single attribute, as is the case with the first normal form version of the INVOICE relation, and the primary key is atomic (that is, has no subparts that make sense by themselves), as all attributes should be, then it is simply not possible for anything to depend on *part* of the primary key. It follows, then, that any first normal form relation that has only a single atomic attribute for its primary key is *automatically* in second normal form.

Looking at the INVOICE LINE ITEM relation, however, second normal form violations should be readily apparent: Product Description and Unit Price depend only on the Product

Number instead of the *combination* of Invoice Number and Product Number. But not so fast! What about price changes? If Acme decides to change its prices, how could you possibly want that change to be retroactive for every invoice you have ever created? After all, an invoice is an official record that you must maintain for seven years, per current U.S. tax laws. This is a common dilemma with fast-changing attributes such as prices. Either you must be able to recall the price at any point in time or you must store the price with the invoice so that you can reproduce the invoice as needed (that is, when the friendly tax auditors come calling).

For simplicity, let's store the price in two places—one being the current selling price and the other being the price at the time the sale was made. Because the latter is a snapshot at a point in time that is not expected to change, there are no anomalies to this seemingly redundant storage. An alternative would be to store a date-sensitive price history somewhere that you could use to reconstruct the correct price for any invoice. (The modeling of time dependent data is discussed in Chapter 10.) That is a practical alternative here, but you would never be able to do that with stock or commodities market transactions, for example. The point is that while the sales price *looks* redundant, there are no *anomalies* to the additional attribute, so it does no harm. Notice that the attribute names are adjusted so that their meaning is abundantly clear.

Once you find a second normal form violation, the solution is to move any attributes that are partially dependent to a new relation where they depend on the *entire* key instead of *part* of the key. Here is our invoice example rewritten into second normal form:

```
INVOICE: Invoice Number (PK), Customer Number, Customer Name,
         Customer Address, Customer City, Customer State,
         Customer Zip Code, Customer Phone, Terms,
         Ship Via, Order Date, Total Order Quantity,
         Total Order Amount

INVOICE LINE ITEM: Invoice Number (PK), Product Number (PK),
         Quantity, Sale Unit Price, Extended Amount

PRODUCT:  Product Number (PK), Product Description,
          List Unit Price
```

The improvement from the first normal form solution is that maintenance of the Product Description now has no anomalies. You can set up a new product independent of the existence of an invoice for the product. If you want to change the Product Description, you may do so by merely changing one value in one row of data. Also, should the last invoice for a particular product be deleted from the database for whatever reason, you won't lose its description (it will still be in the row in the Product relation). *Always* remember that the reason you are normalizing is to eliminate these anomalies.

Third Normal Form: Eliminating Transitive Dependencies

To understand third normal form, you must first understand transitive dependency. An attribute that depends on another attribute that is not the primary key of the relation is said to be *transitively dependent*. Looking at our INVOICE relation in second normal form, you can clearly see that Customer Name is dependent on Invoice Number (each Invoice Number has only one Customer Name value associated with it), but at the same time Customer Name is also dependent on Customer Number. The same can be said of the rest of the customer attributes as well. The problem here is that attributes of another entity (Customer) have been included in our INVOICE relation.

A relation is said to be in *third normal form* if it meets both the following criteria:

- The relation is in second normal form.

- There is no transitive dependence (that is, all the nonkey attributes depend *only* on the primary key).

To transform a second normal form relation into third normal form, simply move any transitively dependent attributes to relations where they depend only on the primary key. Be careful to leave the attribute on which they depend in the original relation as a foreign key. You will need it to reconstruct the original user view via a join.

If you have been wondering about easily calculated attributes such as Extended Amount in the INVOICE LINE ITEM relation, it is actually third normal form that forbids them, but it takes a subtle interpretation of the rule. Because the Extended Amount is calculated by multiplying Sale Unit Price × Quantity, it follows that Extended Amount is *determined by* the combination of Sale Unit Price and Quantity and therefore is *transitively dependent* on those two attributes. Thus, it is third normal form that tells you to remove easily calculated attributes. And in this case, they are simply removed. Using similar logic, you can also remove Total Order Quantity and Total Order Amount from the INVOICE relation because you can simply sum the INVOICE LINE ITEM relation to reproduce the values. A good designer will make a note in the documentation specifying the formula for each calculated attribute so that its value can be reproduced when needed. Another highly effective alternative is to write the SQL that reproduces the original views when you complete a normalization process. It's an excellent way to *test* your normalization because you can use the SQL to *prove* that the original user views can be easily reproduced.

Here is the Acme Industries invoice data rewritten into third normal form:

```
INVOICE: Invoice Number (PK), Customer Number, Terms,
         Ship Via, Order Date

INVOICE LINE ITEM: Invoice Number (PK), Product Number (PK),
         Quantity, Sale Unit Price

PRODUCT: Product Number (PK), Product Description,
         List Unit Price

CUSTOMER: Customer Number (PK), Customer Name,
          Customer Address, Customer City, Customer State,
          Customer Zip Code, Customer Phone
```

Ask the Expert

Q: **In the CUSTOMER entity you just illustrated, aren't City and State transitively dependent on the Zip Code?**

A: Not really. Even if you always have the *complete* nine-digit ZIP code (called "ZIP Plus 4" by the U.S. Postal Service), there is no absolute guarantee that the ZIP code will always contain only one city, county, and state. Yes, the Postal Service publishes a ZIP code list that provides a city, county, and state for each ZIP code, but that only tells you the location of the post office building that serves the ZIP code; it does *not* indicate that all the addresses within that ZIP code are in the listed city, county, and state. In the past, some ZIP codes in the United States have actually crossed state lines. Moreover, thousands of examples exist of different cities and towns sharing the same ZIP codes. Nor can you use ZIP codes to determine the county within the state—roughly 20 percent of U.S. five-digit ZIP codes contain parts of more than one county. So be careful when you assume things. The Postal Service will be the first to tell you that it is not responsible for aligning its zoning system with political boundaries. The only 100 percent reliable way to assign city, county, and state to a U.S. address is to use the complete street address in a ZIP code table that includes street names and ranges of street (building) numbers that apply to that ZIP code. By the way, ZIP is actually an acronym for Zoning Improvement Program, introduced in 1963. But I digress . . . .

Should you then make a Zip Code relation and normalize the City and State out of all your addresses? Or would that be considered overdesign? The question can be answered by going back to the anomalies, because removal of the insert, update, and delete anomalies is the entire reason you normalize data in the first place:

- If a new city is formed, do you need to add it to the database even if you have no customers located there? (This is an insert anomaly.)
- If a city is dissolved, do you have a need to delete its information without losing other data? (This is a delete anomaly.)
- If a city changes its name (this rarely occurs, but it has happened), is it a burden to you to find all the customers in that city and change their addresses accordingly?

If you answered yes to any of these questions, you should normalize the City and State attributes into a table with a primary key of Zip Code. (Note that the city and state names assigned will be the ones for the post office that serves the ZIP code, which are the names the post office prefers, but they may not be the ones preferred by those receiving the mail.) In fact, you can purchase ZIP code data on a regular basis from the U.S. Postal Service or other sources, or you can subscribe to an address cleansing service that will standardize addresses and provide accurate ZIP codes for each one. Furthermore, if you maintain other data by ZIP code, such as shipping rates, you have all the more reason to normalize it. But if not, the Zip Code example is a valuable lesson in why we normalize (or not) and when it may not be as important.

Another argument for not normalizing the Zip Code data is that the data is not stable. The post office is constantly adding and splitting ZIP codes, and whenever cities acquire new territory, the ZIP code list for the city can change. Common sense must prevail at all times.

NOTE
Here is an easy way to remember the rules of first, second, and third normal form: In
a third normal form relation, every nonkey attribute must depend on the key, the whole
key, and nothing but the key, so help me Codd.

Denormalization

As you have seen, normalization leads to more relations, which translates to more tables and
more joins. When database users suffer performance problems that cannot be resolved by
other means, such as tuning the database or upgrading the hardware on which the RDBMS
runs, denormalization may be required. Most database experts consider denormalization
a last resort, if not an act of desperation. With continuous improvements in hardware and
RDBMS efficiencies, denormalization has become far less necessary than in the earlier days
of relational databases. The most essential point is that denormalization is not the same as
not bothering to normalize in the first place. Once a normalized database design has been
achieved, adjustments can be made with the potential consequences (anomalies) in mind.

Possible denormalization steps include the following:

⦿ Recombining relations that were split to satisfy normalization rules

⦿ Storing redundant data in tables

⦿ Storing summarized data in tables

Note also that normalization is intended to remove anomalies from databases that are used
for online transaction-processing systems. Databases that store historical data used solely for
analytical purposes are not as subject to insert, update, and delete anomalies. Chapter 11 offers
more information on analytical databases that hold historical information.

Practice Problems

This section includes two practice problems (in the form of Try This exercises) with solutions
so that you can try normalization for yourself. These are very narrow, scaled-down case
problems that most readers should be able to solve in about an hour each. As you work them,
you will be more successful if you focus just on the views presented and don't worry about
other business processes and data that might be needed. For each case problem, the intent is for
you to produce third normal form relations that support the views presented and then construct
a logical data model, in the form of an entity relationship diagram (ERD), to document the
normalized relations. As you draw the ERDs, keep in mind that they are quite easy to create
once normalization is complete—you simply create a rectangle for each normalized relation
and then draw relationships everywhere a primary key in one relation is used as a foreign
key in another (or the same) relation. These should all be one-to-many relationships, and the
foreign key must always be on the *many* side of the relationship. My solution for each problem
appears in Appendix B.

Try This 6-1 UTLA Academic Tracking

The University of Three Letter Acronyms (UTLA) is a small academic facility offering undergraduate and continuing adult education. Most of the recordkeeping is either manual or done by individuals using personal tools such as spreadsheets. A modernization effort is underway, which includes building integrated application and database systems to perform basic business functions.

The User Views

UTLA wishes to construct a system to track its academic activities, including course offerings, instructor qualifications for the courses, course enrollment, and student grades. The following illustrations show the desired output reports with sample data (these are the user views that should be normalized).

Student Report:

ID	Name	Mailing Address				Home Phone
4567	Helen Wheels	127 Essex Drive	Hayward	CA	94545	510-555-2859
4953	Barry Bookworm	P.O. Box 45	Oakland	CA	94601	510-555-9403
6758	Carla Coed	South Hall #23	Berkeley	CA	94623	510-555-8742

Course Report:

ID	Title	No. Credits	Prerequisite Courses	Description
X100	Concepts of Data Proc.	4	None	This course...
X301	C Programming I	4	X100	Students learn...
X302	C Programming II	6	X301	Continuation of...
X422	Systems Analysis	6	X301	Introduction to...
X408	Concepts of DBMS	6	X301, X422	The main focus...

Instructor Report:

ID	Name	Home Address	Home Phone	Office Phone	Courses
756	Werdna Leppo	12 Main St. Alameda CA 94501	510-555-1234	x-7463	X408, X422
795	Cora Coder	32767 Binary Way Abend CA 21304	510-555-1010	x-5328	X301, X302
801	Tillie Talker	123 Forms Rd. Paperwork CA 95684	510-555-2829	408-555-2047	X100, X422

(continued)

Section Report:

```
Year: 2008     Semester: Spr     Building: Evans     Room: 70     Day(s): Tu     Time(s): 7-10

Instructor: 756, Werdna Leppo     Course: X408     Credits: 6

        Student ID      Student Name            Grade
          4567          Helen Wheels              A
          6758          Carla Coed                B+


Year: 2008     Semester: Spr     Building: SFO     Room: 7     Day(s): We     Time(s): 7-10

Instructor: 756, Werdna Leppo     Course: X408     Credits: 6

        Student ID      Student Name            Grade
          4953          Barry Bookworm            B+
          6758          Carla Coed                A-


Year: 2008     Semester: Spr     Building: Evans     Room: 70     Day(s): M,Fr     Time(s): 7-9

Instructor: 801, Tillie Talker     Course: X100     Credits: 4

        Student ID      Student Name            Grade
```

You cannot design a database without some knowledge of the business rules and processes of an organization. Here are a few such items to keep in mind:

- Only one mailing address and one contact phone number are kept for each student.

- Each course has a fixed number of credits (that is, no variable credit courses are offered).

- Each course may have one or more prerequisite courses. The list of all prerequisites for each course is shown in the Course report.

- Only one mailing address, one home phone number, and one office phone number are kept for each instructor.

- A qualifications committee must approve instructors before they are permitted to teach a particular course. The qualifications (that is, the courses that the committee has determined the instructor is qualified to teach) are then added to the instructor's records, as shown in the Instructor report. The list of qualified courses does not imply that the instructor has actually taught the course but only that he or she is qualified to do so.

- Based on demand, any course may be offered multiple times, even in the same year and semester. Each offering is called a "section," as shown in the Section report.

- Students enroll in a particular section of a course and receive a grade for their participation in that course offering. Should they take the course again at a later time, they receive another grade, and both grades are part of their permanent academic record.

- Although the day, time, building, and room for each section is noted in the Section report, this is done merely to facilitate registering students. The scheduling of classrooms is out of scope for this project.

- The day(s) and time(s) attributes on the Section report are merely text descriptions of the meeting schedule. The building of a meeting calendar for sections is out of scope for this project.

As a convenience, here are the attributes rewritten using the relation listing method, with repeating groups and multivalued attributes enclosed in parentheses:

```
STUDENT REPORT: ID, STUDENT NAME, STREET ADDRESS, CITY, STATE,
                ZIP CODE, HOME PHONE

COURSE REPORT: ID, TITLE, NUMBER OF CREDITS,
               (PREREQUISITE COURSES), DESCRIPTION

INSTRUCTOR REPORT: ID, INSTRUCTOR NAME, STREET ADDRESS,
                   CITY, STATE, ZIP CODE, HOME PHONE,
                   OFFICE PHONE, (QUALIFIED COURSES)

SECTION REPORT: YEAR, SEMESTER, BUILDING, ROOM, DAYS,
                TIMES, INSTRUCTOR ID, INSTRUCTOR NAME,
                COURSE ID, NUMBER OF CREDITS,
                (STUDENT ID, STUDENT NAME, GRADE)
```

Step by Step

1. Study each of the user views in the preceding description, along with the business rules. You may have to make some assumptions if you have questions that the description does not answer.

2. Apply the normalization process described in this chapter, normalizing each view to relations that are in third normal form. Be careful to consolidate the normalized relations you develop as you go. For the purposes of this exercise, no two relations should share the same primary key. (Exceptions to this rule involve supertypes and subtypes because subtypes often have the same primary key as the corresponding supertype.)

3. Clearly indicate the primary key of each relation. Remember that a primary key can be one or more attributes within the relation.

4. Draw a logical data model ERD with one entity (rectangle) for each of your normalized relations and appropriate relationship lines with cardinality clearly noted. This should be quite easy to do once normalization is complete: simply draw a line from each foreign key to the matching primary key and mark the foreign key end of the line as "many" and the primary key end as "one."

(continued)

Try This Summary

In this Try This exercise, you normalized four user views and drew an ERD of your design. My solution appears in Appendix B.

Try This 6-2 Computer Books Company

The Computer Books Company (CBC) buys books from publishers and sells them to individuals via mail and telephone orders. They are looking to expand their services by offering online ordering via the Internet, and in doing so CBC has a compelling need to build a database to hold its business information.

The User Views

Throughout these user views, "sale" and "price" are references to the retail sale of a book to a CBC customer, whereas "purchase" and "cost" are references to the purchase of books from a publisher (CBC supplier). Each user view is described briefly with a list of the attributes in the view following each description. Per our convention, multivalued attributes and repeating groups are enclosed in parentheses.

The Book Catalog lists all the books that CBC has for sale. Each book is uniquely identified by the International Standard Book Number (ISBN). Although an ISBN uniquely identifies a book, it is essentially a surrogate key, so there is no way to tell the edition of a particular book simply by looking at the ISBN. When new editions come out, CBC typically has leftover stock of prior editions and offers them at a reduced price. The previous edition ISBN in the Book Catalog is intended to help the buyer find the prior edition, if one exists. Books are organized by subject, with each book having only one subject. Any book can have multiple authors. (Although the catalog shows only author names, keep in mind that people's names are seldom unique, and nothing would stop two people with the same name from writing two different books.)

Here is the information in the Book Catalog:

```
BOOK CATALOG: SUBJECT CODE, SUBJECT DESCRIPTION, BOOK TITLE,
              BOOK ISBN, BOOK PRICE, PREVIOUS EDITION ISBN,
              PREVIOUS EDITION PRICE, (BOOK AUTHORS),
              PUBLISHER NAME
```

The Book Inventory Report helps the warehouse manager control the inventory in the warehouse. The Recommended Quantity is the reorder point, meaning when on-hand inventory falls below the recommended quantity, it is time to order more books of that title.

```
INVENTORY REPORT: BOOK ISBN, BOOK EDITION CODE, COST,
                  SELLING PRICE, QUANTITY ON HAND,
                  QUANTITY ON ORDER, RECOMMENDED QUANTITY
```

The Customer Book Orders view shows orders placed by CBC customers for purchases of books:

```
CUSTOMER BOOK ORDERS: CUSTOMER ID, CUSTOMER NAME,
                      STREET ADDRESS, CITY, STATE,
                      ZIP CODE (ISBN, BOOK EDITION CODE,
                      QUANTITY, PRICE), ORDER DATE,
                      TOTAL PRICE
```

CBC bills customers as books are shipped, so an unshipped order won't have an invoice. An invoice is created for each shipment. (An order can have zero, one, or more invoices, but each invoice belongs only to one order.) The Book Sales Invoice looks like this:

```
BOOK SALES INVOICE: SALES INVOICE NUMBER, CUSTOMER ID,
                    CUSTOMER NAME, CUSTOMER STREET ADDRESS,
                    CUSTOMER CITY, CUSTOMER STATE,
                    CUSTOMER ZIP CODE, (BOOK ISBN, TITLE,
                    EDITION CODE, (BOOK AUTHORS), QUANTITY,
                    PRICE, PUBLISHER NAME),
                    SHIPPING CHARGES, SALES TAX
```

The Master Billing Report helps the Collections and Customer Service departments manage customer accounts. A system for recording customer payments against invoices is out of scope for the current project, but the CBC project sponsors do want to keep a running balance showing what each customer owes CBC. As invoices are generated, a database trigger will be used to automatically add invoice totals to the Balance Due. As payments are received, the CBC staff will manually adjust the Balance Due. The Master Billing Report attributes are as follows:

```
MASTER BILLING REPORT: CUSTOMER ID, CUSTOMER NAME, STREET ADDRESS,
                       STREET ADDRESS, CITY, STATE, ZIP CODE,
                       PHONE, BALANCE DUE
```

Each time CBC buys books from a publisher, the publisher sends an invoice to CBC. To assist in managing inventory cost, CBC wishes to store the Purchase Invoice information and report it using this view:

```
PURCHASE INVOICE: PUBLISHER ID, PUBLISHER NAME,
                  STREET ADDRESS, CITY, STATE, ZIP CODE,
                  PURCHASE INVOICE NUMBER, INVOICE DATE,
                  (BOOK ISBN, EDITION CODE, TITLE,
                  QUANTITY, COST EACH, EXTENDED COST),
                  TOTAL COST
```

Note that Extended Cost is calculated as Cost Each × Quantity.

(continued)

Step by Step

1. Study each of the user views in the preceding description, along with the business rules. You might have to make some assumptions if you have questions that the description does not answer.

2. Apply the normalization process described in this chapter, normalizing each view to relations that are in at least third normal form. Be careful to consolidate the normalized relations you develop as you go. For the purposes of this exercise, no two relations should share the same primary key unless they are a supertype and subtype.

3. Clearly indicate the primary key of each relation. Remember that a primary key can be one or more attributes within the relation.

4. Draw a logical data model ERD with one entity (rectangle) for each of your normalized relations and appropriate relationship lines with cardinality clearly noted. This is actually quite easy once normalization is complete: simply draw a line from each foreign key to the matching primary key and mark the foreign key end of the line as "many" and the primary key end as "one."

Try This Summary

In this Try This exercise, you normalized six user views that were more complicated than the previous Try This exercise and drew an ERD of your design. My solution appears in Appendix B.

Chapter 6 Self Test

Choose the correct responses to each of the multiple-choice and fill-in-the-blank questions. Note that there may be more than one correct response to each question.

1. Normalization

   A Was developed by E.F. Codd

   B Was first introduced with five normal forms

   C First appeared in 1972

   D Provides a set of rules for each normal form

   E Provides a procedure for converting relations to each normal form

2. The purpose of normalization is

   A To eliminate redundant data

   B To remove certain anomalies from the relations

    C To provide a reason to denormalize the database

    D To optimize data-retrieval performance

    E To optimize data for inserts, updates, and deletes

3. When implemented, a third normal form relation becomes a(n) _____.

4. The insert anomaly refers to a situation in which

    A Data must be inserted before it can be deleted

    B Too many inserts cause the table to fill up

    C Data must be deleted before it can be inserted

    D A required insert cannot be done due to an artificial dependency

    E A required insert cannot be done due to duplicate data

5. The delete anomaly refers to a situation in which

    A Data must be deleted before it can be inserted

    B Data must be inserted before it can be deleted

    C Data deletion causes unintentional loss of another entity's data

    D A required delete cannot be done due to referential constraints

    E A required delete cannot be done due to lack of privileges

6. The update anomaly refers to a situation in which

    A A simple update requires updates to multiple rows of data

    B Data cannot be updated because it does not exist in the database

    C Data cannot be updated due to lack of privileges

    D Data cannot be updated due to an existing unique constraint

    E Data cannot be updated due to an existing referential constraint

7. The roles of unique identifiers in normalization are

    A They are unnecessary

    B They are required once you reach third normal form

    C All normalized forms require designation of a primary key

    D You cannot normalize relations without first choosing a primary key

    E You cannot choose a primary key until relations are normalized

8. Writing sample user views with representative data in them is

    A The only way to normalize the user views successfully

    B A tedious and time-consuming process

    C An effective way to understand the data being normalized

    D Only as good as the examples shown in the sample data

    E A widely used normalization technique

9. Criteria useful in selecting a primary key from among several candidate keys are

    A Choose the simplest candidate

    B Choose the shortest candidate

    C Choose the candidate most likely to have its value change

    D Choose concatenated keys over single attribute keys

    E Invent a surrogate key if that is the best possible key.

10. First normal form resolves anomalies caused by _____.

11. Second normal form resolves anomalies caused by _____.

12. Third normal form resolves anomalies caused by _____.

13. In general, violations of a normalization rule are resolved by

    A Combining relations

    B Moving attributes or groups of attributes to a new relation

    C Combining attributes

    D Creating summary tables

    E Denormalization

14. A foreign key in a normalized relation may be

    A The entire primary key of the relation

    B Part of the primary key of the relation

    C A repeating group

    D A nonkey attribute in the relation

    E A multivalued attribute

15. Proper handling of multivalued attributes when converting relations to first normal form usually prevents subsequent problems with _____.

Chapter 7

Beyond Third Normal Form

Key Skills & Concepts

- Boyce-Codd Normal Form

- Fourth Normal Form

- Fifth Normal Form

- Domain Key Normal Form

- Resolving Supertypes and Subtypes

- Generalizing Attributes

- Alternatives for Reference Data

This chapter addresses additional considerations not covered by third normal form. While third normal form resolves most of the anomalies found in business systems, there can be other issues. The section "Advanced Normalization" covers normalization forms designed to mitigate anomalies that are sometimes found in entities that are already in third normal form, including Boyce-Codd normal form, fourth normal form, fifth normal form, and domain key normal form. The section "Resolving Supertypes and Subtypes" addresses design alternatives for handling supertypes and subtypes in structures that comply with normalization rules. The section "Generalizing Attributes" presents an alternative design technique when subtypes and attributes are expected to radically vary over time. And finally, the section "Alternatives for Reference Data" explores techniques for handling all the reference tables produced by the normalization processes.

Advanced Normalization

Since the original introduction of normalization, various authors have offered advanced versions. Third normal form will cover well over 90 percent of the cases you will see in business information systems, and it's considered the "gold standard" in business systems. However, once you have mastered third normal form, additional normal forms are worth knowing because you will occasionally come across the anomalies the additional forms address.

Boyce-Codd Normal Form

Boyce-Codd Normal Form (BCNF), developed by Raymond F. Boyce and E.F. Codd in 1974, is a stronger version of third normal form. It addresses anomalies that occur when a nonkey attribute is a *determinant* of an attribute that is part of the primary key (that is, when an attribute that is part of the primary key is functionally dependent on a nonkey attribute).

Customer	Product Line	Support Specialist
W. Coyote	Springs	R.E. Coil
W. Coyote	Straps	B. Brown
W. Coyote	Helmets	C. Bandecoot
W. Coyote	Rockets	R. Goddard
USAF	Rockets	R. Goddard
S. Gonzalez	Springs	R.E. Coil
S. Gonzalez	Straps	B. Brown
S. Gonzalez	Rockets	E. John
L. Armstrong	Helmets	S.D. Osborne

Table 7-1   The Customer Support Specialist Assignment Entity

As an example, assume that Acme Industries assigns multiple product support specialists to each customer, and each support specialist handles only one particular product line. Table 7-1 shows sample data for an entity named Customer Support Specialist Assignment that assigns specialists to customers. In practice, Customer ID and Support Specialist (Employee) ID would be used instead of the customer and support specialist names, but their names are used here for better illustration of the issue.

In this example, you must concatenate the Customer and Product Line attributes to form a primary key. However, because a given support specialist supports only one product line, it is also true that the Support Specialist attribute determines the Product Line attribute. The data model shown in Figure 7-1 graphically illustrates the anomaly in the Customer Support Assignment data shown in Table 7-1.

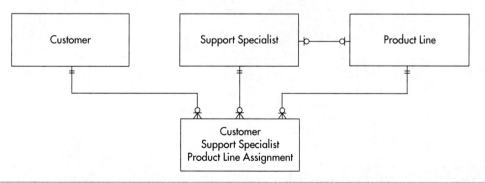

Figure 7-1   Data model with BCNF issue

Data modelers should always scrutinize intersection entities that have more than two parents—more often than not, they represent a violation of one of the forms of normalization. In this case, the anomaly stems from the enforcement of the business rule that a support specialist can handle only one product line. The one-to-many relationship between the Product Line and Support Specialist entities seems to handle it, but as shown, nothing prevents a row in the Customer Support Specialist Assignment entity from containing the name of a product line that is other than the one assigned to the support specialist contained in the same row. Given this design, we would have to either write a trigger to enforce this business rule or leave it up to the applications that update the database to do so. It is clear from Figure 7-1, however, that the fundamental error is the inclusion of Product Line in the Customer Support Specialist Assignment entity. It should be inherited from Support Specialist instead.

If the Customer Support Specialist Assignment relation used a surrogate primary key instead of combining Customer and Product Line for the primary key, the third normal form violation—a nonkey attribute determining another nonkey attribute (Support Specialist determining Product Line in this case)—would have been obvious. However, the normalization error was masked by making Product Line part of the primary key. This is why BCNF is considered a *stronger* version of third normal form.

The BCNF has two requirements:

- The relation (entity) must be in third normal form.

- No determinants can exist that are not either the primary key or a candidate key for the table. That is, a nonkey attribute may not uniquely identify (determine) any other attribute, including one that participates in the primary key.

The solution is to split the unwanted determinant to a different table, just as you would with a third normal form violation. Figure 7-2 shows the modified data model. In this case,

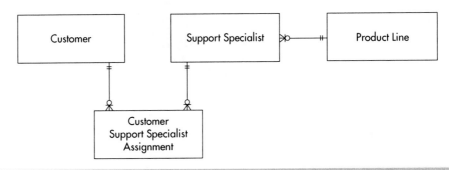

Figure 7-2 Data model in Boyce-Codd normal form

Customer	Support Specialist
W. Coyote	R.E. Coil
W. Coyote	B. Brown
W. Coyote	C. Bandecoot
W. Coyote	R. Goddard
USAF	R. Goddard
S. Gonzalez	R.E. Coil
S. Gonzalez	B. Brown
S. Gonzalez	E. John
L. Armstrong	S.D. Osborne

Table 7-2 The Customer Support Specialist Assignment Entity

we already had a relationship between Product Line and Support Specialist. Otherwise, we would need to establish it. Note that BCNF specifically addresses anomalies caused by overlapping candidate keys.

In tabular form, the entities and data look like those shown in Tables 7-2 and 7-3 (again, names have been substituted for the IDs to make the data easier to visualize).

Fourth Normal Form

Once in BCNF, remaining normalization problems deal almost exclusively with entities where every attribute is a candidate key. One such anomaly surfaces when two or more multivalued attributes are included in the same entity. Suppose, for example, you want to

Support Specialist	Product Line
B. Brown	Straps
C. Bandecoot	Helmets
E. John	Rockets
R.E. Coil	Springs
R. Goddard	Rockets
S.D. Osborne	Helmets

Table 7-3 The Support Specialist Entity with Product Line Assignment

track both office skills and language skills for our employees. You might come up with an entity such as this one:

Employee ID	Office Skill	Language Skill
1001	Typing, 40 wpm	Spanish
1001	10 key	French
1002	Spreadsheets	Spanish
1002	10 key	German

You can form a primary key for this entity by choosing the combination of either Employee ID and Office Skill, or Employee ID and Language Skill. That leaves you with either of these two alternatives for third normal form entities:

```
EMPLOYEE SKILL: EMPLOYEE ID (PK), OFFICE SKILL (PK),
                LANGUAGE SKILL

EMPLOYEE SKILL: EMPLOYEE ID (PK), LANGUAGE SKILL (PK),
                OFFICE SKILL
```

Both the alternatives shown are in third normal form, and both pass BCNF as well. The problem, of course, is that an implied relationship exists between office skills and language skills. Does the first tuple for employee 1001 imply that he or she can type only in Spanish? And does the second tuple imply that he or she can work only a French 10-key pad? If we construct a data model as shown in Figure 7-3, the three-way intersection entity Employee Skill graphically shows the anomaly. Again, three-way intersection entities need careful scrutiny. While some such entities are legitimate, many present issues with advanced normal forms (those beyond third normal form). Although the model looks at a glance as if it illustrates the BCNF issue shown in Figure 7-1, the difference is that the three parent entities (Office Skill, Employee, and Language Skill) are really independent of one another with no relationship between any of them.

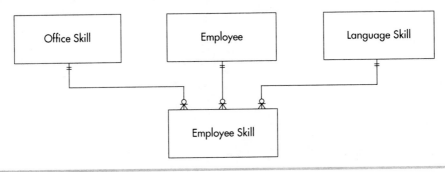

Figure 7-3 Data model with fourth normal form issue

Entities such as these are rare in real life because when experienced designers resolve multivalued attribute problems to satisfy first normal form, they move each multivalued attribute to its own entity rather than combining them as shown here. So, with some strict interpretation of first normal form procedures, this can be avoided altogether. Also, if you are going to apply the rules of fifth normal form, it covers the anomalies addressed by fourth normal form in terms that are much easier to understand, so you can skip this step altogether. However, should you encounter a fourth normal form violation, the remedy is simply to put each multivalued attribute in a separate entity, such as these:

EMPLOYEE OFFICE SKILL: EMPLOYEE ID (PK), OFFICE SKILL (PK)

EMPLOYEE LANGUAGE SKILL: EMPLOYEE ID (PK), LANGUAGE SKILL (PK)

Figure 7-4 shows the corrected (fourth normal form) data model.

Fifth Normal Form

Fifth normal form is very easy to understand. You simply keep splitting entities, stopping only when one of the following conditions is true:

- Any further splitting would lead to entities where the original view cannot be reconstructed with joins.

- The only splits left are trivial. *Trivial splits* occur when resulting entities have a primary key consisting only of the primary key or one of the candidate keys of the original entity.

It is interesting to note that, unlike other normal forms, fifth normal form specifies a desired end state instead of a specific anomaly to be mitigated. While fifth normal form seems to forbid all three-way relationships, some of these are legitimate. Problems arise only when the entities can be split into simpler, more fundamental relationships.

To most practitioners, fifth normal form is synonymous with *fully normalized*. However, in recent years, database management guru C.J. (Chris) Date, along with Hugh Darwen and Nikos Lorentzos, proposed a sixth normal form that deals with temporal and interval data in

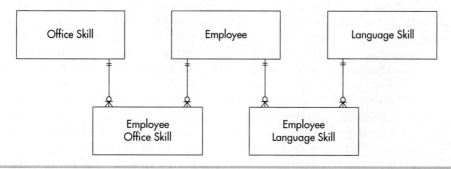

Figure 7-4 Data model in fourth normal form

the book *Temporal Data and the Relational Model* (Morgan Kaufmann, 2003). It remains to be seen whether it will be widely adopted.

Domain-Key Normal Form (DKNF)

Ron Fagin introduced domain-key normal form (DKNF) in the research paper "A Normal Form for Relational Databases That Is Based on Domains and Keys" published in *ACM Transactions on Database Systems* (September 1981). The theory is that an entity is in DKNF if and only if every constraint on the entity is a result of the definitions of domains and keys. Although Fagin was able to prove that entities in DKNF have no modification anomalies, he provided no procedure or step-by-step rules to achieve it. The dilemma then is that designers have no solid indication of when DKNF has been achieved for an entity. Nor is the notion that constraints are a consequence of keys obvious. This is likely why DKNF is not in widespread use and is not generally expected in the design of databases for business applications. Academic interest in it has also faded.

Resolving Supertypes and Subtypes

During the normalization process, designers often revisit the specialization versus generalization trade-offs they made during the conceptual design phase in order to better tune their logical model. Unfortunately, there are no firm rules for resolving the trade-off. Therefore, generalization versus specialization becomes one of the topics that prevent database design from becoming an exact science. The general guideline to follow (in addition to common sense) is that the more the various subtypes share common attributes and relationships, the more the designer should be inclined to combine the subtypes into the supertype.

Let's look at an example. Assume for a moment that an existing database includes a single Customer entity containing basic information about all customers, and now the Customer Service Department at Acme Industries has requested database and application enhancements that will allow it to record and track more information about customers. In particular, the department is interested in knowing the type of customer (such as individual person, sole proprietorship, partnership, or corporation) so that correspondence can be addressed appropriately for each type. Figure 7-5 shows the logical data model that was developed on the basis of the new requirements.

In IE notation, the type or category is shown using a symbol that looks like a circle with a line under it. Therefore, you know that Individual Customer and Commercial Customer are subtypes of Customer because of the symbol that appears in the line that connects them. Also note that they share the exact same primary key and that in the subtypes, the primary key of the entity is also a foreign key to the supertype entity. This makes perfect sense when you consider the fact that an Individual Customer entity *is* a Customer, meaning that any occurrence of the Individual Customer entity would have a tuple in the Customer entity as well as a matching tuple in the Individual Customer entity. Usually an attribute in the supertype entity indicates which subtype is assigned to each entity occurrence (tuple). Once this is implemented in tables, database users can use the type attribute to know where to look for (that is, which

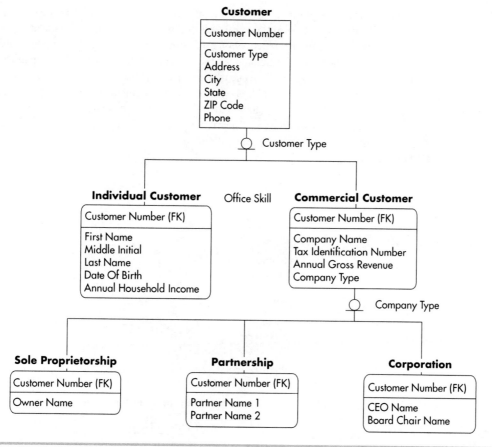

Figure 7-5   Customer subclasses

subtype table contains) the remainder of the information about each entity occurrence (each row). Such an attribute is called the *type discriminator* and is usually named next to the type symbol on the ERD. Therefore, Customer Type is the type discriminator that indicates whether a given Customer is an Individual Customer or a Commercial Customer. Similarly, Company Type is the type discriminator that indicates whether a given Commercial Customer is a sole proprietorship, partnership, or corporation.

As you might imagine, this IE notation is not the only format used in ERDs for supertypes and subtypes. However, it is the most commonly used method. Another popular format is to draw the subtype entities within the supertype entity (that is, subtype entity rectangles drawn inside the corresponding supertype entity's rectangle). Although this format makes it visually clear that the subtypes really are just a part of the supertype, it has practical limitations when the entities are broken down into many levels.

As mentioned, finding the right level of specialization is a significant database design challenge. In reviewing the logical design as proposed in Figure 7-5, the database design team noticed something: The only difference among the Sole Proprietorship, Partnership, and Corporation subtypes is in the way that the names of key people in those types of companies appear as attributes. Moreover, the use of two nearly identical attributes for the names of the co-owners in the Partnership subtype could be considered a repeating attribute, and therefore a first normal form violation. The design team elected to generalize these names into the Commercial Customer entity, but in doing so, they recognized the first normal form problems and decided to place them into a separate entity called Commercial Customer Principal. This led to the ERD shown in Figure 7-6.

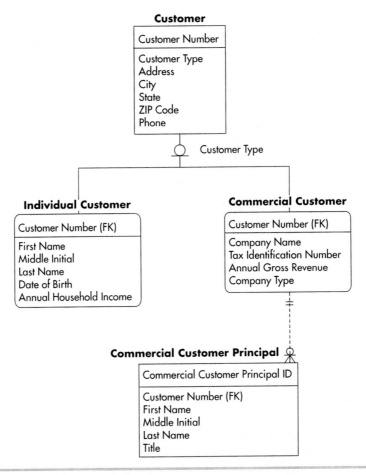

Figure 7-6 Customer subtypes, version 2

Clearly this is a simpler design that will result in fewer tables when it is physically implemented. It offers a very big win, because not only is there no loss of function when you consolidate the subtypes into the supertype, but you actually have *more* function available because you can add as many names as you want to any type of commercial customer. Notice that although I folded the subtypes Sole Proprietorship, Partnership, and Corporation into the supertype Commercial Customer, I left the Company Type attribute in Commercial Customer. This is important because the business users likely still want to know what type of commercial customer is represented by each row in the Commercial Customer table.

Further study by the design team helped them realize the similarity between the name attributes now contained in the Commercial Customer Principal entity and those contained in the Individual Customer entity. In discussing options further with the Customer Service Department, the design team uncovered a few cases for which it would be desirable for multiple contact names to be recorded for individual customers as well as for commercial customers. For example, customers that have legal disputes often request that all contact go through an attorney. With that information, the design team decided to generalize these names and move Commercial Customer Principal up to be a child of Customer and name it Customer Contact so that it could be used to hold the information about either a principal (owner, co-owner, partner, officer) of the customer or any other contact person for the customer that the Customer Service Department might find useful. The design team further realized that contact names would be more useful if a phone number was included. The Phone attribute was left in the Customer entity because it is intended to hold the general phone number for the customer. The phone number in the Customer Contact entity is intended to hold the phone for an individual contact person. The resultant logical design is shown in Figure 7-7.

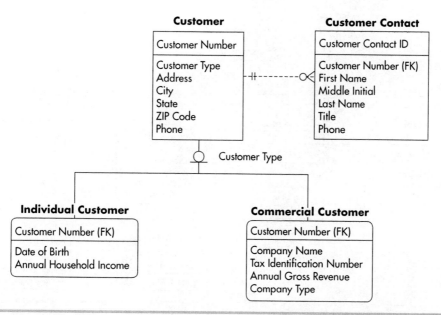

Figure 7-7 Customer subtypes, version 3

The fact that all three of the designs presented (Figures 7-5, 7-6, and 7-7) are workable should underscore the generalization versus specialization dilemma: No one "right" answer exists. The art to database design, then, is to arrive at the design that best fits what is known about the expected uses of the database. This is best done by comparing the relative strengths and weaknesses of each alternative design. And there is no better vehicle for communicating the alternatives than the ERD.

Generalizing Attributes

In some situations, precisely following the normalization process can lead to logical models that are impractical to implement. This section explores an example of one such situation and a solution developed by generalizing some of the attributes.

Figure 7-8 shows a data model for an online product catalog that might be used for a web-based shopping application. Notice the subtypes beneath the Product entity, one for each product line. The Product Line Code attribute in the Product entity is the type discriminator that indicates which subtype holds the additional information for a given Product tuple (row) based on the product line.

Figure 7-8 shows only four product lines. It is reasonable to expect more to be added as the business grows or as a result of mergers and acquisitions. If the business sponsors confirm that product lines are volatile (subject to change), implementing this model has

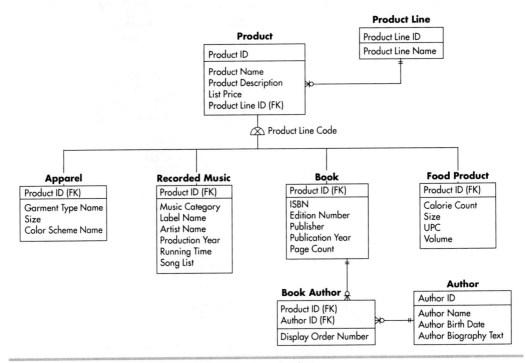

Figure 7-8   Logical model for an online product catalog

serious maintenance consequences. If the structure is flattened, placing all the attributes of the subtypes (product lines) into the Product entity, we will be required to add multiple new attributes to the entity (and corresponding columns to any physical database table built from the model) each time a new product line is added. And of course, attributes will have to be removed, although perhaps not immediately, whenever a product line is discontinued. On the other hand, if we implement the structure as is (retaining the Product entity as a table and creating a separate table for each product line), or if we implement only the subtypes, creating a table for each subtype (product line) and repeating the product attributes in each product line table, we now must add a new table each time a new product line is added, and (eventually) remove tables for discontinued product lines. When the application logic changes for either alternative are considered (changing the application to recognize new columns or new tables when product lines are added), it should be clear that neither is viable.

Another consideration is the volatility of the attributes assigned to each subtype. Figure 7-8 includes only a representative sample of the attributes that might be included in each subtype. I'm sure that you can easily imagine some additional attributes for each, such as a name and/or description of the material used for each apparel item. And if you can easily think of them, so can your business users, which means that you can expect the list of attributes required for each subtype to vary over time just as the required subtypes of a product will.

The fundamental problem here is that the number and nature of the attributes vary considerably from one subtype to another and the number and nature of the subtypes themselves are expected to vary a lot over time. One of the patterns that experienced modelers know about is a generalized model where attributes of the subtype become independently defined properties that can be assigned to supertype entity instances as needed. This structure is commonly used in object-oriented databases and in databases designed to hold various types of metadata, including those used to hold data model metadata for popular commercial data modeling tools. This pattern is especially useful when the same property can be used by multiple subtypes. Notice, for example, that both the Apparel and Food Product subtypes include the Size attribute. Figure 7-9 shows the model from Figure 7-8 with the subtype attributes converted into generic properties that can be assigned to products by product line.

To help you follow the discussion that follows, Figure 7-10 shows a few rows of sample data for each entity represented in Figure 7-9.

Comparing the model in Figure 7-9 with the one in Figure 7-10, notice the following:

- The Product Line and Product entities are the same in both models.

- The entities for the product line subtypes (Apparel, Recorded Music, Book, and Food Product) do not exist in Figure 7-10. However, as with the model shown in Figure 7-9, the list of valid product lines is determined by the Product Line entity.

- The Property Type entity contains the name and data type for each attribute. Each distinct attribute from the product line subtypes can be represented by an occurrence of the Product Type entity (a row in the physical table). The Property Data Type attribute is necessary because we no longer have the luxury of assigning a specific data type to each attribute. However, by recording the intended data type (string, integer, date, and so forth) with the property type, we can assist the application logic in properly converting each property for display on a web page or report.

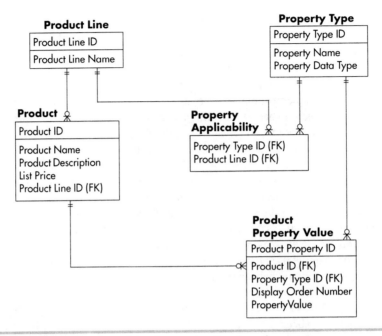

Figure 7-9 Alternative logical model using generalized attributes

Product Line

Prod. Line ID	Prod. Line Desc.
101	Apparel
104	Food Products

Property Type

Prop. Type ID	Prop. Name	Prop. Data Type
P10001	Size	String
P10005	Garment Type Name	String
P10012	Calorie Count	Integer

Property Type Applicability

Prod. Line ID	Prop. Type ID
101	P10001
101	P10005
104	P10001
104	P10012

Product

Prod. ID	Prod. Name	Prod. Description	List Price	Prod. Line ID
1254678	ComfoSteer Glove	Men's leather driving glove	22.99	101
3549076	CalDry Apricots	Dried California apricots	3.25	104

Product Property Value

Prod. Prop. ID	Prod. ID	Prop. Type ID	Display Order Num.	Prop. Value
33341461	1254678	P10001	2	Large
86743573	1254678	P10005	1	Men's gloves
77303926	3549076	P10001	1	6 oz.
96901490	3549076	P10012	2	110

Figure 7-10 Sample data showing use of generalized attributes

- The Property Applicability entity is an intersection entity intended to assist the application with controlling the assignment of property types to product instances. To that end, it shows the valid combinations of product lines and property types so that the application can restrict the addition of property type values to a given product to only the ones listed as valid for the product line. This design could be enhanced to include other information such as whether the property type is mandatory and whether multiple values of the property type can be assigned to a single product instance.

- The Product Property Value entity assigns property types and values to each product occurrence. The Property Value attribute holds the data for the property, such as the size or garment type. I added attribute Display Order Number to allow the business user to control the order in which the properties for any given product instance are displayed, and of course creative individuals will think of even more attributes that can be added.

Looking back at Figure 7-8, you may be wondering what happened to the Author and Book Author entities that were used to assign the list of authors to each occurrence of the Book subtype. The answer is that they can be implemented as properties! This can be accomplished by adding a property type for the Author ID, adding the property type to Property Applicability to show it as valid for the Book product line, and then adding one or more tuples (rows) to the Product Property Value entity (table) for each Product entity instance that is in the Book product line. The specific intersection entity between the Book and Author entities is lost and the database cannot record direct relationships as a result, but it is still possible to write an SQL query that finds the Author ID values associated with a given book and uses them to join to the Author table. It's just more complicated than before. Note that the same technique can be used if we want to associate multiple artists with instances of the Recorded Music product line.

As you have no doubt seen, this technique has some distinct advantages:

- Product lines can be added and removed without changing the data model, database tables or application logic.

- Properties can be added and removed without changing the data model, database tables, or application logic.

- The properties assigned to a given product instance can be easily changed.

- In short, this appears to provide the ultimate in design flexibility.

Given that this technique offers such terrific flexibility, why not use it for all of our databases? The answer is that generalization has its disadvantages, including:

- The specific data types of the attributes are lost when generic properties are used. The application logic becomes responsible for validating that the data is in the correct format and for any conversions required between the way the property is displayed and the way it is stored in the database. In addition, database functions such as date arithmetic (for example, calculating the number of days between two dates) and calculating averages cannot be performed by the database engine without first applying a conversion function to the property value. A partial workaround to this is to provide multiple attributes with varying data types in the Product Property Value entity, but then the application must know which one applies to each property.

- Specific relationships to children of the original subtypes are lost. Application logic must manage, for example, finding the authors associated with a product instance that represents a book.

- As mentioned, generalized models are often more difficult to understand. Within data processing, flexibility and complexity are indeed directly proportional.

Alternatives for Reference Data

This section covers alternatives for handling reference data that is usually normalized into reference entities (tables in a physical model). A *reference table,* sometimes called a lookup table or a code table, is one used to translate code values into names or descriptions for the code. For example, a State table can be used to translate the two-character U.S. state and territory codes into proper names for the states and territories, such as MD for the state of Maryland. Most often, these code tables have a primary key composed of the code value and the name or description of the code as the only other attribute.

Common Code Structures

As you no doubt noticed, the normalization process generates a lot of reference tables. For example, the Office Skill and Language Skill entities in Figure 7-4 fit the definition of reference tables. However, normalization may not generate all the reference tables that might be useful. Any text name or description should be considered for replacement with an identifier (code or surrogate key) that becomes a foreign key to a reference table. The reason is that most names and descriptions tend to change over time and replacing them with a stable identifier isolates any update to a single row in a single table. Another way to look at it is that if the identifier were in the original relation (along with the name or description), the name or description would be recognized as transitively dependent on the identifier, and the normalization process would yield a reference entity (table).

A large model can have dozens of reference tables, so some modelers prefer to replace them with a generalized structure that consolidates all the reference tables. Figure 7-11 shows

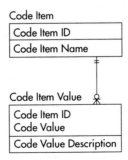

Figure 7-11 Generalized reference data structure

Code Item

Code Item ID	Code Item Name
2456	Gender
2480	US State/Possession

Code Item
Value

Code Item ID	Code Value	Code Value Description
2456	F	Female
2456	M	Male
2480	AL	Albama
2480	AK	Alaska
2480	AS	American Samoa
⋮	⋮	⋮

Figure 7-12   Sample data rows for structure shown in Figure 7-11

the data model for such a generalized structure. And to help you see how the structure would be used, Figure 7-12 shows a few sample data rows for each of two code attributes, Gender and US State / Possession, which would be two separate reference tables if specialized structures were used.

The obvious advantage of this approach is simplification of the model. A less obvious advantage is that the generalized structure provides the basis for handling other functions in a common manner, such as translation of code values across systems and translation of text descriptions into other human languages. However, there are some disadvantages as well:

- Common reference structures are somewhat more complex to use.

- It may take more joins to use a common reference structure.

- It is not practical to use database constraints to ensure that a proper code value is referenced from the common structure. For example, using the generalized reference data structure shown in Figure 7-11, it is nearly impossible to construct a referential constraint that will prevent a foreign key for a gender code from incorrectly referencing a row that belongs to some other code set, such as state code.

Crosswalk Tables

Once a common reference structure has been established, it is easy to expand it to solve additional problems. One such expansion is the addition of a *crosswalk* table, which is a structure used to map code values from different coding systems (usually different source application systems) to a standard set of values. For example, multiple sets of language codes were developed prior to the establishment of ANSI/ISO standards and if you have legacy application systems using the old values, you need a way to map the old values to a standard set. The model shown in Figure 7-13 adds a Source System reference table that shows

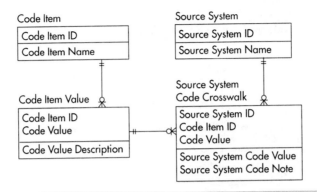

Figure 7-13 Generalized reference structure with crosswalk added

application or coding systems used and a Source System Code Crosswalk system that pairs up code values from a source system with values used in the Code Item Value table.

Notice that the Source System Code Crosswalk table acts as an intersection table between Source System and Code Item Value, implementing a many-to-many relationship between the two. Not only can a Code Item Value row have rows from many source systems, but also there can be multiple related rows from the same source system. This provides maximum flexibility, but at the expense of additional complexity. This is a typical trade-off in computerized systems—some might even say that flexibility leads to complexity.

Language Translation Tables

In application systems that must support multiple human languages, a common structure for storing translations of descriptions of code values becomes a necessity. Figure 7-14 shows the generalized structure from Figure 7-13 with two additional entities (tables) added to accommodate translations of the text descriptions.

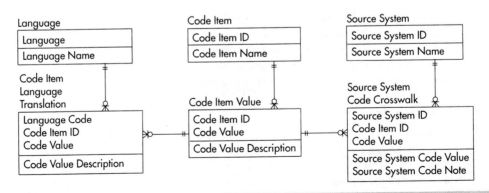

Figure 7-14 Generalized reference structure with language translations added

The Language table is a reference table that holds codes and names of the languages the application must support. An alternative design is to put the list of languages in the Code Item and Code Item Value tables. The advantage of this approach is that the language names themselves can be translated into the names used in other languages (for example, English translates to Inglés in Spanish and Anglais in French). However, the disadvantage is that this arrangement is more difficult to understand.

The Code Item Language Translation table is an intersection between Language and Code Item Value used to store the Code Value Description for the code value from the Code Item Value table, but translated into the language from the Language table. In this way, any code value can have any number of language translations.

Try This 7-1   Complex Logical Data Model

In this Try This exercise you will create a complex logical data model from requirements given in the exercise instructions. By complex, I mean a data model that contains supertypes, subtypes and the use of roles when subtypes are not appropriate.

Step by Step

1. Study these requirements from Acme Industries, a fictitious manufacturing company:

   - Collect and store this information about organizations that have a relationship with Acme Industries:

     - Company name

     - Web address (URL)

     - Postal addresses with type (shipping, mailing, etc.)

     - Telephone numbers with device type (telephone, fax, etc.) and usage type (general, customer service, sales, etc.)

   - Collect and store this information about people who have a relationship with Acme Industries:

     - Name (given, middle, and family)

     - E-mail addresses with type (personal, work, etc.)

     - Postal addresses with type (home, work, etc.)

     - Telephone numbers with device type (telephone, cell, pager, fax, etc.) and usage type (personal, work, etc.)

(continued)

- Organizations to be included are Customers, Suppliers, or Brokers (outside agencies that market on behalf of Acme Industries).

  - Brokers have their own employees, who are called Sales Agents.

  - Sales Agents must be included in the database.

- People to be included are Employees, Sales Agents (employees of Brokers), and External Contacts.

  - Employees can be part time or full time.

  - Employees can be contract (temporary) or permanent.

  - Employees can be assigned to work as Sales Representatives, as Customer Service Representatives, or in some other capacity. A history of all past employee work assignments is required.

  - All employees are assigned a work location along with their work role: Sales Representatives always work in a sales office; Customer Service Representatives always work in a call center.

  - Sales Representatives are assigned to a sales district based on their geographic location.

  - Sales Representatives are assigned to one or more customers (independent of their sales office or sales region assignment).

2. Determine the entities, including supertypes and subtypes.

  - When entities are broken into subtypes, each instance of the entity must fit into one and only one subtype. Given this rule, some subtypes will have to be represented in other ways, such as roles or relationships.

  - Consider the use of the Party supertype (see Chapter 5) to simplify generalization of elements common to both Organizations and Individuals.

  - For this exercise, reference entities need not be included.

3. Draw the data model.

  - Include attributes mentioned in the requirements and other attributes that add clarity to the usage of the supertypes, subtypes, and intersection entities you included. However, there is no need to populate the model with every possible attribute.

  - Draw relationships using the Information Engineering (IE) notation.

Try This Summary

In this Try This exercise, you evaluated requirements and developed a complex data model that included supertypes, subtypes, and the use of roles. As with most design efforts, there isn't a single correct solution, but I offer my solution in Appendix B for comparison with your own.

Chapter 7 Self Test

1. For a relation to be in Boyce-Codd normal form, it must

    A Be in domain key normal form

    B Be in third normal form

    C Be in fourth normal form

    D Be in fifth normal form

    E Have no determinants that are not either the primary key or a candidate key

2. Fourth normal form problems can be avoided during resolution of first normal form problems by

    A Placing all candidate keys in separate entities

    B Placing all multivalued attributes in common reference table structures

    C Placing all multivalued attributes in separate entities

    D Removing constraints that are not a result of the definitions of domains and keys

    E Using roles to resolve all multivalued attributes

3. When choosing the level of generalization versus specialization in a model, you should

    A Find the one correct solution

    B Find the solution that is in the highest normal form

    C Select the alternative with the most subtypes

    D Strive for the best fit with known and expected requirements

    E Select the simplest alternative

4. Advantages of generalized reference data structures include which of the following?

    A They are easier for business users to understand.

    B They help to simplify data models by consolidating many small reference tables into a single structure.

    C Database constraints can be used to prevent values from other code sets from being accidentally selected.

    D They provide support for additional functions such as language translation.

    E They are more normalized than specialized reference tables.

5. Advantages of specialized reference data structures include which of the following?

   A They are easier for business users to understand.

   B They require more joins than generalized reference data structures.

   C Database constraints can be used to prevent values from other code sets from being accidentally selected.

   D They provide support for additional functions such as language translation.

   E They are more normalized than generalized reference tables.

6. Intersection tables involving more than two parent tables

   A Should be carefully scrutinized by the data modeler

   B Are perfectly okay in all cases

   C Are always considered to be modeling errors

   D Can be an indication of an anomaly addressed by one of the advanced forms of normalization

   E Are highly recommended because they simplify data models

7. Boyce-Codd normal form deals with anomalies caused by _____.

8. Fourth normal form deals with anomalies caused by _____.

9. Instead of dealing with a specific type of anomaly, fifth normal form specifies _____.

10. Domain key normal form deals with anomalies caused by _____.

11. Most business systems require that you normalize only as far as _____.

12. In IE notation, the type or category symbol looks like _____.

13. An attribute used to indicate which subtype a particular occurrence of an entity falls into is known as a(n) _____.

14. A table used to translate code values from one system to another is known as a(n) _____ table.

Chapter 8

Physical Database Design

Key Skills & Concepts

- The Physical Design Process

- Designing Tables

- Integrating Business Rules and Data Integrity

- Adding Indexes for Performance

- Designing Views

Once the logical design phase of a project is complete, it is time to move on to physical design. Other members of a typical project team will define the hardware and system software required for the application system. We will focus on the database designer's physical design work, which is transforming the logical database design into one or more physical database designs. For situations in which an application system is being developed for internal use, it is normal to have only one physical database design for each logical design. However, if the organization is a software vendor, for example, the application system must run on all the various platform and RDBMS versions that the vendor's customers use, and that requires multiple physical designs. This chapter covers each of the major steps involved in physical database design.

The Physical Design Process

The physical design phase of a database project requires a profound shift in the topics on which the database designer must focus as well as the skills and experience required in order to be successful. In many organizations a database administrator (DBA) handles all or part of the physical database design after a carefully planned and executed handoff of the design work completed by the data modeler. However, in smaller organizations, the data modeler and the DBA might be the same person.

The physical design involves the transformation of the results of the logical database design (largely the logical data model) into a physical database design, which includes a physical data model. Eventually, however, the goal of the physical database design effort is to produce the actual database, usually through SQL data definition language (DDL) scripts created by the data modeler and/or DBA and run in the DBMS of choice to create all the required database objects. Thus the focus (at least for a relational database) must be on tables and columns along with other supporting objects such as indexes. (These supporting objects are explained a bit later in this chapter.)

The skills required to produce a physical design that conforms to the logical design and yields acceptable performance include not only an understanding of the logical model and the design principles used to create the logical design that is the starting point for the physical database design, but also the following:

- The features of the target DBMS, particularly table storage and indexing options

- DBMS tuning options and trade-offs

- The operating system on which the DBMS will run

- The hardware on which the database server will run

- Physical storage mechanisms available on the particular platform. By *platform*, I mean a particular combination of hardware and operating system software

The inputs to the physical design process include the following:

- **Logical database design**   This is the primary output of the logical design process, including the logical model selected for promotion to the physical design.

- **Process models**   Also from the logical design process, this gives the physical design team a sense of the timing and frequency of inserts, updates, and deletes for each database table. Furthermore, the process model provides an overall sense of the balance between query and modification. A database optimized for read-only queries will not perform as well for updates, and vice versa.

- **CRUD matrix**   This provides the best indication of the database access each process requires from the various database objects.

- **Data requirements**   These are initially developed during the Requirements Gathering phase but are augmented during logical design. The requirements should cover data retention; expected data volumes by object; security and privacy rules; and expectations for data availability (days and hours when the data must be available) and freshness (how current the data in the database must be).

- **Performance requirements**   These are the specifications of required *response time* (the elapsed time between the submission of a query or transaction and the return of results to the submitter), and *throughput* (the number of queries or transactions that can be processed in a given time period, such as orders processed per minute).

- **Target DBMS**   This is the vendor brand and version on which the database will be installed. Any optional DBMS features that are required should also be specified.

- **Disk space constraints**   If the database must fit within a finite amount of disk storage, or if the storage costs must fit a particular budget, the constraint must be communicated to the physical designers.

- **Development schedule**   Since the database design must be completed in time for the developers to begin testing, the timing of the completion of the physical design and the creation of the initial database is critical to the on-time completion of the overall project.

Designing Tables

The first step in physical database design is to map the normalized relations shown in the logical design to tables. The importance of this step should be obvious, because tables are the primary unit of storage in relational databases. However, if adequate work was put into the logical design, then translation to a physical design is much easier. As you work through this chapter, keep in mind that Chapter 2 contains an introduction to each component in the physical database model. For relational databases, the physical database objects (tables, constraints, indexes, views, and so on) are usually created using SQL that is generated from the physical data model and then adjusted by the DBA. However, the SQL language is outside the scope of this book. Briefly, the table design process goes as follows:

1. Each normalized relation becomes a table. A common exception to this occurs when supertypes and subtypes are involved, as discussed in the next section.

2. Each attribute within the normalized relation becomes a column in the corresponding table. Keep in mind that the column is the smallest division of meaningful data in the database, so columns should not have subcomponents that make sense by themselves. For each column, the following must be specified:

   - *A unique column name within the table.* Generally, the attribute name from the logical design should be adapted as closely as possible. However, adjustments may be necessary to work around database reserved words and to conform to naming conventions for the particular RDBMS being used, such as the maximum name length supported by the RDBMS.

   - *A data type, and, for some data types, a length and perhaps a precision (number of numeric digits) and scale (number of digits to the right of the decimal point).* Data types vary from one RDBMS to another, which is one reason that different physical designs are needed for each RDBMS to be used.

   - *Whether column values are required or not.* This takes the form of a NULL or NOT NULL clause for each column. Be careful with defaults—they can fool you. For example, when this clause is not specified, Oracle assumes NULL, but Sybase and Microsoft SQL Server assume NOT NULL (although this default behavior can be changed for an instance or database). It's always better to specify such things and be certain of what you are getting.

   - *Check constraints.* These may be added to columns to enforce simple business rules. For example, a business rule specifying that the unit price on an invoice must always be greater than or equal to zero can be implemented with a check constraint, but a business rule requiring the unit price to be lower in certain states cannot use a check constraint. Generally, a check constraint is limited to comparison of a column value with a single value, a range or list of values, or other column values in the same row of table data.

3. The unique identifier of the relation is defined as the primary key of the table. Columns participating in the primary key must be specified as NOT NULL, and in most RDBMSs, the definition of a primary key constraint causes automatic definition of a unique index on the primary key column(s). Foreign key columns should have a NOT NULL clause if the relationship is mandatory; otherwise, they may have a NULL clause.

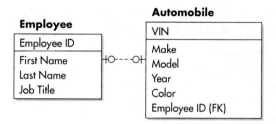

Figure 8-1   One-to-one relationship between Employee and Automobile

4. Any other sets of columns that must be unique within the table may have a unique constraint defined. As with primary key constraints, unique constraints in most RDBMSs cause automatic definition of a unique index on the unique column(s). However, unlike primary key constraints, a table may have *multiple* unique constraints, and the columns in a unique constraint may contain null values (that is, they may be specified with the NULL clause).

5. Relationships among the normalized relations become referential constraints in the physical design. For those rare situations for which the logical model contains a one-to-one relationship, you can implement it by placing the primary key of one of the tables as a foreign key in the other (do this for only *one* of the two tables) *and* placing a unique constraint on the foreign key to prevent duplicate values. For example, Figure 8-1 (copied from Figure 2-5 in Chapter 2) shows a one-to-one relationship between Employee and Automobile, and I chose to place EMPLOYEE_ID as a foreign key in the AUTOMOBILE table. I should also place a unique constraint on EMPLOYEE_ID in the AUTOMOBILE table so that an employee may be assigned only to one automobile at any point in time.

Ask the Expert

Q: **For a one-to-one relationship, why should we place a foreign key in only one of the two tables?**

A: The problem with placing a foreign key on both sides of a one-to-one relationship is that it would actually establish two relationships (one for each foreign key) and the redundant relationship could easily lead to data inconsistency. In the Employee–Automobile example, if we place EMPLOYEE_ID in the AUTOMOBILE table and VIN in the EMPLOYEE table, the DBMS cannot guarantee that the foreign key values will always be consistent. For example, the row for employee 125 might contain the VIN for a particular vehicle, but when you look at the row for that vehicle, it might contain a different employee, say 206.

Q: **I see. Does it then matter which of the two tables in the one-to-one relationship has the foreign key defined in it?**

A: Assuming a unique index (or unique constraint) is placed on the foreign key column, there really isn't a performance difference. However, there may be a slight advantage to putting the foreign key in the table that is accessed more frequently.

6. Physical storage characteristics must be selected and added to the physical data model. There are a number of considerations, including:

- **Tablespace assignment**   A *tablespace* (sometimes called a *file group*) is a logical container for physical database files. Each tablespace is composed of one or more physical files. Smaller tables can be grouped into common tablespaces, while the largest tables should have their own dedicated tablespaces. In some DBMSs the *block size* (physical record size) for the data files can be specified at the tablespace level, allowing the designer to select the tablespace for a table based on the desired block size. For tables that are frequently joined, placement in common tablespaces with row interleaving (if supported by the DBMS) can offer significant performance advantages because the rows to be joined are already in the correct physical sequence in the data files. Many DBMS products also support tablespace assignment for indexes.

- **Index Organized Tables (IOT)**   For simple tables such as reference code tables that only have a primary key (code) and description columns, many DBMSs offer an option to fold the table data (the descriptions) into the primary key index. The obvious performance advantage is random retrieval of entire rows using a single access to the index.

- **Free space**   As rows of data are maintained in tables, they tend to grow in size. Sometimes this yields rows that are too large to fit back in the same physical record in the file. Moving records around in the file to accommodate a newly expanded record would be a performance killer, so most DBMS products migrate (move) the row to some other place in the file, typically either the end of the file or a special overflow area. This tends to fragment the files, meaning that table rows are no longer stored in logical sequence, making extra work (and costing additional time) when the rows are accessed. To prevent this, the designer can leave unused space (called *free space*) in the files when tables are initially loaded with data. Free space parameters vary a lot across RDBMSs, but generally the choices are leaving a prescribed percentage of each physical record (block) free and/or leaving every *n*th physical record as free space. Also, many RDBMSs support free space parameters for indexes.

- **Data compression**   For RDBMSs that support it, data compression can save a substantial amount of disk space without a significant performance penalty. As you might guess, compression is most effective for longer text columns and columns that have patterns of repeating characters.

- **Clustering**   Some RDBMSs support *clustering,* where the RDBMS stores the rows in a prescribed physical sequence. Often the clustering is based on an index defined on the table. By default, some DBMS products such as SQL Server automatically cluster on the first index defined on the table unless another option is explicitly stated. Clustering can improve join performance when child table rows are clustered on the foreign key columns as well as query performance when the search condition contains a less-than or greater-than operator. The trade-off is that rows sometimes have to be moved around to make room for newly inserted rows while maintaining the clustering sequence.

7. Large tables (that is, those that exceed several gigabytes in total size) should be partitioned if the RDBMS being used supports it. *Partitioning* is a database feature that permits a table to be broken up into multiple physical components, each stored in separate data files, in a manner that is transparent to the database user. Typical methods of breaking tables into partitions use a range or list of values for a particular table column (called the *partitioning column*) or use a randomizing method known as *hashing* that evenly distributes table rows across available partitions. The benefits of breaking large tables into partitions include easier administration (particularly for backup and recovery operations) and improved performance, achieved when the RDBMS can run an SQL query in parallel against all (or some of) the partitions and then combine the results. Partitioning is solely a physical design issue that is never addressed in logical designs. After all, a partitioned table is still *one* table. There is wide variation in the way database vendors have implemented partitioning in their products, so you need to consult your RDBMS documentation for more details.

8. Another technique for large tables is to split them into multiple separate tables. Unfortunately, some call this table partitioning, which confuses the concept with the one I just covered. For this reason, I use the term *table splitting* for dividing a single logical table into multiple physical tables. Table splits take two forms:

   - **Vertical splitting**   The process of placing subsets of a table's columns into separate tables. Vertical splitting is useful when some columns are only used by particular processes or applications, or perhaps at a particular geographic location. The other potential use is when the table rows are just too large to be supported by the DBMS, in which case the splits are considered extension tables. The downside is the need to join the rows back together to get a comprehensive view of the original table's data. Vertical splits should *not* be used as a means of achieving column level access privileges (that is, preventing some users from accessing columns they should not see)—this is best done using views or RDBMS column-level security (if supported).

   - **Horizontal splitting**   The process of placing subsets of a table's rows in separate tables. In contrast to vertical splitting, horizontal splitting yields multiple tables with the same column definitions. Horizontal splitting is useful when subsets of rows are used by particular processes or applications, especially if those processes or applications can use a different database server. The downside is the need to access multiple tables in order to reconstruct the original table when required. Horizontal splitting should *not* be used to implement row-level security—this is best done using views or RDBMS row-level security features (if available).

9. *Table replication* (the duplication of all or part of a table on another database server) may be necessary in order to satisfy high availability or fast access requirements. Most modern RDBMS products support such features.

10. New table columns and/or new tables may be added to meet requirements for audit data (such as the user ID who last updated the data along with the date and time of the update and a reason code). It is also not unusual to add new tables to support data capture, reporting, security controls, and various application processes.

11. The logical model may be for a complete database system, whereas the current project may be an implementation of a subset of that entire system. When this occurs, the physical database designer will select and implement only the subset of tables required to fulfill current needs.

Let's have a look at a simple example. Figure 8-2 shows the logical model for the Acme Industries invoice introduced in Chapter 6.

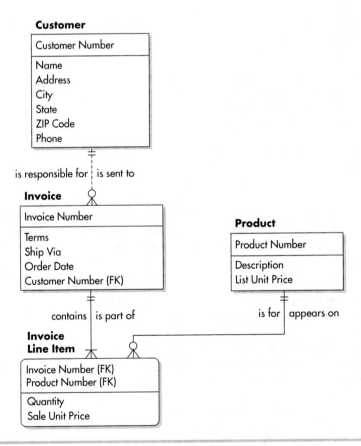

Figure 8-2 Logical model for Acme Industries invoice

CUSTOMER

CUSTOMER_NUMBER	NUMBER(5)	NOT NULL
NAME	VARCHAR(25)	NOT NULL
ADDRESS	VARCHAR(255)	NOT NULL
CITY	VARCHAR(50)	NOT NULL
STATE	CHAR(2)	NOT NULL
ZIP_CODE	VARCHAR(10)	NOT NULL
PHONE	VARCHAR(15)	

FK_CUSTOMER_INVOICE

INVOICE

INVOICE_NUMBER	NUMBER(7)	NOT NULL
TERMS	VARCHAR(20)	NULL
SHIP_VIA	VARCHAR(10)	NULL
ORDER_DATE	DATE	NOT NULL
CUSTOMER_NUMBER (FK)	NUMBER(5)	NOT NULL

PRODUCT

PRODUCT_NUMBER	VARCHAR(10)	NOT NULL
DESCRIPTION	VARCHAR(100)	NOT NULL
LIST_UNIT_PRICE	NUMBER(7,2)	NOT NULL

FK_INVOICE_INVOICE_LINE_ITEM   FK_PRODUCT_INVOICE_LINE_ITEM

INVOICE_LINE_ITEM

INVOICE_NUMBER (FK)	NUMBER(7)	NOT NULL
PRODUCT_NUMBER (FK)	VARCHAR(10)	NOT NULL
QUANTITY	NUMBER(5)	NOT NULL
SALE_UNIT_PRICE	NUMBER(7,2)	NOT NULL

Figure 8-3 Physical model for Acme Industries invoice

Figure 8-3 shows the physical table design I created from the logical design. Notice the following modifications:

- The logical names were shifted to uppercase and spaces were replaced with underscores. While some RDBMSs support mixed-case names, I prefer uppercase names with no special characters other than the underscore used to separate words because of universal support across RDBMS products.

- A data type and either length or precision and scale (as appropriate) was added to each column.

- A NULL or NOT NULL specification was added to each column.

- The verb phrases on the logical model were replaced with the names I assigned to the foreign key constraints.

As you can see, this is a very straightforward transformation that can easily be automated. In fact, all the popular data modeling tools support the automated transformation of logical models to physical models, and some allow the data modeler to build the logical and physical models in tandem.

Try This 8-1 Drawing a Physical Data Model

In this Try This exercise, you will draw a physical data model ERD that demonstrates most of the concepts presented thus far, including entities (tables), relationships, recursive relationships, and supertypes and subtypes.

Step by Step

1. Draw a table for PERSON with columns PERSON_ID (primary key), FIRST_NAME, LAST_NAME, BIRTH_DATE, and GENDER. Leave room for two more columns, which you will be adding in the next step.

2. Draw two one-to-many recursive relationships: one for the person's father and one for the person's mother. Remember that recursive relationships use the same table as both the parent and the child. In this case, the relationships should be optional in both directions because you won't have every person's parents in the database and not all persons have children. The PERSON table will need two foreign keys to support the recursive relationships: one for the PERSON_ID of the father and another for the PERSON_ID of the mother.

3. Draw a dependent table called MARRIAGE with columns PERSON_ID_1, PERSON_ID_2, MARRIAGE_DATE, and END_DATE. To be unique under all circumstances, the primary key must be composed of the first three columns (while rare, there are cases where a person married the same other person more than once). PERSON_ID_1 and PERSON_ID_2 will be the foreign keys for the two people who are married.

4. Draw two one-to-many relationships from PERSON to MARRIAGE—one where PERSON_ID_1 is the foreign key and the other where PERSON_ID_2 is the foreign key. These relationships are mandatory-optional (every marriage must have two people, but some people were never married).

5. Draw an EMPLOYEE table with columns PERSON_ID (primary key), EMPLOYEE_ID, HIRE_DATE, and TERMINATION_DATE.

6. Draw a CUSTOMER table with columns CUSTOMER_NUMBER (primary key), NAME, ADDRESS, CITY, STATE, ZIP_CODE, and PHONE.

7. Draw a CUSTOMER_CONTACT table with columns PERSON_ID (primary key) and CUSTOMER_ID.

8. Draw the lines and symbol(s) necessary to make EMPLOYEE and CUSTOMER_CONTACT subtypes of PERSON.

9. Draw a one-to-many mandatory-optional relationship from CUSTOMER to CUSTOMER_CONTACT, making CUSTOMER_ID in CUSTOMER_CONTACT the foreign key.

Try This Summary

In this Try This exercise, you created five tables and five relationships (two of them recursive), and you made two tables subtypes of another table. My solution appears in Appendix B.

Implementing Supertypes and Subtypes

Most data modelers tend to specify every conceivable subtype in conceptual and logical data models. This is not really a problem, because the conceptual model and logical design are supposed to encompass not only where things currently stand, but also where things are likely to end up in the future. The designer of the physical database therefore has some decisions to make in choosing to implement or not implement the supertypes and subtypes depicted in the logical model. The driving motivators here should be reasonableness and common sense. These, along with input from the application designers and business users about their intended uses of the database, will lead to the best decisions.

Figure 8-4 shows a Customer entity with two subtypes: Individual Customer and Commercial Customer (part of a data model that we examined in Chapter 7). You have basically three choices for physically implementing such a logical design, and we will explore each in the subsections that follow.

Implementing Subtypes As Is

This is called the "three table" solution because it involves creating one table for the supertype and one table for each of the subtypes (two in this example). This design is most appropriate when many attributes are particular to individual subtypes. In our example, only two attributes are particular to the Individual Customer subtype (Date of Birth and Annual Household Income), and four are particular to the Commercial Customer subtype. Figure 8-5 shows the physical design for this alternative.

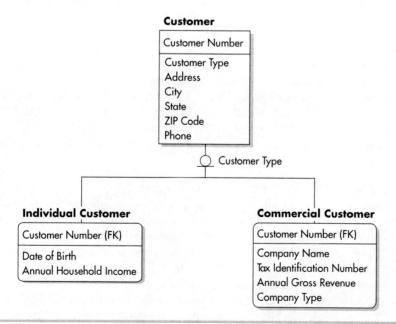

Figure 8-4   Customer entity with Individual Customer and Commercial Customer subtypes

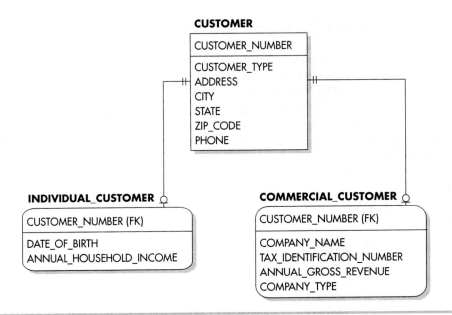

Figure 8-5 Customer subclasses: three-table physical design

This design alternative is favored when many common attributes (located in the supertype table) as well as many attributes particular to one subtype or another (located in the subtype tables) are used. The other factor is relationships—when the supertype and one or more subtypes have many relationships, it may be easier to use this alternative rather than reconcile the relationships to a different arrangement. In one sense, this design is simpler than the other alternatives because no one has to remember which attributes and relationships apply to which subtype. On the other hand, it is also more complicated to use, because the database user must join the CUSTOMER table either to the INDIVIDUAL_CUSTOMER table or the COMMERCIAL_CUSTOMER table, depending on the value of CUSTOMER_TYPE. The data-modeling purists on your project team are guaranteed to favor this approach, but the application programmers who must write the SQL to access the tables may take a counter position.

Implementing Each Subtype as a Discrete Table

This is called the "two-table" solution because it involves creating one table for each subtype and including all the columns from the supertype table in each subtype. At first, this may appear to involve redundant data, but in fact no redundant storage exists, because a given customer can be only one of the two subtypes. However, some columns are redundantly defined. Figure 8-6 shows the physical design for this alternative.

This alternative is favored when very few attributes and relationships are common between the subtypes. In our example, the situation is further complicated because of the CUSTOMER_ CONTACT table, which is a child of the supertype table (CUSTOMER). You cannot (or at least *should* not under most circumstances) make a table the child of two different parents based on the same foreign key. Therefore, if we eliminate the CUSTOMER table, we must create two

INDIVIDUAL_CUSTOMER

CUSTOMER_NUMBER
ADDRESS
CITY
STATE
ZIP_CODE
PHONE
DATE_OF_BIRTH
ANNUAL_HOUSEHOLD_INCOME

COMMERCIAL_CUSTOMER

CUSTOMER_NUMBER
ADDRESS
CITY
STATE
ZIP_CODE
PHONE
COMPANY_NAME
TAX_IDENTIFICATION_NUMBER
ANNUAL_GROSS_REVENUE
COMPANY_TYPE

Figure 8-6   Customer subclasses: two-table physical design

versions of the CUSTOMER_CONTACT table—one as a child of INDIVIDUAL_CUSTOMER and the other as a child of COMMERCIAL_CUSTOMER. Although this alternative may be a viable solution in some situations, the complication of the CUSTOMER_CONTACT table makes it a poor choice in this case.

Collapsing Subtypes into the Supertype Table

This is called the "one-table" solution because it involves creating a single table that encompasses the supertype and both subtypes. Figure 8-7 shows the physical design for this alternative. Constraints are required to enforce the optional columns. As columns that are mandatory in subtypes (including foreign keys used to establish relationships) are consolidated into the supertype table, they usually must be defined to allow null values because they don't apply for all subtypes. For the CUSTOMER_TYPE value that signifies "Individual,"

CUSTOMER

CUSTOMER_NUMBER
CUSTOMER_TYPE
ADDRESS
CITY
STATE
ZIP_CODE
PHONE
COMPANY_NAME
TAX_IDENTIFICATION_NUMBER
ANNUAL_GROSS_REVENUE
COMPANY_TYPE
DATE_OF_BIRTH
ANNUAL_HOUSEHOLD_INCOME

Figure 8-7   Customer subclasses: one-table physical design

DATE_OF_BIRTH and ANNUAL_HOUSEHOLD_INCOME would be allowed to (or required to) contain values, and COMPANY_NAME, TAX_IDENTIFICATION_NUMBER, ANNUAL_ GROSS_INCOME, and COMPANY_TYPE would be required to be null. For the CUSTOMER_ TYPE value that signifies "Commercial," the behavior required would be just the opposite.

NOTE
The constraints mentioned here might be implemented in the database using check constraints or triggers, discussed later in this chapter, or in application logic. The decision of which method to use depends a lot on the capabilities of the DBMS.

This alternative is favored when relatively few attributes and relationships are particular to any given subtype. In terms of data access, it is clearly the simplest alternative, because no joins are required. However, it is perhaps more complicated in terms of logic, because you must always keep in mind which attributes (including foreign keys) apply to which subtype (that is, which value of CUSTOMER_TYPE in this example). With only two subtypes, and a total of six subtype-determined attributes between them, this seems a very attractive alternative for this example.

Naming Conventions
Naming conventions are important because they help promote consistency in the names of tables, columns, constraints, indexes, and other database objects. Every organization should develop a standard set of naming conventions (with variations as needed when multiple RDBMSs are in use), publish it, and enforce its use. The conventions offered here are suggestions based on current industry best practices.

Table Naming Conventions
Here are some suggested naming conventions for database tables:

- Table names should be based on the name of the entity they represent. They should be descriptive, yet concise.

- Table names should be unique across the entire organization (that is, across all databases), except where the table is an exact duplicate of another (that is, a replicated copy).

- Some designers prefer singular words for table names, whereas others prefer plural names (for example, CUSTOMER versus CUSTOMERS). Oracle Corporation recommends singular names for entities and plural names for tables (a convention I have never understood). I prefer singular names for both entities and tables. However, it doesn't matter which convention you adopt as long as you are *consistent* across *all* your tables, so do set one or the other as your standard.

- Do not include words such as "table" or "file" in table names.

- Use only uppercase letters, and use an underscore to separate words. Not all RDBMSs have case-sensitive object names, so mixed-case names limit applicability across multiple vendors. Many RDBMS products, including Oracle and DB2, support mixed-case names in SQL but fold all of them into uppercase when they are processed. The names in the catalog metadata are stored in uppercase, and when you look at them later with one of the popular DBA or developer tools, they become difficult to decipher. For example, a table created with the name EmpJobAsmtHistory would be displayed as EMPJOBASMTHISTORY.

- Use abbreviations when necessary to shorten names that are longer than the RDBMS maximum (typically 30 characters or so, but there is considerable variation among RDBMS products). Actually, it is a good idea to stay a few characters short of the RDBMS maximum to allow for suffixes when necessary. All abbreviations should be placed on a standard list and the use of nonstandard abbreviations discouraged.

- Avoid limiting names such as WEST_SALES. Some organizations add a two- or three-character prefix to table names to denote the part of the organization that owns the data in the table. However, this is not considered a best practice because it can lead to a lack of data sharing. Moreover, placing geographic or organizational unit names in table names plays havoc every time the organization changes.

Column Naming Conventions

Here are some suggested naming conventions for table columns:

- Column names should be based on the attribute name as shown in the logical data model. They should be descriptive, yet concise.

- Column names must be unique within the table, but, where possible, it is best if they are unique across the entire organization. Some conventions make exceptions for common attributes such as City, which might describe several entities such as Customer, Employee, and Company Location.

- Use only uppercase letters, and use an underscore to separate words. Not all RDBMSs have case-sensitive object names, so mixed-case names limit applicability across multiple vendors.

- Prefixing column names with entity names is a controversial issue. Some prefer prefixing names. For example, in the CUSTOMER table, they would use column names such as CUSTOMER_NUMBER, CUSTOMER_NAME, CUSTOMER_ADDRESS, CUSTOMER_CITY, and so forth. Others (including me) prefer to prefix *only* the primary key column name (for example, CUSTOMER_NUMBER), which leads easily to primary key and matching foreign key columns having exactly the same names. Still others prefer no prefixes at all, and end up with a column name such as ID for the primary key of every single table.

- Use abbreviations when necessary to shorten names that are longer than the RDBMS maximum (typically 30 characters or so). All abbreviations should be placed on a standard list and the use of nonstandard abbreviations discouraged.

- Regardless of any other convention, most experts prefer that foreign key columns always have exactly the same name as their matching primary key column. This helps other database users understand which columns to use when coding joins in SQL.

Constraint Naming Conventions

In most RDBMSs, the error message generated when a constraint is violated contains the constraint name. Unless you want to field questions from database users every time one of these messages shows up, you should name the constraints in a standard way that is easily understood by the database users. Most database designers prefer a convention similar to the one presented here.

Constraint names should be in the format *TNAME_TYPE_CNAME,* where:

- *TNAME* is the name of the table on which the constraint is defined, abbreviated if necessary.

- *TYPE* is the type of constraint:

  - PK for primary key constraints.

  - FK for foreign key constraints.

  - UQ for unique constraints.

  - CK for check constraints.

- *CNAME* is the name of the column on which the constraint is defined, abbreviated if necessary. For constraints defined across multiple columns, another descriptive word or phrase may be substituted if the column names are too long (even when abbreviated) to make sense.

Index Naming Conventions

Indexes that are automatically defined by the RDBMS to support primary key or unique constraints are typically given the same name as the constraint name, so you seldom have to worry about them. For other types of indexes, it is wise to use a naming convention so that you know the table and column(s) on which they are defined without having to look up anything. The following is a suggested convention.

Index names should be in the format *TNAME_TYPE_CNAME,* where:

- *TNAME* is the name of the table on which the index is defined, abbreviated if necessary.

- *TYPE* is the type of index:

  - UX for unique indexes.

  - IX for nonunique indexes.

- *CNAME* is the name of the column on which the index is defined, abbreviated if necessary. For indexes defined across multiple columns, another descriptive word or phrase may be substituted if the column names are too long (even when abbreviated) to make sense.

Any abbreviations used should be documented in the standard abbreviations list.

View Naming Conventions

View names present an interesting dilemma. The object names used in the FROM clause of SQL statements can be for tables, views, or synonyms. A *synonym* is an alias (nickname) for a table or view. So how does the DBMS know whether an object name in the FROM clause is a table or view or synonym? Well, it doesn't until it looks up the name in a metadata table that catalogs all the objects in the database. This means, of course, that the names of tables, views, and synonyms must come from the same *namespace,* or list of possible names. Therefore, a view name must be unique among all table, view, and synonym names.

Because it is useful for at least some database users to know whether they are referencing a table or a view, and as an easy way to ensure that names are unique, it is common practice to give views distinctive names by employing a standard that appends *VW* to the beginning or end of each name, with a separating underscore. Again, the exact convention chosen matters a lot less than choosing *one* standard convention and sticking to it for all your view names. Here is a suggested convention:

- All view names should end with _VW so they are easily distinguishable from table names.

- View names should contain the name of the most significant base table included in the view, abbreviated if necessary.

- View names should describe the purpose of the views or the kind of data included in them. For example, CALIFORNIA_CUSTOMERS_VW and CUSTOMERS_BY_ZIP_CODE_ VW are both reasonably descriptive view names, whereas CUSTOMER_LIST_VW and CUSTOMER_JOIN_VW are much less meaningful.

- Any abbreviations used should be documented in the standard abbreviations list.

Integrating Business Rules and Data Integrity

Business rules determine how an organization operates and uses its data. Business rules exist as a reflection of an organization's policies and operational procedures and because they provide control. *Data integrity* is the process of ensuring that data is protected and stays intact through defined constraints placed on the data. We call these *database constraints* because they prevent changes to the data that would violate one or more business rules. The principal benefit of enforcing business rules using data integrity constraints in the database is that database constraints cannot be circumvented. Unlike business rules enforced by application programs, database constraints are enforced no matter *how* someone connects to the database. The only way around database constraints is for the DBA to remove or disable them. On the other hand, developers often prefer to control the rule enforcement themselves rather than relegating them to a DBA, and some rules are best tested before sending the data to the database for processing. In rare cases, usually involving the most important business rules, you might even want to enforce them in both places—in the database, because the rule cannot be circumvented, and in the application, so the user gets fast feedback when he or she violates the rule.

Business rules are implemented in the database as follows:

- NOT NULL constraints
- Primary key constraints
- Referential (foreign key) constraints
- Unique constraints
- Check constraints
- Data types, precision, and scale
- Triggers

The subsections that follow discuss each of these implementation techniques and the effects of the constraints on database processing. Figure 8-8 shows two tables taken from Figure 8-3 with one slight modification—the addition of a CUSTOMER_PO_NUMBER column, which is needed to illustrate an important concept. I use these tables as examples throughout this discussion.

CUSTOMER

CUSTOMER_NUMBER	NUMBER(5)	NOT NULL
NAME	VARCHAR(25)	NOT NULL
ADDRESS	VARCHAR(255)	NOT NULL
CITY	VARCHAR(50)	NOT NULL
STATE	CHAR(2)	NOT NULL
ZIP_CODE	VARCHAR(10)	NOT NULL
PHONE	VARCHAR(15)	

FK_CUSTOMER_INVOICE

INVOICE

INVOICE_NUMBER	NUMBER(7)	NOT NULL
TERMS	VARCHAR(20)	NULL
SHIP_VIA	VARCHAR(10)	NULL
ORDER_DATE	DATE	NOT NULL
CUSTOMER_PO_NUMBER	VARCHAR(20)	NULL
CUSTOMER_NUMBER (FK)	NUMBER(5)	NOT NULL

Figure 8-8 CUSTOMER and INVOICE tables with CUSTOMER_PO_NUMBER

NOT NULL Constraints

As you have already seen, business rules that state which attributes are required translate into NOT NULL clauses on the corresponding columns in the table design. In fact, the NOT NULL clause is how we define a NOT NULL constraint on table columns. Primary keys must always be specified as NOT NULL (Oracle will automatically do this for you, unlike most other RDBMS products). And, as already mentioned, any foreign keys that participate in a mandatory relationship should also be specified as NOT NULL.

In our example, if we attempt to insert a row in the INVOICE table and fail to provide a value for any of the columns that have NOT NULL constraints (that is, the INVOICE_NUMBER, ORDER_DATE, and CUSTOMER_NUMBER columns), the insert will fail with an error message indicating the constraint violation. Also, if we attempt to update any existing row and set one of those columns to a NULL value, the update statement will fail.

Primary Key Constraints

Primary key constraints require that the column(s) that make up the primary key contain unique values for every row in the table. In addition, primary key columns must be defined with NOT NULL constraints. A table may have only one primary key constraint. Most RDBMSs will automatically create an index to assist in enforcing the primary key constraint.

In our sample INVOICE table, if we attempt to insert a row without specifying a value for the INVOICE_NUMBER column, the insert will fail because of the NOT NULL constraint on the column. If we instead try to insert a row with a value for the INVOICE_NUMBER column that already exists in the INVOICE table, the insert will fail with an error message that indicates a violation of the primary key constraint. This message usually contains the constraint name—which is why it is such a good idea to give constraints meaningful names. Finally, assuming the RDBMS in use permits updates to primary key values (some do not), if we attempt to update the INVOICE_NUMBER column for an existing row and we provide a value that is already used by another row in the table, the update will fail.

Referential (Foreign Key) Constraints

The referential constraint on the INVOICE table defines CUSTOMER_NUMBER as a foreign key to the CUSTOMER table. It takes some getting used to, but referential constraints are always defined on the child table (that is, the table on the "many" side of the relationship). The purpose of the referential constraint is to make sure that foreign key values in the rows in the child table *always* have matching primary key values in the parent table.

In our INVOICE table example, if we try to insert a row without providing a value for CUSTOMER_NUMBER, the insert will fail due to the NOT NULL constraint on the column. However, if we try to insert a row and provide a value for CUSTOMER_NUMBER that does not match the primary key of a row in the CUSTOMER table, the insert will fail due to the referential constraint. Also, if we attempt to update the value of CUSTOMER_NUMBER for an existing row in the INVOICE table and the new value does not have a matching row in the CUSTOMER table, the update will fail, again due to the referential constraint.

Always keep in mind that referential constraints work in both directions, so they can prevent a child table row from becoming an "orphan," meaning it has a value that does not match a primary key value in the parent table. Therefore, if we attempt to delete a row in the CUSTOMER table that has INVOICE rows referring to it, the statement will fail because it would cause child table rows to violate the constraint. The same is true if we attempt to update the primary key value of such a row. However, many RDBMSs provide a feature with referential constraints written as ON DELETE CASCADE, which causes referencing child table rows to be *automatically* deleted when the parent row is deleted. Of course, this option is not appropriate in all situations, but it is nice to have when you need it.

Ask the Expert

Q: You mentioned that ON DELETE CASCADE is not appropriate in all situations. When would it be appropriate?

A: ON DELETE CASCADE is appropriate when the child table rows cannot exist without the parent table rows, a situation known as an *existence dependency*. For example, a line item on an invoice cannot exist without the invoice itself, so it is logical to delete the line items automatically when an SQL statement attempts to delete the invoice. However, this option can be dangerous in other situations. For instance, it would be dangerous to set up the database so that invoices were deleted automatically when someone attempted to delete a customer; because invoices are financial records, it would be safer to force someone first to explicitly delete the invoices. Naturally, these are business rule decisions that depend on requirements, and there are other options to consider, such as marking a row as logically deleted using a status code or end date.

Unique Constraints

Like primary key constraints, unique constraints ensure that no two rows in the table have duplicate values for the column(s) named in the constraint. However, unique constraints have two important differences:

- Although a table may have only one primary key constraint, it may have as many unique constraints as necessary.

- Columns participating in a unique constraint do not have to have NOT NULL constraints on them.

As with a primary key constraint, an index is automatically created to assist the DBMS in efficiently enforcing the constraint.

In our example, a unique constraint can be defined on the CUSTOMER_NUMBER and CUSTOMER_PO_NUMBER columns, to enforce a business rule that states that customers may use a PO (purchase order) number only once. You should realize that the *combination* of the values in the two columns must be unique. Many invoices can exist for any given CUSTOMER_NUMBER, and multiple rows in the INVOICE table can have the same PO_NUMBER (we cannot prevent two customers from using the same PO number, nor do we wish to). However, no two rows for the same customer number may have the same PO number.

As with the primary key constraint, if we attempt to insert a row with values for the CUSTOMER_NUMBER and PO_NUMBER columns that are already in use by another row, the insert will fail. Similarly, we cannot update a row in the INVOICE table if the update would result in the row having a duplicate combination of CUSTOMER_NUMBER and PO_NUMBER.

Check Constraints

Check constraints are used to enforce business rules that restrict a column to a list or range of values or to some condition that can be verified using a simple comparison to a constant, calculation, or a value of another column in the same row. Check constraints may *not* be used to compare column values between different rows, whether in the same table or not. Check constraints are written as conditional statements that must always be true. The terminology comes from the fact that the database must always "check" the condition to make sure it evaluates to true before allowing an insert or update to a row in the table.

In our example, a check constraint can be defined that requires the INVOICE_NUMBER to be greater than 0. This enforces a business rule that requires positive invoice numbers. Keep in mind that the condition is checked only when we insert or update a row in the INVOICE table, so it will not be applied to existing rows in the table (should there be any) when the constraint is added. With the constraint in force, if we attempt to insert or update a row with an INVOICE_NUMBER set to zero or a negative number, the statement will fail. And remember that there is always a balance to be found regarding which business rules are enforced in the database versus application logic versus both.

Data Types, Precision, and Scale

The data type assigned to the table columns automatically constrains the data to values that match the data type. For example, anything placed in a column defined with the DATE data type, such as the ORDER_DATE column, must be a valid date. Furthermore, you cannot put nonnumeric characters in numeric columns. However, you can put just about anything in a character column.

For data types that support the specification of the precision (maximum size) and scale (positions to the right of the decimal point), these specifications also constrain the data. You simply cannot put a character string or number larger than the maximum size for the column into the database. Nor can you specify decimal positions beyond those allowed for in the scale of a number.

In our example, CUSTOMER_NUMBER must contain only numeric digits and cannot be larger than 99,999 (five digits) or smaller than –99,999 (again, five digits). Also, because the scale is 0, it cannot have decimal digits (that is, it must be an integer). It may seem silly to allow negative values for CUSTOMER_NUMBER, but no SQL data type restricts a column only to positive integers. However, it is easy to restrict a column only to positive numbers using a check constraint if such a constraint is required.

Triggers

A *trigger* is a unit of program code that executes automatically based on some event that takes place in the database, such as inserting, updating, or deleting data in a particular table. Triggers must be written in a language supported by the RDBMS. For Oracle, this is either a proprietary extension to SQL called PL/SQL (Procedural Language/SQL) or Java (available in Oracle8*i* or later). Sybase and Microsoft SQL Server support triggers written in Transact-SQL, and recent versions of SQL Server also support triggers written in Common Language Runtime (CLR). Some RDBMSs have no support for triggers, whereas others support a more general programming language such as C. Trigger code must either end normally, which allows the SQL statement that caused the trigger to fire to end normally, or it must raise a database error, which in turn causes the SQL statement that caused the trigger to fire to fail as well.

Triggers can enforce business rules that cannot be enforced via database constraints. Because they are written using a full-fledged programming language, they can do just about anything that can be done with a database and a program (some RDBMSs do place restrictions on triggers). Deciding whether a business rule should be enforced in normal application code or through the use of a trigger is not always easy. Application developers typically want control of such things, but on the other hand, the main benefit of triggers is that they run automatically and cannot be circumvented (unless the DBA removes or disables them), even if someone connects directly to the database, bypassing the application.

A common use of triggers in RDBMSs that do not support ON DELETE CASCADE in referential constraints is to carry out the cascading delete. For example, if we want invoice line items to be automatically removed from the INVOICE_LINE_ITEM table when the corresponding invoice in the INVOICE table is deleted, we could write a trigger that carries that out. The trigger would be set to fire when a delete from the INVOICE table occurs. It would then issue a delete for all the child rows related to the parent invoice (those matching the primary key value of the invoice being deleted) and then end normally, which would permit the original invoice delete to complete (because the referencing child rows will be done by this time, the delete will not violate the referential constraint).

Adding Indexes for Performance

Indexes provide a fast and efficient means of finding data rows in tables, much like the index at the back of a book helps you to quickly find specific references. Although the implementation in the database is more complicated than this, it's easiest to visualize an index as a table with one column containing the key value and another containing a pointer to where the row with that key value physically resides in the table, in the form of a row ID or a relative block address (RBA). For nonunique indexes, the second column contains a list of matching pointers.

Indexes provide faster searches than scanning tables for two reasons: First, index entries are considerably shorter than typical table rows, so many more index entries fit per physical file block than the corresponding table rows. Therefore, when the database must scan the index sequentially looking for matching rows, it can get a lot more index entries with a single read to the file on disk than a corresponding read to the file holding the table. Second, index entries are always maintained in key sequence, which is not at all true of tables. The RDBMS software can take advantage of this by using binary search techniques that remarkably reduce search times and the resources required for searching. However, there is no guarantee that queries will use available indexes. The RDBMS optimizer determines the best way to process the query, and poorly written queries can preclude the use of indexes. While some RDBMS products support hints that attempt to influence the optimizer's index selection, these are generally not recommended because they are proprietary and may stop working when the RDBMS is upgraded to a new version.

There are no free lunches, however, and indexes come with a price—they take up space and must be maintained. Storage space seems less of an issue with every passing day, because storage devices keep getting cheaper. However, they still cost something, and they require maintenance and must be backed up. Most RDBMS vendors provide tools to help calculate the storage space required for indexes. These will assist you in estimating storage requirements. The more important consideration is maintenance of the index. Whenever a row is inserted into a table, every index defined on that table must have a new entry inserted as well, except that null values are never indexed. As rows are deleted, index entries must also be removed. And when columns that have an index defined on them are updated, the index must be updated as well. It's easy to forget this point because the RDBMS does this work automatically, but every index has a detrimental effect on the performance of inserts, updates, and deletes to table data. In essence, this is a typical trade-off, sacrificing a bit of performance when table data is changed for considerable gains in SELECT statement performance. An additional performance consideration is that indexes must be rebuilt whenever a table is reorganized, a process where the data is backed up, the table emptied, and the data reloaded in order to put rows back in the desired sequence.

Here are some general guidelines regarding the use of indexes:

- Keep in mind that most RDBMSs automatically create indexes on key columns in primary key constraints and unique constraints.

- Indexes on foreign keys can markedly improve the performance of joins.

- Indexes that contain all the columns used in a query allow the RDBMS to handle the query without accessing any table rows. These index-only queries are usually very efficient.

- Consider using indexes on columns that are frequently referenced in WHERE clauses.

- Indexes on long variable character columns are seldom very helpful at improving overall performance.

- While most RDBMS products support indexes on nullable columns, if the columns contain a lot of null values, the index will not be as useful.

- The larger the table, the less you want any database query to have to scan the entire table (in other words, the more you want *every* query to use an index).

- The more a table is updated, the fewer the number of indexes you should have on the table, particularly on the columns that are updated most often.

- For relatively small tables (less than 1,000 rows or so), sequential table scans are probably more efficient than indexes. Most RDBMSs have optimizers that decide when an index should be used, and typically they will choose a table scan over an index until at least a few hundred rows exist in the table.

- For tables with relatively short rows that are most often accessed using the primary key, consider the use of an *index organized table* (on RDBMSs that support such a table), where all the table data is stored in the index. This can be a highly efficient structure for lookup tables (tables containing little more than code and description columns).

- Consider the performance consequences carefully before you define more than two or three indexes on a single table.

- B-tree (balanced tree) indexes (the default type of index in nearly every RDBMS) only provide a performance benefit when they are selective. *Index selectivity* is a ratio of the number of distinct values a column has divided by the number of rows in a table. For example, if a table has 1,000 rows and a column has 800 distinct values, the selectivity of the index is 0.8, which is considered good. However, a column such as gender that has only two distinct values (M and F) has very poor selectivity (.002 in a 1,000-row table). Unique indexes always have a selectivity of 1.0, which is the best possible.

- For columns with few distinct values, some RDBMS products support bitmap indexes. A *bitmap index* uses arrays of bits to represent whether data values in table rows match particular values. They offer lightening fast searches of tables but perform so poorly when updated that most RDBMS products do not attempt to update them as table data is maintained, but instead only support periodic rebuilds of the index. For this reason, bitmap indexes are most appropriate for analytical databases where the data is updated infrequently. A more detailed explanation of bitmap indexes can be found in Chapter 11.

Designing Views

As covered in Chapter 2, views can be thought of as virtual tables. They are, however, merely stored SQL statements that do not themselves contain any data. Data can be selected from views just as it can from tables, and with some restrictions, data can be inserted into, updated in, and deleted from views. Here are the restrictions:

- For views containing joins, any insert, update, or delete statements issued against the view must reference only one table.

- Inserts are not possible using views where any required (NOT NULL) column has been omitted.

- Any update against a view may reference only columns that directly map to base table columns. Calculated and derived columns may not be updated.

- Appropriate privileges are required (just as with base tables).

- Various other product-specific restrictions apply to view usage, so the RDBMS documentation should always be consulted.

Views can be designed to provide the following advantages:

- In some RDBMSs, views provide a performance advantage over ordinary SQL statements. Views are precompiled, so the resources required to check the syntax of the statement and prepare it for processing are saved when views are repeatedly referenced. However, there is no such advantage with RDBMSs that provide an automatic SQL statement cache, as Oracle does. Moreover, poorly written SQL can be included in a view, so putting SQL in a view is not a magic solution to performance issues.

- Similarly, in some RDBMSs, stored procedures can outperform views. (A *stored procedure* is a program that is written in a language supported by the RDBMS and stored in the database. They are invoked with an SQL statement and can optionally return a result set much as a view does.) Stored procedures can do a lot more data manipulation than can be accomplished in a view.

- Views may be tailored to individual department needs, providing only the rows and columns needed, and perhaps renaming columns using terms more readily understood by the particular audience.

- Views can provide alternative representations of the data, such as concatenated names, formatted date and time fields, codes replaced with text descriptions, and even language translations.

- Because views hide the real table and column names from their users, they insulate users from changes to those names in the base tables.

- Data usage can be greatly simplified by hiding complicated joins and calculations from the database users. For example, views can easily calculate ages based on birth dates, and they can summarize data in nearly any way imaginable.

- Security needs can be met by omitting rows and columns that users are not supposed to see. Some RDBMS products permit column-level security, where users are granted privileges by column as well as by table, but using views is far easier to implement and maintain. Moreover, a WHERE clause in the view can filter rows easily.

- Views can be used to reestablish supertypes and subtypes that were not implemented. Similarly, tables that were split or merged can be reestablished.

Once created, views must be managed like any other database object. If many members of a database project are creating and updating views, it is very easy to lose control. Moreover, views can become invalid as maintenance is carried out on the database, so their status must be reviewed periodically.

Try This 8-2 Mapping a Logical Model to a Physical Database Design

Implementing subtypes and supertypes in relational databases is perhaps the most challenging part of physical database design. This Try This exercise gives you an opportunity to practice this essential skill. The following illustration shows part of the logical model for part of an HR (human resources) application. The steps in this exercise walk you through converting this model to a physical data model.

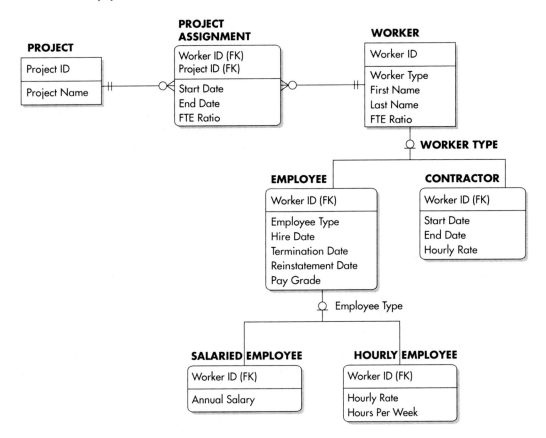

Step by Step

1. Given that the Salaried Employee and Hourly Employee entities have so few attributes, it seems best to collapse them into the Employee relation. Move the Annual Salary, Hourly Rate, and Hours Per Week attributes to Employee.

2. On further analysis, you notice that both the Employee and Contractor entities now have an Hourly Rate attribute. Therefore, you need to move Hourly Rate to the Worker entity.

3. After discussion with the business analysts working on your project, you conclude that Hours Per Week can easily be derived from the FTE (Full Time Equivalency) Ratio in the Worker entity. For example, an FTE of 0.5 means the person works 20 hours per week (40 * 0.5 = 20). This was simply missed in earlier analysis passes because Hours Per Week was two layers down the subtype hierarchy from FTE Ratio. You can simply remove Hours Per Week from the model.

4. After discussion regarding the Employee and Contract subtypes, you conclude that they should remain as separate entities (tables) in the physical model. Too many distinct attributes exist between the two subtypes to consider combining them into the Worker entity. At the same time, pushing the Worker supertype into the two subtypes is not an attractive option because the many-to-many relationship between Worker and Project applies to both subtypes and therefore would have to be redundantly (and awkwardly) implemented if the Worker entity were eliminated. Create one-to-one relationships between Worker and Employee and between Worker and Contractor.

5. Shift all the table and column names to uppercase with underscores between words so that they can be used as object names in any relational database.

Try This Summary

In this Try This exercise, you stepped through the considerations that are typical in converting a logical model containing supertypes and subtypes to a physical model. My solution is shown in Appendix B.

You may have noticed that this particular design does not handle storage of historical data. For example, if a contract employee finished a contract and then returned some time later for another contract, you could not hold both contracts in the database at the same time, because you have only one set of start and end dates per employee. Similarly, if an employee leaves for a time and is rehired at a later time, you cannot hold both employment engagements in the database at the same time. This is typical of modern OLTP (online transaction processing) databases, where you expect to have a different database such as a data warehouse to hold the historical data. Data warehouses and other data structures for OLAP (online analytical processing) are covered in Chapter 11.

Chapter 8 Self Test

1. When you're designing tables,

    A   Each normalized relation becomes a table

    B   Each attribute in the relation becomes a table column

    C   Relationships become check constraints

    D   Unique identifiers become triggers

    E   Primary key columns must be defined as NOT NULL

2. Supertypes and subtypes

   A Must be implemented exactly as specified in the logical design

   B May be collapsed in the physical database design

   C May have the supertype columns folded into each subtype in the physical design

   D Usually have the same primary key in the physical tables

   E Apply only to the logical design

3. Table names

   A Should be based on the attribute names in the logical design

   B Should always include the word "table"

   C Should use only uppercase letters

   D Should include organization or location names

   E May contain abbreviations when necessary

4. Column names

   A Must be unique within the database

   B Should be based on the corresponding attribute names in the logical design

   C Must be prefixed with the table name

   D Must be unique within the table

   E Should use abbreviations whenever possible

5. Referential constraints

   A Define relationships identified in the logical model

   B Are always defined on the parent table

   C Require that foreign keys be defined as NOT NULL

   D Should have descriptive names

   E Name the parent and child tables and the foreign key column

6. Check constraints

   A May be used to force a column to match a list of values

   B May be used to force a column to match a range of values

   C May be used to force a column to match another column in the same row

D May be used to force a column to match a column in another table

E May be used to enforce a foreign key constraint

7. Data types

A Prevent incorrect data from being inserted into a table

B Can be used to prevent alphabetic characters from being stored in numeric columns

C Can be used to prevent numeric characters from being stored in character format columns

D Require that precision and scale be specified also

E Can be used to prevent invalid dates from being stored in date columns

8. View restrictions include which of the following?

A Views containing joins can never be updated.

B Updates to calculated columns in views are prohibited.

C Privileges are required in order to update data using views.

D If a view omits a mandatory column, inserts to the view are not possible.

E Any update involving a view may reference columns only from one table.

9. Some advantages of views are

A Views may provide performance advantages

B Views may insulate database users from table and column name changes

C Views may be used to hide joins and complex calculations

D Views may filter columns or rows that users should not see

E Views may be tailored to the needs of individual departments

10. Indexes

A May be used to assist with primary key constraints

B May be used to improve query performance

C May be used to improve insert, update, and delete performance

D Are usually smaller than the tables they reference

E Are slower to sequentially scan than corresponding tables

11. General rules to follow regarding indexes include which of the following?

    A The larger the table, the more important indexes become.

    B Indexing foreign key columns often helps join performance.

    C Columns that are frequently updated should always be indexed.

    D The more a table is updated, the more indexes will help performance.

    E Indexes on very small tables tend not to be very useful.

12. Business rules are implemented in the database using _____.

13. Two key differences between unique constraints and primary key constraints are _____ and _____.

14. Relationships in the logical model become _____ in the physical model.

15. Constraint names are important because _____.

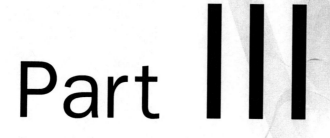

Part III

Design Alternatives

Chapter 9

Alternatives for Incorporating Business Rules

Key Skills & Concepts

- Anatomy of a Business Rule
- Implementing Business Rules in Data Models
- Limitations on Implementing Business Rules in Data Models
- Functional Classification of Business Rules

This chapter explores business rules, methods for implementing business rules in data models, and the limitation on implementing business rules in data models.

The Anatomy of a Business Rule

In "Defining Business Rules—What Are They Really" (www.businessrulesgroup.org/first_paper/br01c0.htm, July 2000), the Business Rules Group defines a business rule as follows. "A business rule is a statement that defines or constrains some aspect of the business. It is intended to assert business structure or to control or influence the behavior of the business."

This is a more precise definition than the one I offered in Chapter 2. It is also a broader definition because it incorporates not only constraints but also definitions. As shown in Figure 9-1, the Business Rules Group defines the following categories of business rules:

- **Term**   A word or phrase that has a single definition. The same definition may point to multiple words or phrases, but each word or phrase must have one and only one definition.
- **Fact**   A statement that relates terms to each other, describes a thing or a role it plays, or provides some other description.
- **Derivation**   An attribute that is derived from other attributes.
- **Constraint**   A condition that prescribes the values a relationship or attribute must have, or a rule that prevents record updates until a required condition is met. To avoid confusion with physical database constraints, the term *assertion* is sometimes used for this category of business rules.

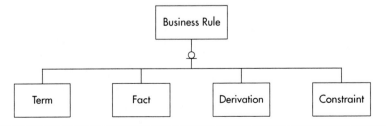

Figure 9-1   Business rule categories

The Origin of Business Rules

Obviously, business rules must be identified and validated in order to be useful in a data model. Identification comes from reviewing process models and requirements and asking the right questions. Validation that business rules are accurately represented in data models is handled by reviewing the models that are complete (or nearly so) with subject matter experts (SMEs) and business users.

Here are some of the sources of business rules:

- **Business users and SMEs**   Comments and descriptions given in requirements meetings, data modeling working sessions, and other workshops

- **Process models**   Process documentation for existing applications as well as the design for the proposed application

- **Documents**   Manuals, forms, application documentation, and the like

- **Business policies**   Rules set forth by an organization's senior management

- **Laws and regulations**   Rules set forth in federal, state and local laws

- **Audit recommendations**   Best practices and recommendations from the organization's internal and external auditors

- **Established best practices**   Policies and procedures published by governments, regulatory agencies, trade associations, standards bodies, and other organizations

- **Certification rules and guidelines**   Rules and guidelines with which the organization must comply in order to receive industry or trade group certifications

Implementing Business Rules in Data Models

Terms and facts are the primary categories of business rules that can be represented in data models. Derivations can only be partially represented in that the results of derivations can be shown in data models as attributes. The limitations on implementing business rules in the constraints category are discussed in the section "Limitations on Implementing Business Rules in Data Models" later in this chapter.

Implementing Terms

As shown in Figure 9-2, terms fall into these three categories:

- **Entity Name**   The name of an entity in the data model.

- **Attribute Name**   The name of an attribute in the data model (typically acting as a descriptor for the entity).

- **Other Business Term**   A term that represents some other aspect of the enterprise that will not be addressed as a formal entity or attribute. Most often these are common business or industry terms that are used in descriptions of entities, attributes, or process logic.

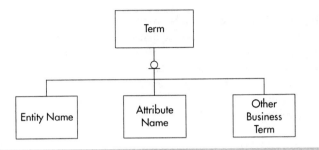

Figure 9-2 Term categories

For example, gross margin is a common business term that would be used in combination with other words or phrases to form attribute names in a data model. And HMO (health maintenance organization) is a common health care industry term that can be used to form entity and attribute names in a data model.

Figure 9-3 shows a data model with selected terms (entity names and attribute names) called out.

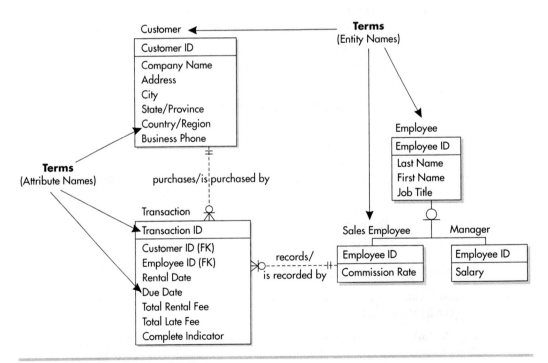

Figure 9-3 Data model with terms

Implementing Facts

As shown in Figure 9-4, facts fall into three categories:

- **Relationships**   A business relationship between two objects, or a *role* that one object plays with respect to another. For example, a customer would play the role of purchaser in a transaction, while an employee would play the role of seller. Relationships establish referential constraints in the data model.

- **Attributes**   A fact that characterizes or describes an object in some way. This is basically the same definition as that of an attribute in a data model. Note that the name of the attribute is considered a term, while the attribute itself is considered a fact. Parts of the attribute definition establish constraints in the data model, including the data type, allowable values (if they fit into a check constraint), uniqueness (primary key or alternate key), and other constraints that can be implemented in a trigger or in application logic.

- **Supertypes/subtypes**   A fact that requires each occurrence of a subtype to have a corresponding supertype occurrence. Subtypes can be used to document limitations on which entity instances can be associated with each other. Therefore, including subtypes in conceptual and logical models is useful even when you have no intention of implementing them in the physical model.

Figure 9-5 shows a data model with selected facts (attributes, relationships/roles and subtypes) called out. Note that each relationship between two entities in a data model consists of two facts, one representing the relationship/role in each direction. For example, the relationship between the Sales Employee and Transaction entities in Figure 9-5 is an implementation of two business rule roles, one stating that an employee records zero, one, or more transactions, and the other stating that each transaction is recorded by one and only one employee. The pair of roles is represented in the data model as a single line with symbols and/or text identifying the two roles.

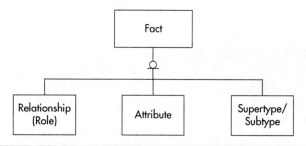

Figure 9-4   Fact categories

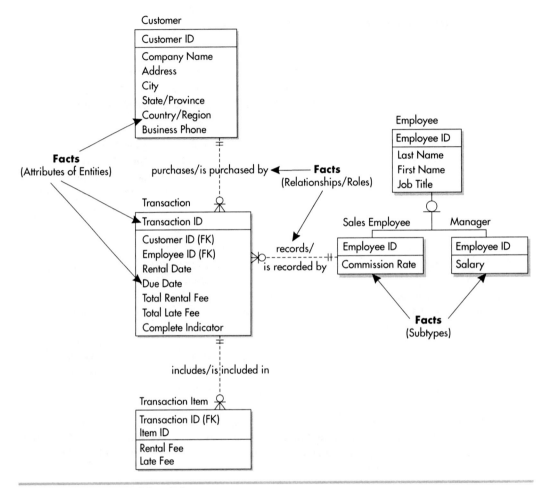

Figure 9-5 Data model with facts

Implementing Derivations

As mentioned earlier, derivations cannot be completely represented in data models. For example, in Figure 9-5, the Total Rental Fee and Total Late Fee attributes could be considered derivations because they are calculated by summing the individual Rental Fee and Late Fee attribute values from the associated Transaction Item rows.

While we can show the results of the derivation in the form of the attributes that store the results, the data model provides no mechanism for indicating that the attributes are in fact derived, not to mention any information about how the derivation takes place.

Ask the Expert

Q: You said that data models don't provide a way to show which attributes are derived or how they are derived. Isn't this important information that needs to be captured and recorded somewhere?

A: Yes indeed. Most practitioners add this information to the text description of the attribute. In cases where a derived attribute is removed during normalization, the description and derivation information can be handled in a view definition. In a UML model, a note can be added to the diagram to include the formula for the derived attribute.

Limitations on Implementing Business Rules in Data Models

Recall that constraints are business rules that determine the values an attribute or relationship can (or must) have. Data models drawn using entity relationship diagrams provide limited support for constraints.

There are myriad methods for documenting business rules that cannot be included in a data model. These methods include decision trees and tables, data flow diagrams, function hierarchies, pseudocode, and various UML constructs. Moreover, business rules implemented in application logic can be documented along with the application. Finally, there is a lot to be said for plain language descriptions because they are so easily understood.

Implementing Constraints

As shown in Figure 9-6, entity relationship models provide support for the following forms of constraints:

- **Optionality** May be shown in terms of whether an attribute or relationship is mandatory. However, entity relationship diagrams cannot show an attribute or relationship that is only mandatory under certain circumstances or an attribute that is optional when the object is initially created but becomes mandatory at a later time. For example, an employee benefits account can be created without a beneficiary, but when any life insurance option is activated, a beneficiary becomes mandatory. The model cannot show the circumstances under which an attribute becomes mandatory—it can only show whether the attribute is optional or mandatory (NULL or NOT NULL). Relationship optionality is specified in the data model by whether the foreign key attributes are optional or mandatory.

- **Cardinality** Shows the maximum number of occurrences that are possible for a given entity. However, only a fixed value can be shown, such as one (no symbol or a hash mark across the line), many (crow's foot), or some specific number (a number next to the line end). It is not possible to show variable cardinality such as an account that can have one, two, or many owners depending on the type of account.

- **Unique identifiers**   May be shown in the form of one or more unique constraints (each formed using one or more attributes), one of which is marked as the primary identifier or primary key.

- **Exclusive subtypes**   May be shown using a specific symbol, usually a variation of the general subtype symbol being used. In Figure 9-6, the circle with a line under it is the symbol for an exclusive subtype.

- **Domains**   May be shown, but only in the form of the data type for an attribute. (Recall that a domain is a specification of the values that a particular attribute can have.) Note that some data modeling tools and DBMS products support user-defined types that can be used to specify a more precise domain.

Constraints That Cannot Be Shown in Entity Relationship Models

Thus far in this chapter I have presented constraints that can be represented to some degree in an entity relationship data model. However, there are many more types of constraints that can only be represented outside of a data model. Often this problem is exacerbated by the tendency of experienced data modelers to generalize models in an attempt to make them less vulnerable to changes in business rules.

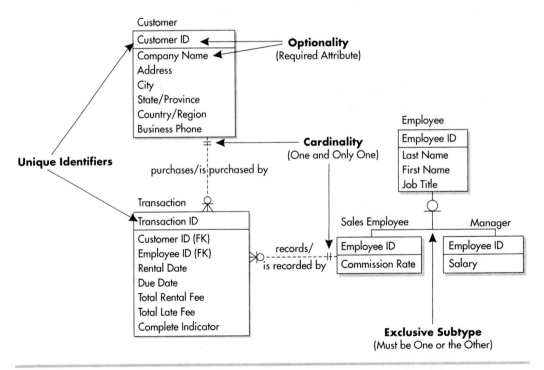

Figure 9-6   Data model with constraints

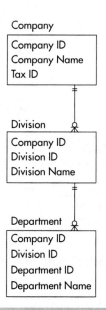

Figure 9-7 Data model of organizational hierarchy

For example, consider the data model shown in Figure 9-7, which represents business rules for these cardinalities (among others):

- A company may have zero, one or more divisions.

- Each division must belong to one and only one company.

- A division may have zero, one, or more departments.

- Each department must belong to one and only one division.

The problem with such a rigid structure should be obvious. Business organizations are prone to change, and any change to the structure shown in Figure 9-7 that adds a new organizational unit type or relaxes one of the rules requires a database design change. For example, if an organization using this structure decided to add regions as an organizational unit between divisions and departments, the data model and any database built from it would require modification.

The obvious solution to most practitioners is to employ a generic organizational structure like the one shown in Figure 9-8. This model is far more flexible, but at the expense of explicit specification and enforcement of the cardinalities listed earlier. For example, the data model shown in Figure 9-8 (and any database built from it) cannot prevent a department from being associated with a company instead of a division, while the structure shown in Figure 9-7 can. An additional issue is that organizational units could be organized into an infinite loop. These issues must be handled by the applications that maintain the database rather than constraints implemented directly in the database.

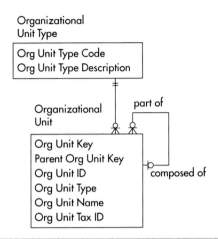

Figure 9-8 Data model of a generic organizational structure

Functional Classification of Business Rules

An alternative (and perhaps more common) way to classify business rules is by function. This section provides an overview of business rules and their implementation in data models from the functional perspective. Keep in mind that while data and process modelers should strive to uncover and document all applicable business rules, not all rules are appropriate for implementation in the database.

Definitional Rules

Definitional rules determine the definition of entities and attributes. The most common of these are the data type, precision, and scale (where applicable) of the attributes. However, the text description of each entity and attribute can include other information that cannot be directly implemented in the definition of the object.

Data Validation Rules

Data validation rules determine the required characteristics of data that is to be stored. For example, a rule that employees must be at least 18 years old is a data validation rule that can be associated with the Birth Date attribute in the Employee entity.

For attributes restricted to a discrete list of values, such as a gender code that can only have the values *F* or *M*, a check constraint or a foreign key to a reference table can be used to implement the rule. For attributes restricted to nondiscrete values, such as a purchase price that must be zero or a positive number, a reference table is not a viable alternative, so implementation in the database can be done with either a check constraint or a trigger, depending on complexity. If subtypes are rolled up into the supertype table, it is important to determine for each subtype which attributes should have values and which should not.

Data validation rules are best discovered by analyzing each entity and asking about restrictions on adding new instances, the values assigned to each attribute, changing attribute values, and on deleting instances.

Data Derivation Rules

Data derivation rules are the methods by which derived data items are calculated. For example, the Total Sale attribute in an order should have a data derivation rule that specifies how the data value is determined.

The best way to discover data derivation rules is to analyze the output of each process as well as any derived attributes in screens, reports, web pages, forms, and other types of user views.

Cardinality Rules

Cardinality rules determine how many of one entity or attribute can be associated with some other entity or attribute. For example, the Customer-Order relationship should have a cardinality rule that specifies that a customer can have many orders while each order belongs to one and only one customer.

For attributes, cardinality rules are reflected in the placement of the attribute (that is, which entity can hold the entity while complying with first normal form) and whether the attribute is allowed to be null or not. For entities, cardinality rules are reflected in the cardinality of the relationships in which the entity participates. However, rules requiring specific cardinality, such as "managers must have at least two but no more than six subordinates," cannot be enforced completely by relationships. Cardinality rules are determined by checking the cardinality of each attribute and relationship with business users and SMEs.

Referential Integrity Rules

Referential integrity rules require that foreign key values always have a matching key value in the parent entity. For example, a Customer ID attribute in an Order entity should always have a matching customer with the same Customer ID in the Customer entity.

Referential integrity rules are implicit in the relationships defined in the data model. As with cardinality rules, referential integrity rules are determined by checking the cardinality of each relationship with business users and SMEs.

Process Rules

Process rules determine what processing the system must do in particular circumstances. For example, a process rule might state that no shipments can be made to customers who have overdue accounts. Other common process rules specify which roles can perform certain operations and data values that depend on other values, such as an end effective date that must be greater than the begin effective date.

Except for the data that is supported by or created by the processes, process rules are generally out of scope for the data modeler. These rules will be handled in application logic and therefore are in the domain of the process modeler(s) and application developer(s).

Try This 9-1 Modeling Business Rules

In this Try This exercise, you will analyze a series of business rules and create a logical data model for an academic application.

Step by Step

1. Analyze the following business rules for a community college that requires a new database application to track student interactions with academic tutors.

   - Each course is identified by a unique Course ID as well as a unique Course Title.

   - Courses can be offered multiple times each year. When there is sufficient demand, the course may be offered multiple times in the same semester.

   - Each course offering is assigned one instructor and one tutor. Instructors and tutors can be assigned to multiple course offerings during the same semester.

   - Students enroll in one or more course offerings and receive both a numeric raw score and a letter grade for their academic performance.

   - Tutors can be students, faculty members, or other persons who are neither students nor faculty.

   - At least one contact method must be stored for each instructor, tutor, and student, but any person may have multiple contact methods. The contact information can be in the form of a mailing address, a telephone number, or an e-mail address.

   - A contact event occurs whenever a tutor and a student communicate, whether in person or via a contact method (e-mail, telephone, or postal mail). Each contact event includes the contact method used to contact the tutor as well as the method used by the tutor to respond. For example, a student might e-mail a tutor, and the tutor may choose to respond by phone or in person.

2. Determine the required entities, attributes, and relationships. Feel free to add additional attributes that add to the clarity of the model.

3. Normalize to at least third normal form.

4. Draw the logical model.

Try This Summary

In this Try This exercise, you took a set of business rules and created a logical data model in third normal form.

✓ Chapter 9 Self Test

1. A _____ is a word or phrase that has a single definition.

2. A _____ is a statement that relates terms to each other.

3. A _____ is an attribute that is derived from other attributes.

4. A _____ is a condition that prescribes the values a relationship or attribute must have.

5. _____ shows the maximum number of occurrences that are possible for a given entity.

6. A _____ is a specification of the values that a particular attribute may have.

7. _____ rules determine how many of one entity or attribute can be associated with some other entity or attribute.

8. _____ rules require that foreign key values always have a matching key value in the parent entity.

9. _____ rules determine what processing the system must do in particular circumstances.

10. _____ rules determine the definition of entities and attributes.

11. _____ rules determine the required characteristics of data that is to be stored.

12. The Business Rules Group defines which of the following categories of business rules?

   A Term

   B Entity

   C Fact

   D Derivation

   E Constraint

13. Origins of business rules include which of the following?

   A Laws and regulations

   B Business policies

   C Certification rules and guidelines

   D Process models

   E User views

14. A term can fall into which of these categories?

   A Attribute name

   B Relationship

   C Entity name

   D Supertype/subtype

   E Other business term

15. A fact can fall into which of these categories?

   A Attribute name

   B Attribute

   C Relationship

   D Supertype/subtype

   E Entity name

16. An entity relationship model supports which of the following forms of constraints?

   A Unique identifiers

   B Domains

   C Exclusive subtypes

   D Cardinality

   E Optionality

Chapter 10

Alternatives for Handling Temporal Data

Key Skills & Concepts

- Temporal Data Structures

- Calendar Data Structures

- Business Rules for Temporal Data

Most data models must handle temporal (time dependent) data in one form or another, be it past data values (history), future data values (records that are not to take effect until some point in the future), attaching a time zone to an event such as a flight or an online meeting, or audit trails to account for old and new values as the database is updated. This chapter explores alternatives for handling such temporal data.

Temporal Data Structures

Although many practitioners would find comfort in adopting an organization-wide standard method for handling temporal data, such an approach is not in the best interest of the organization. If a rudimentary standard is adopted, it will prove to be inadequate in some circumstances, and yet a comprehensive standard will prove to be overkill for many data models. Adding temporal structures to everything in the model will needlessly over-complicate the entire model. Therefore, the modeler must have a toolkit of patterns and techniques for handling temporal data requirements and must apply them uniquely to each situation.

To be successful in any data modeling effort, the requirements must be clear. When accounting for time, you may find it useful to categorize data in the same way that data warehouse and dimensional database guru Ralph Kimball categorizes data in dimensional data structures (which are presented in Chapter 11):

- **Type 1** No history—when an attribute is changed, the new value is simply written over the existing value.

- **Type 2** Complete history—every previous value of the attribute must be retained

- **Type 3** Limited history—only a finite number of previous values of the attribute must be retained, including the case where only the current and one previous value are required

When Does Time Matter?

Obviously, time must be accounted for when the requirements and business rules call for it. But at what point in data model development (conceptual modeling, logical modeling, or physical modeling) should we concentrate on handling temporal data requirements? The answer is in all of them to some degree.

Some business applications such as a scheduling system for airline flights have such profound and obvious time requirements that temporal structures should appear even in the conceptual model. However, by no means should this push you into adding temporal structures to everything in the model. In conceptual models, time-related components should appear only in entities where time is of direct interest to the business. Leave the handling of basic reporting on history to the logical and/or physical models.

The transformation of the conceptual model to a logical model is a reasonable place to account for time. If you develop rules and standard patterns for handling temporal data, it may even be possible to handle the temporal data requirements in a systematic if not mechanical manner.

You may also find some opportunities to handle temporal data requirements solely in the physical data model. For example, a requirement for standard audit attributes for tracking who changed each row of data along with when and why it was changed can easily be handled in the physical model by mechanically adding the required columns to each applicable table. In fact, this can be a huge advantage because the logical model does not need to show the same attributes in every (or nearly every) entity. However, as shown in the next section of this chapter, be aware that adding temporal data often changes the cardinality of relationships, and in those cases, the temporal data should be included in the logical model so that relationships match between the logical and physical models.

Another consideration is the application itself. Generally speaking, online transaction processing (OLTP) applications (the applications that control and track the day-to-day operation of the business, such as order processing, manufacturing control, and human resources) need mostly current state information. On the other hand, online analytical processing (OLAP) applications such as data warehouses and data marts are all about tracking history, so a date and/or time is necessary for just about everything in an OLAP model. Modeling for analytical databases is covered in detail in Chapter 11. This chapter focuses on general techniques applicable to data models that support either OLTP or OLAP applications.

Adding History to Data Structures

Many practitioners believe that adding history to an existing data structure changes every one-to-one relationship to one-to-many and every one-to-many relationship to many-to-many. However, while this rule is generally true, it only applies to transferable relationships as data modeling expert Graeme Simsion has frequently pointed out. Recall that a *transferable* relationship is one where the related entity occurrence (row of data, physically speaking) can be reassigned to a different occurrence, such as an employee being transferred from one department to another.

Figure 10-1 shows a partial conceptual model for an automobile dealership. Employees are organized into departments, some employees (the sales representatives and their managers) are assigned a vehicle to drive, and some employees have employment contracts. Note that there are two relationships between the Department and Employee entities, one for membership in the department and the other for the manager of the department, with each department having only one manager at any point in time.

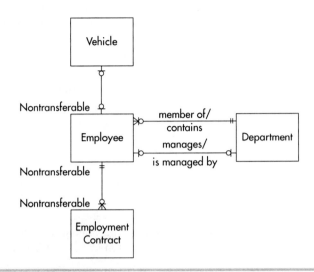

Figure 10-1 Conceptual model without history

No history is included in the model shown in Figure 10-1. A database implemented from this model will not be capable of showing which vehicle was previously assigned to an employee, or which department an employee used to work in, or who the previous manager of a department was. In the case of employment contracts, multiple contracts are possible for each employee because some employees serve multiple roles, each of which could have a contract. For example, sales supervisors are also sales representatives, so they have a contract that spells out the terms of their supervisory role as well as a contract that spells out the terms of their sales role, including quotas and commissions.

Since nontransferable relationships do not change when history is added, I noted three places where relationships are nontransferable in Figure 10-1. First, company policy requires that only one employee use a vehicle from the inventory, and for no more than a month before it is placed back in inventory. Once used by an employee, the vehicle may not be used by another employee before it is sold. While an employee can be assigned another vehicle out of inventory when they turn in the one they have been using, the vehicle cannot be reassigned to another employee. Therefore the Vehicle-Employee relationship is nontransferable on the Employee end. Second, an employee is never required to adhere to the terms of an employee contract for another employee, nor is an employment contract reassigned to another employee when someone leaves the dealership. Therefore the Employee-Employment Contract relationship is nontransferable on both ends.

Figure 10-2 shows the conceptual model from Figure 10-1 with history added to all relationships. Take a moment and compare the relationship cardinality changes between Figure 10-1 and Figure 10-2.

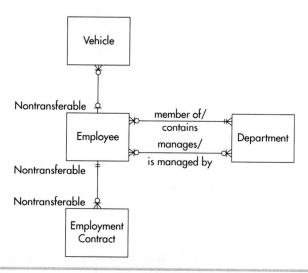

Figure 10-2   Conceptual model with history added

Note the following cardinality changes:

- The Vehicle-Employee relationship has changed from one-to-one to one-to-many in order to show the history of which vehicles have been assigned to each employee. There can be only one employee per vehicle over time because of the company policy prohibiting reassignment of a vehicle to additional employees.

- The Department-Employee relationship labeled "member of/contains" has changed from one-to-many to many-to-many in order to show the history of departments in which each employee has worked.

- The Department-Employee relationship labeled "manages/is managed by" has changed from one-to-one to many-to-many in order to show the history of departments a person has managed as well as the history of who has managed each department.

- The Employee-Employment Contract relationship has not changed because the relationship is nontransferable on both ends.

In terms of attributes, there are three basic methods for handling temporal data: adding an effective date to the primary key (or natural key) of an entity, adding history tables to applicable entities, and adding a data structure to log changes to the data.

Adding Effective Dates

Figure 10-3 shows a logical model for the Employee-Department relationships with an intersection table that includes an effective date in the primary key. Since both the relationships between the Employee and Department entities have become many-to-many

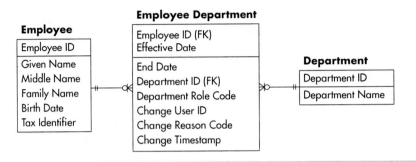

Figure 10-3 Logical model with effective date in the primary key

when adjusted to handle history as shown in Figure 10-3, they can now be implemented with the same intersection table. In essence, I have decided to handle department members and department managers as two different roles implemented by a common relationship.

For the primary key, I have chosen Employee ID and Effective Date. An employee can only be assigned to one department at a time, therefore adding Department ID to the key does not contribute to the uniqueness of the primary key. Adding the End Date to the primary key does not contribute to uniqueness unless an employee can have multiple assignments on the same day. However, it would be easier to handle that situation by changing Effective Date to Begin Timestamp (a combination of the date and time with as much time granularity as necessary—seconds being enough for most business systems). The Department Role Code attribute indicates whether the employee is a member of the department or the department manager (which in this company includes being a member).

For those that prefer surrogate keys, a simple attribute named something like Employee Department SK could be used as the primary key, which would make Employee ID and Effective Date nonkey attributes. However, when you do this, you must remember to also include a unique constraint (sometimes called an alternate key constraint in popular data modeling tools) because you must ensure that the combination of attributes that forms the natural key is always unique. (I have gotten in the habit of using SK [for surrogate key] as the class word suffix for surrogate key attribute names because it helps me remember that the primary key is not the natural key of the entity.)

Notice that I also added three commonly used audit attributes to the Employee Department entity: Change User ID to record the identifier of the database user (whether a person or an application) that added or changed the data, Change Reason Code to indicate the reason the data was changed, and Change Timestamp to record the moment in time when the data was changed. I recommend that you work with your auditors to come up with a standard set of attributes such as these that you can add to every entity in your OLTP data models so that audit data is uniformly available. As mentioned, you might also consider adding attributes such as these to physical models instead of logical ones.

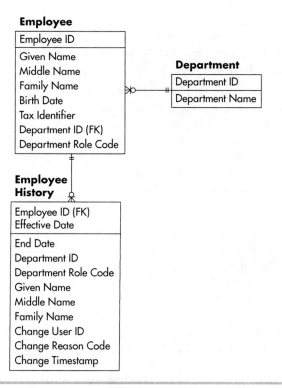

Employee

Employee ID
Given Name
Middle Name
Family Name
Birth Date
Tax Identifier
Department ID (FK)
Department Role Code

Department

Department ID
Department Name

Employee History

Employee ID (FK)
Effective Date
End Date
Department ID
Department Role Code
Given Name
Middle Name
Family Name
Change User ID
Change Reason Code
Change Timestamp

Figure 10-4   Logical model with history table

Adding History Tables

An alternative to adding dates to primary or natural keys is to add history tables. Figure 10-4 shows the model from Figure 10-3 adjusted to use a history table. Often we add history structures such as this one only to physical models, which is why the term "history table" is commonly used for this structure rather than a logical term such as "history entity."

Note the following changes to the data model:

- The Department-Employee relationship is back to one-to-many, but the Department Role Code has been added so that only one relationship is required to show both department members and managers.

- The Employee entity shows the current department assignment using Department ID as a foreign key.

- The Employee History table was added as a child of Employee. Employee History has the combination of Employee ID and Effective Date as its primary key, and it contains Department ID and Department Role in order to show previous department assignments. The audit columns contained in the Employee Department entity were moved to the Employee History table as well.

● You may have noticed that I left Birth Date and Tax Identifier out of the Employee History table. This was done because, at least in theory, these values should never change once set to the correct values. However, if experience showed that they do change over time, they could be added to the table.

● As a bonus, I chose to use the same table to track changes to employee names, so the previous values of the Given Name, Middle Name, and Family Name attributes are also included. It would be unusual for the employee's name and department assignment to be changed at the same time, or even for all three parts of their name to change at the same time, so the name and department assignment attributes must all be optional (NULL in the physical model) to allow attributes that did not change to be null in the history table. This is an easy way to tell what changed and what did not when reviewing rows in the history table.

When implementing history tables, a discussion needs to take place regarding what happens when a row is added to the base table (the Employee table in this example). Should a history table row be written when a new employee is added, or only after an existing employee is changed for the first time? Some organizations prefer the history table to be self-contained, including a row for inserts with an appropriate reason code; others prefer to include only updates and deletes in the history table.

Figure 10-5 shows a hybrid approach where an effective-dated intersection table is used to show current, future, and historical employee department assignments while the Employee Name History table is used to show the history of changes to employee name components.

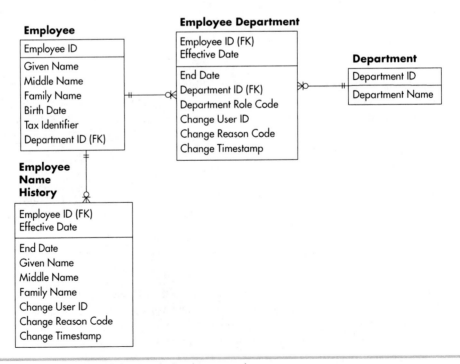

Figure 10-5 Logical model using hybrid approach

A distinct advantage to the effective-dated intersection table is that it can easily contain future values by setting the effective date to a future value. This seems a very reasonable alternative in this case. It is likely that the organization will know of department transfers and department manager changes in advance of the effective date (at least sometimes). However, the organization has no control over employee name changes and thus will likely not know about them until after the fact.

Adding a Change Log Structure

Some practitioners prefer to simplify their data models by creating a generic logging structure instead of specialized log tables. Figure 10-6 shows a commonly used pattern that can be used for such logging.

The Event entity can be used to record events that take place in the organization. The definition of the event is up to the organization and can be as simple as an ordinary business transaction such as hiring a sales employee or assigning a vehicle to an existing employee. On the other hand, the event can be a major undertaking such as a complete reorganization or a merger with another organization.

The Event Change entity is intended to capture all the individual data value changes associated with a particular event. In this design, each data value change requires a separate row in the Event Change table, so if a person changed both their first and last names at the same time, there would be two Event Change rows—one for each change. There are many possible alternative designs. A generalized facility such as this one works best when

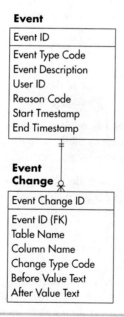

Figure 10-6 Event log structure

all database changes are captured using one comprehensive process such as a set of stored procedures that apply all the updates to the tables or a commercial change data capture (CDC) product that captures changes from database logs shortly after they occur.

A generalized logging structure such as the one shown in Figure 10-6 has the following advantages:

- The data models are simpler than models using effective-dated entities and/or history tables.

- Generalized logging structures can be populated by DBMS audit facilities or third-party auditing software that uses facilities in the DBMS such as transaction logs or SQL statement caches to obtain the information about changes.

- Generalized logging structures seldom require changes when the database structure is changed.

Processing Rules for History

Tracking history in the database complicates processing somewhat. In particular, the following rules must be observed in order to maintain the integrity of the history:

- Once written, history and log records should never be updated. If something was changed in error, there should be either a subsequent change to correct the error or a reversal transaction to back out the error, each with appropriate history.

- If natural keys change, we must have a way to tie history or log records back to the original record that was updated. A common way to achieve this is to log the old and new values of the natural keys that were changed.

- For numeric data, some logging mechanisms track the net change amount instead of the old and new values. However, this method cannot be used if null values are involved, and obviously it cannot be used for nonnumeric data.

- When history tables are used and some data in the base table is more volatile than other data, consider using multiple history tables with the more volatile attributes handled by a different history table than the more stable attributes.

- For data that is time dependent, consider adding a timestamp, a sequence number, or a version number so that you can put the data in proper sequence.

Handling Deletions

Deletions must be handled in a consistent manner. This is especially important when records are to be purged from the OLTP database. Obviously, for records where laws and regulations require record-keeping for a period of time (such as seven years for records related to U.S. taxes), there must be long-term retention of the records in a data warehouse or some form of archival system. In fact, your organization's archival requirements will likely drive your handling of deletions because you cannot archive records once they have been deleted.

There are a number of workable alternatives for handling deletions:

- Records that have been end-dated could be considered deleted and therefore eligible to be archived and purged from the OLTP database after a preset period of time, say 90 days.

- A status code column can be added to the table that is set to a particular value when the record has been logically deleted. The archive and purge process can use this code value to select records to be removed.

- Some organizations prefer a very explicit indication of deletions and use separate audit columns to track the "who, why, and when" regarding the deletion. Figure 10-7 shows the structure from Figure 10-5 modified to show separate audit columns for insert, update,

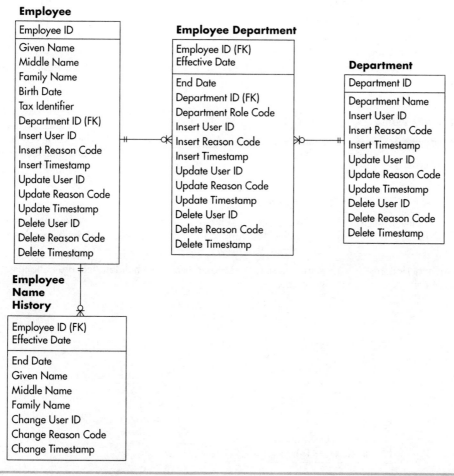

Figure 10-7 Logical model using separate audit columns for insert, update, and delete

and delete operations in each of the base tables. The insert and delete columns are not needed in the Employee Name History table because it only tracks name changes (the names are inserted and deleted at the same time as the rest of the data in the Employee table). The trade-off here is that although you can now keep insert and delete audit information separate from the last change information, there are now a lot of audit columns in each table.

Whichever approach you choose, you should not be making the decision alone. You should be working with the organization's audit and legal departments to come up with requirements and an approach that everyone agrees fully meets those requirements.

Calendar Data Structures

Occasionally you will find the need to implement a calendar function in a business application to keep track of such events as company holidays or beginning and ending dates for fiscal months or quarters. Figure 10-8 shows a simple model for a calendar data structure.

The Holiday entity contains one row for each recurring holiday that the company observes. The attributes are described in the following table:

Attribute Name	Description
Holiday ID	A unique identifier for a recurring holiday. The data value can be an arbitrary value or a mnemonic code, whichever the organization prefers.
Holiday Name	The text name of the holiday, such as "Memorial Day" or "Independence Day."
Holiday Recurrence Description	A text description of the recurrence rule for the holiday. For Memorial Day in the U.S., for example, the recurrence description would read "Last Monday in May."
National Holiday Indicator	A true/false (or yes/no) indicator for holidays that are nationally observed.

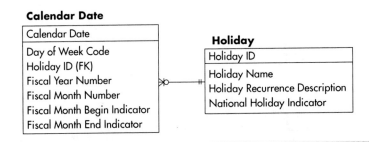

Figure 10-8 Calendar data structure

The Calendar Date entity contains one row per date of interest to the organization. (Note that it would be unwise to use the name Date because the word "date" is a reserved word in many SQL implementations.) Calendar Date can be populated with a tuple (row) for every day of every year in recent history and the near future if necessary, and this is a common practice in OLAP data models. Alternatively, it can be sparsely populated by omitting dates that are of no interest, such as weekend days. The attributes are described in the following table:

Attribute Name	Description
Calendar Date	A valid date of interest to the organization. In the corresponding physical model, the data type for the column should be a valid date data type for the DBMS, preferably one that stores only the date without a time component.
Holiday ID	The foreign key to the Holiday entity just described. If the date does not represent a holiday in the Holiday entity, the value must be NULL.
Fiscal Year Number	The four-digit number representing the fiscal year for the date. (For organizations where the fiscal year is not the same as the calendar year.)
Fiscal Month Number	The two-digit number representing the fiscal month within the fiscal year. The value 01 would represent the first fiscal month of the year, and 12 the last.
Fiscal Month Begin Indicator	A true/false (or yes/no) indicator as to whether the Calendar Date is the first day of a fiscal month. (An alternative design is to add a separate entity that contains a tuple for each fiscal month along with its start and end date.)
Fiscal Month End Indicator	A true/false (or yes/no) indicator as to whether the Calendar Date is the last day of a fiscal month. (An alternative design is to use a query to calculate the last day of the month by subtracting one day from the begin date of the following month, but the design shown here is much more obvious.)

When an entity such as Calendar Date is added to a data model, it is tempting to make every date in every other entity a foreign key to the Calendar Date entity. In practice, however, this unnecessarily clutters the diagram and (at a physical database level) results in needless lookups to the Calendar Date table as the DBMS confirms that a matching row exists as each date value is recorded in the database. Every modern relational DBMS has data types for dates or date/time combinations, and the dates recorded using these data types are automatically validated by the DBMS and rejected if they prove to be invalid date values. Therefore, there is little added value to creating dozens or perhaps hundreds of extraneous referential constraints on date attributes.

Business Rules for Temporal Data

Whenever temporal data is added to a data model, it is important to make sure the business rules properly describe how the data is to be handled. This is especially true when pairs of begin and end dates are used to specify the time period in which particular records are to be considered effective.

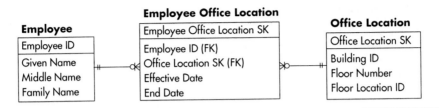

Figure 10-9 Employee Office Location model

These rules are best understood in the context of an example. Figure 10-9 contains a simple model for the assignment of employees to office locations. (The term "office" is used here in the generic sense—it can be any location where an employee can be assigned to work, including a desk in an open area, a partially enclosed cubicle, or a fully enclosed private or semiprivate office.) Each location where an employee can work is assigned an identifier that is unique within the floor of the building that contains the office location (Floor Location ID). These identifiers can change from time to time as work spaces are rearranged, so a stable surrogate key (Office Location ID) is assigned to each combination of Building ID, Floor Number, and Floor Location ID. The assignment of an employee to an office location is recorded in the Employee Office Location entity along with effective dates for the assignment.

These are the specific business rules that must be addressed:

- *Are overlapping periods permitted?* Specifically, can a new row for the same employee be recorded that has an effective date that falls between the effective date and end date for an existing Employee Office Location row for the same employee? Also, can a new row for the same office location be recorded that has an effective date that falls between the effective date and the end date for an existing Employee Office Location row for the same Office Location? In a more general sense, we are asking if an employee can be assigned multiple locations at the same time and if a location can be assigned multiple employees at the same time.

- *An End Date value should not be earlier than an Effective Date value in the same row. Should this rule be enforced, and if so, how?* This rule could easily be enforced with a check constraint in the database or in application logic, or perhaps both. There are trade-offs to each approach as discussed in previous chapters.

- *Should the Effective Date be tested to make sure it is not earlier than some logical point such as the employee's hire date?* If such a rule is enforced, it will have to be done in application logic because check constraints can only test values that are in the same row.

- *Should the End Date be tested to make sure it is not later than some logical point such as the employee's termination date?* Again, if this rule is enforced, it will have to be done in application logic.

- *Are gaps in time acceptable, or should application logic ensure that the begin date of a new Employee Office Location row for an employee be exactly one calendar day later than the end date of the previous Employee Office Location row (assuming there is one)?* This rule will seem silly for this example, but it could be very important if the assignment was to a pay rate instead of to something like an office location.

● *Are consecutive rows for the same employee and office location acceptable?* By consecutive rows, I mean two Employee Office Location rows with the same values of Employee ID and Office Location ID where the Effective Date in one row is exactly one day later than the End Date in the other.

● *Can assignments be made for less than one day? If so, what grain is needed (hour, minute, second, millisecond, etc.)?* Obviously the answer to this question directly affects the data type required for the Effective Date and End Date attributes, not to mention the attribute names. A related question is how much later than the End Date value should the Effective Date of the next related row be? Uniform assignment of effective dates and end dates is essential.

Try This 10-1   Adding History to Data Structures

In this Try This exercise, you will take an existing data structure designed to handle only current data values and modify it so that it can also handle past and future data values.

Step by Step

1. Study the data structure for the generalized product catalog data structure introduced in Chapter 7. Figure 7-9 showing the data model is reproduced here, and the sample data from Figure 7-10 is reproduced in the illustration that follows this one.

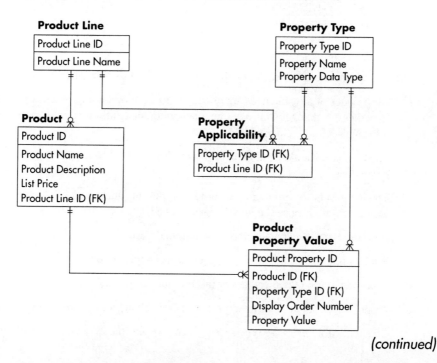

(continued)

Product Line

Prod. Line ID	Prod. Line Desc.
101	Apparel
104	Food Products

Property Type

Prop. Type ID	Prop. Name	Prop. Data Type
P10001	Size	String
P10005	Garment Type Name	String
P10012	Calorie Count	Integer

Property Type Applicability

Prod. Line ID	Prop. Type ID
101	P10001
101	P10005
104	P10001
104	P10012

Product

Prod. ID	Prod. Name	Prod. Description	List Price	Prod. Line ID
1254678	ComfoSteer Glove	Men's leather driving glove	22.99	101
3549076	CalDry Apricots	Dried California apricots	3.25	104

Product Property Value

Prod. Prop. ID	Prod. ID	Prop. Type ID	Display Order Num.	Prop. Value
33341461	1254678	P10001	2	Large
86743573	1254678	P10005	1	Men's gloves
77303926	3549076	P10001	1	6 oz.
96901490	3549076	P10012	2	110

2. Change the data model to accommodate the following business rules:

- All product catalog changes are effective as of the beginning of a business day (whether the change is introducing a new item, discontinuing an item, or changing information for an existing item).

- The database should be able to show valid values for product catalog data as of any given date.

- The identifiers for product lines, product types, products, and product property values are never reused once the item is discontinued.

- A product line may be added or discontinued as of any date.

- Product line names are rarely changed, but changes do occur.

- A property type may be added or discontinued as of any date.

- Property type names and data types are rarely changed, but changes do occur.

- The applicable property types for a given product line may change as of any date.

- A product may be added or discontinued as of any date.

- Changes to product information, particularly list prices, are common.

- Changes to product property value information are common.

Try This Summary

In this Try This exercise, you took an existing data model that was designed to handle only current data and modified it so that it is capable of handling past and future values as well as current values. There are countless valid solutions to this exercise. I chose adding effective and end dates to the existing entities over the use of history tables or a generalized log largely because of the need to be able to quickly show valid data as of any selected date. However, valid solutions can be designed using either of those methods. My solution appears in Appendix B.

Chapter 10 Self Test

1. Methods for adding temporal data to a data model include

    A Changing all relationships to many-to-many

    B Adding history tables

    C Adding an effective date to the primary key

    D Adding a data structure to log changes

    E Adding an effective date to the natural key

2. Commonly used audit attributes include

    A A code for the reason a change was made

    B The end date of the currently effective transaction

    C The date and time (timestamp) when the change occurred

    D The identifier of the database user who made the change

    E The begin date of the currently effective transaction

3. Advantages of generalized logging structures include

    A They can handle past, present, and future data values

    B They seldom require changes when the database structure is changed

    C Current data values can be included

    D Data can be obtained using DBMS logging facilities or third-party auditing software

    E Data models are simpler than those using effective-dated entities and history tables

4. Recording the net change amount instead of old and new data values is applicable for which of the following?

    A Numeric data

    B Nonnumeric data

    C Data elements where null values are permitted

    D All of the above

    E None of the above

5. Methods for handling deletion of effective-dated data include which of the following?

    A Adding a new record with a new effective date and a status of "deleted"

    B End-dating the existing record

    C Setting a status code in the existing record with a status of "deleted"

    D Physically deleting the current record and logging the deletion

    E All of the above

6. Business rules for temporal data should address

    A Whether consecutive rows for the same logical data combination should be permitted

    B Whether overlapping time periods should be permitted

    C How to handle end dates that are earlier than the effective date in the same record

    D Whether gaps in time are acceptable

    E Whether the begin date should be after some logical starting point

7. Adding temporal structures to everything in the model will _____.

8. In _____ models, time-related components should appear only in entities where time is of direct interest to the business.

9. A requirement for standard audit attributes can be easily handled in the _____ model by mechanically adding the attributes to every applicable data structure.

10. Adding temporal data to an existing data model often changes the _____ of the relationships.

11. Generally, only _____ relationships change when temporal data is added to an existing model.

12. A distinct advantage of effective-dated keys as opposed to history tables or generic audit structures is the ability to handle _____.

Chapter 11

Modeling for
Analytical Databases

Key Skills & Concepts

- Data Warehouses
- Data Marts
- Modeling Analytical Data Structures
- Loading Data into Analytical Databases

Before we look at data modeling for analytical databases, a conceptual overview is in order. Starting in the 1980s, businesses recognized the need for keeping historical data and using it for analysis to assist in decision making. It was soon apparent that data organized for use by day-to-day business transactions was not as useful for analysis. In fact, storing significant amounts of history in an *operational* database (a database designed to support the day-to-day transactions of an organization) could have serious detrimental effects on performance. William H. (Bill) Inmon pioneered work in a concept known as *data warehousing,* in which historical data is periodically trimmed from the operational database and moved to a database specifically designed for analysis. It was Inmon's dedicated promotion of the concept that earned him the title "father of data warehousing."

The popularity of the data warehouse approach grew with each success story. In addition to Inmon, others made significant contributions, notably Ralph Kimball, who developed specialized database architectures for analytical databases (covered in the section "Data Warehouse Architecture," later in this chapter). E.F. (Ted) Codd added his endorsement to the data warehouse approach and coined two important terms in 1993:

- **Online transaction processing (OLTP)**   Systems designed to handle high volumes of transactions that carry out the day-to-day activities of an organization
- **Online analytical processing (OLAP)**   Analysis of data (often historical) to identify trends that assist in making strategic decisions regarding the business

Up to this point, the chapters of this book have dealt almost exclusively with OLTP databases. This chapter, on the other hand, is devoted exclusively to modeling for OLAP databases.

Data Warehouses

Using Bill Inmon's definition, a *data warehouse* is a subject-oriented, integrated, time-variant, and nonvolatile collection of data intended to support management decision making. Here are some important properties of data warehouses:

- They are organized around major subject areas of an organization, such as sales, customers, suppliers, and products. OLTP systems, on the other hand, are typically organized around major processes, such as payroll, order entry, billing, and so forth.

- They are integrated from multiple operational (OLTP) data sources.

- They are not updated in real time, but periodically, based on an established schedule. Data is pulled from operational sources as often as needed, such as daily, weekly, monthly, and quarterly.

The potential benefits of a well-constructed data warehouse are significant, including the following:

- Competitive advantage

- Increased productivity of corporate decision makers

- Potential high return on investment as the organization finds the best ways to improve efficiency and/or profitability

However, there are significant challenges to creating an enterprise-wide data warehouse, including the following:

- Underestimation of the resources required to load the data

- Hidden data integrity problems in the source data

- Omitting data, only to find out later that it is required

- Ever-increasing end-user demands (each new feature spawning ideas for even more features)

- Consolidating data from disparate data sources

- High resource demands (huge amounts of storage; queries that process millions of rows)

- Ownership of the data

- Difficulty in determining what the business really wants or needs to analyze

- "Big bang" projects that seem never-ending

OLTP Systems Compared with Data Warehouse Systems

Data warehouse systems and OLTP systems are fundamentally different. Here is a comparison:

OLTP Systems	Data Warehouse Systems
Hold current data	Hold historical data—new data must integrate with the old in the same data structures
Store detailed data as required by business transactions	Store detailed data along with lightly and highly summarized data—data is typically translated, reformatted, accumulated. and combined
Data is dynamic—updates to existing data are common	Data is static, except for periodic additions—once added data is almost never updated
Database queries are short-running and access relatively few rows of data	Database queries are long-running and access many rows of data
Stability and maintainability are important design concerns	Performance is often more important than maintainability
Database queries usually submitted by application programs	Database queries usually submitted by end-user query and analysis tools
High transaction volume	Medium to low transaction volume
Repetitive processing; predictable usage pattern	Ad hoc and unstructured processing; unpredictable usage pattern
Transaction driven; support day-to-day operations	Analysis driven; support strategic decision making
Process oriented	Subject oriented
Serve a large number of concurrent users	Serve a relatively low number of managerial users (decision makers)
Are designed with the emphasis on normalization	Are designed with far less focus on normalization because update anomalies don't exist (although normalization does offer some useful efficiencies)

Data Warehouse Architecture

Two schools of thought reign as to the best way to organize OLTP data into a data warehouse: the *summary table approach* and the *star schema approach*. The following subsections take a look at each approach, along with the benefits and drawbacks of each. As you might imagine, there has been much debate regarding which approach is the best overall. The good news for data modelers is that your skills are required no matter which approach is taken.

Summary Table Architecture

Inmon originally developed the summary table data warehouse architecture. This data warehouse approach involves storing data not only in detail form, but also in summary tables so that analysis processes do not have to summarize the same data continually. This is an obvious violation of the principles of normalization, but because the data is historical—and therefore is not expected to change after it is stored—the data anomalies (insert, update, and delete) that drive the need for normalization simply don't exist. Figure 11-1 shows the summary table data warehouse architecture.

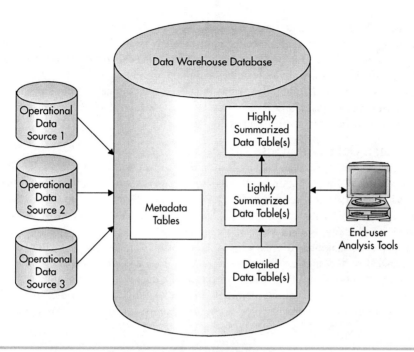

Figure 11-1   Summary table data warehouse architecture

Data from one or more operational data sources (databases or flat file systems) is periodically moved into the data warehouse database. A major key to success is determining the appropriate level of detail that must be carried in the database and anticipating the necessary levels of summarization. Using Acme Industries as an example, if the subject of the data warehouse is sales, it may be necessary to keep every single invoice, or it may be necessary to keep only those invoices that exceed a certain amount—or perhaps only those that contain certain products. If requirements are not understood, it is unlikely that the data warehouse project will be successful. Failure rates of data warehouse projects are higher than most other types of IT projects, and the most common cause of failure is poorly defined requirements.

In terms of summarization, we might summarize the transactions by month in one summary table and by product in another. At the next level of summarization, we might summarize the months by quarter in one table and the products by department in another. An *end user* (the person using the analysis tools to obtain results from the OLAP database) might look at sales by quarter and notice that one particular quarter doesn't look quite right. The user can expand the quarter of concern and examine the data for the months within it. This process is known as "drilling down" to more detailed levels. The user may then choose a particular month of interest and drill down to the detailed transactions for that month.

The metadata (data about data) shown in Figure 11-1 is very important and, unfortunately, often a missing link. Ideally, the metadata defines every data item in the data warehouse, along with sufficient information so that its source can be tracked all the way back to the original source data in the operational database. The biggest challenge with metadata is that, lacking standards, each vendor of data warehouse tools has stored metadata in its own way. When multiple analysis tools are in use, metadata must usually be loaded into each one of them using proprietary formats. For end-user analysis tools (also called OLAP tools or business intelligence tools), not only are tools embedded in major relational database products such as SQL Server and Oracle, but literally dozens of specialized commercial products are available, including Business Objects (now owned by SAP), Cognos (an IBM company), Actuate, Hyperion (now owned by Oracle), and many more.

Star Schema Data Warehouse Architecture

Kimball developed a specialized database structure known as the *star schema* for storing data warehouse data. His contribution to OLAP data storage is significant, including founding Red Brick Systems in 1986 and serving as its CEO until 1992. Red Brick, the first DBMS devoted exclusively to OLAP data storage, used the star schema. In addition, Red Brick offered SQL extensions specifically for data analysis, including moving averages, this year versus last year, market share, and ranking. Informix acquired Red Brick's technology, and later IBM acquired Informix, so IBM now markets the Red Brick technology as part of its data warehouse solution. Figure 11-2 shows the basic architecture of a data warehouse using the star schema.

The star schema uses a single detailed data table, called a *fact table,* surrounded by supporting reference data tables called *dimension tables,* forming a starlike pattern.

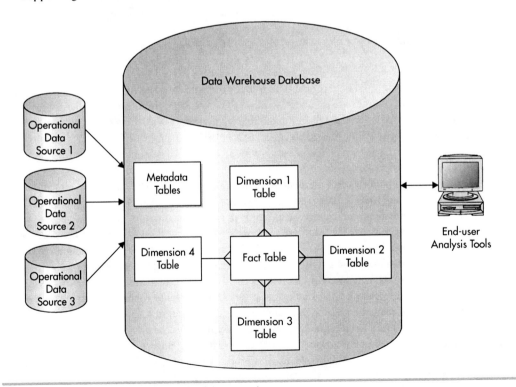

Figure 11-2 Star schema data warehouse architecture

Compared with the summary table data warehouse architecture, the fact table replaces the detailed data tables, and the dimension tables logically replace the summary tables. Aside from the primary key, each attribute in the fact table must be either a *fact* (a metric that can be summarized) or a foreign key to a dimension table. Keep in mind that facts must be additive, such as quantities, scores, time intervals, and currency amounts. A new star schema is constructed for each additional fact table. Dimension tables have a one-to-many relationship with the fact table, with the primary key of the dimension table appearing as a foreign key in the fact table. However, dimension tables are not necessarily normalized because they may have an entire hierarchy, such as layers of an organization or different subcomponents of time, compressed into a single table. The dimension tables may or may not contain summary information, such as totals, but they generally should not contain facts.

Ask the Expert

Q: I've heard that star schemas can be very difficult to use when analysis requires combining data from multiple fact tables. Is there a way around these issues?

A: Yes, indeed, but the solution is to design the dimensions correctly rather than employing workarounds after the data warehouse is implemented. If, for example, the time dimension in one schema uses calendar months, and another uses fiscal months, it may be impossible to combine them unless individual days are somehow available. The trick is to use what Kimball calls *conformed dimensions,* which are dimensions that have identical structure, attributes, domain values, definitions, and concepts. Following that tenet, every time dimension in the database would be identically defined, perhaps by calendar day, which can easily be rolled up to calendar or fiscal weeks, months, and quarters.

Using our prior Acme Industries sales example, the fact table would contain the invoices from the table, and typical dimension tables would be time (days, months, quarters, and perhaps years), products, and organizational units (departments, divisions, and so forth). In fact, time and organizational structure appear as dimensions in most star schemas. As you might guess, the keys to success in star schema OLAP databases are getting the fact table right and using only conformed dimensions. Here's a list of the considerations that influence the design of the fact table:

- The required time period (how often data will be added and how long history must remain in the OLAP database)

- Storing every transaction versus statistical sampling

- Columns in the source data table(s) that are not necessary for OLAP

- Columns that can be reduced in size

- The best uses of intelligent (natural) and surrogate (dumb) keys

- Partitioning of the fact table

Over time, some variations of the star schema emerged:

- **Snowflake schema** A variant in which dimensions are allowed to have dimensions of their own. The name comes from the entity-relationship diagram's resemblance to a snowflake. If you fully normalize the dimensions of a star schema, you end up with a snowflake schema. For example, the time dimension at the first level could track days, with a dimension table above it to track weeks, one above that to track months, one above that one to track quarters, and so forth. Similar arrangements could be used to track the hierarchy of an organization (departments, divisions, and so on).

- **Starflake schema** A hybrid arrangement containing a mixture of (denormalized) star and (normalized) snowflake dimensions.

Multidimensional Databases

Multidimensional databases evolved from star schemas. They are sometimes called multidimensional OLAP (MOLAP) databases. A number of specialized multidimensional database systems are on the market, including Oracle Express, Microsoft SQL Server Analysis Services, and Oracle Essbase. MOLAP databases are best visualized as cubes, where each dimension forms a side of the cube. To accommodate additional dimensions, the cube (or set of cubes) is simply repeated for each.

Figure 11-3 shows a four-column fact table for Acme Industries. Product Line, Sales Department, and Quarter are dimensions, and they would be foreign keys to a dimension table in a star schema. Quantity contains the number of units sold for each combination of Product Line, Sales Department, and Quarter.

Figure 11-4 shows the multidimensional equivalent of the table shown in Figure 11-3. Note that Sales Department, Product Line, and Quarter all become edges of the cube, with the single fact Quantity stored in each grid square. The dimensions displayed may be changed by simply rotating the cube.

When the dimensions contain data that mutates over time, such as a product being moved from one product family to another, we call this a *slowly changing dimension*. These present a special challenge when designing multidimensional schemas. Several solution methods, known as *types* of slowly changing dimensions, are listed in the following table:

Method Type	Description
1	Old data is overwritten with new data, so no tracking of history occurs.
2	A new row is created every time any data in the dimension changes, which provides unlimited history. A version number or effective dates are included in each row to record the sequence of the changes.
3	Multiple columns are provided for each attribute for which changes must be tracked, with each new value written into the next available column for the attribute. Naturally, the amount of history is limited to the number of columns provided.
4	Current data is kept in one table, and a history table is used to record some or all of the previous data values.

Product Line	Sales Department	Quarter	Quantity
Helmets	Corporate Sales	1	2250
Helmets	Corporate Sales	2	2107
Helmets	Corporate Sales	3	5203
Helmets	Corporate Sales	4	5806
Helmets	Internet Sales	1	1607
Helmets	Internet Sales	2	1812
Helmets	Internet Sales	3	4834
Helmets	Internet Sales	4	5150
Springs	Corporate Sales	1	16283
Springs	Corporate Sales	2	17422
Springs	Corporate Sales	3	21288
Springs	Corporate Sales	4	32768
Springs	Internet Sales	1	12
Springs	Internet Sales	2	24
Springs	Internet Sales	3	48
Springs	Internet Sales	4	48
Rockets	Corporate Sales	1	65
Rockets	Corporate Sales	2	38
Rockets	Corporate Sales	3	47
Rockets	Corporate Sales	4	52
Rockets	Internet Sales	1	2
Rockets	Internet Sales	2	1
Rockets	Internet Sales	3	6
Rockets	Internet Sales	4	9

Figure 11-3 Four-column fact table for Acme Industries

You can find more information on slowly changing dimensions in the many articles published on the Internet.

Data Marts

A *data mart* is a subset of a data warehouse that supports the requirements of a particular department or business *function*. In part, data marts evolved in response to some highly visible multimillion-dollar data warehouse project failures. When an organization has little experience building OLTP systems and databases, or when requirements are very sketchy, a scaled-down project such as a data mart is a far less risky approach. Here are a few characteristics of data marts:

- Focus on one department or business process

- Do not normally contain any operational data

- Contain much less information than a data warehouse

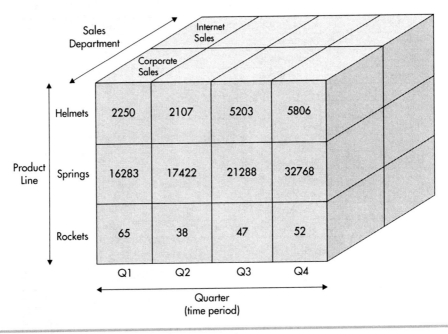

Figure 11-4 Three-dimension cube for Acme Industries

Here are some reasons for creating a data mart:

- Data may be tailored to a particular department or business function.

- Overall costs are lower than that of a full data warehouse.

- Project is lower risk than a full data warehouse project.

- A limited number of end-user analysis tools (usually just one) allow data to be tailored to the particular tool to be used.

- For departmental data marts, the database may be placed physically near the department, reducing network delays.

Three basic strategies can be used to build data marts:

- *Build the enterprise-wide data warehouse first, and use it to populate data marts.* The problem with this approach is that you will never get to build the data marts if the data warehouse project ends up being canceled or put on indefinite hold.

- *Build several data marts and build the data warehouse later, integrating the data marts into the enterprise-wide data warehouse at that time.* This is a lower-risk strategy, at least in terms of delivery, because it does not depend on completion of a major data warehouse project. However, it may cost more because of the rework required to integrate the data marts after the fact. Moreover, if several data marts are built containing similar data without a common data warehouse to integrate all the data, the same query may yield different results depending on the data mart used. Imagine, for example, the finance department quoting one revenue number and the sales department another, only to find they are both correctly quoting their data sources.

- *Build the data warehouse and data marts simultaneously.* This sounds great on paper, but when you consider that the already complex and large data warehouse project now has the data marts added to its scope, you begin to appreciate the enormity of the project. In fact, this strategy practically *guarantees* that the data warehouse project will be the never-ending project from hell.

Ask the Expert

Q: Are data marts built using summary tables or star schemas?

A: Data marts are built almost exclusively using star schemas. This is most likely because almost all the popular end-user analysis tools expect star schemas, including pivot tables supported by spreadsheet tools such as Microsoft Excel.

Modeling Analytical Data Structures

Now that I have introduced you to the architecture of OLAP data structures, we need to explore how they are designed and modeled. This section covers OLAP database requirements, data warehouse modeling, and data mart modeling.

OLAP Database Requirements

Considering the significantly different ways that OLTP and OLAP databases are used, it should come as no surprise that OLAP requirements are markedly different from OLTP requirements. Typical requirements for OLAP databases include the following:

- **Data redundancy**   Redundant data can be included without update anomaly issues. The most important trade-off is performance versus space requirements. For example, code descriptions can be stored with codes in the base table (a violation of third normal form) in order to avoid a join to look up the description when satisfying a query.

- **Flexibility**   The design should accommodate changes in source database structures whenever possible. This can be quite a challenge in environments where the OLTP applications and databases undergo major change, such as replacement of a major application with a new version or (worse yet) an entirely different product.

- **Data availability** Requirements should limit the data to be included. The alternative of including everything is expensive and usually wasteful in terms of both computer and human resources. Be sure you consider data beyond the organization's operational databases. For example, international standard codes and descriptions can be acquired from ANSI and ISO, and industry-specific data such as medical classification coding systems (designed for grouping data for analysis) can be acquired from third-party sources.

- **Performance** As stated, OLAP databases typically have fewer queries that run longer compared with OLTP databases. However, the performance of the processes that load data according to a prearranged schedule are equally important because in most OLAP systems there is a limited window in which they must complete so that current data is available for workers during prime work hours.

- **Data reuse** Most OLAP data is loaded from OLTP databases and is thus reused. Moreover, data warehouse data is typically reused in data marts. If the data warehouse is relational, then normalizing its data structures often makes reuse of the data in data marts easier to accomplish. Similarly, if the data warehouse is dimensional, then conformed dimensions promote reusability.

- **Business rules** Unlike OLTP databases, OLAP databases generally do not enforce business rules. However, business rules play an important role in determining the data structures required for analysis.

- **Stability** The OLAP database designer must anticipate the buildup of history as new data is added while data structures in the operational databases that feed the data warehouse continue to evolve. It's essential to design structures that can be expanded without having to change existing history.

- **Usability** The data structures, particularly the data marts, need to be easily understood by business users. Overgeneralization often leads to confusion.

Data Warehouse Modeling

Although there are vocal proponents of using star schemas and/or multidimensional databases for data warehouses, the majority of organizations use the relational approach. However, regardless of approach, data modeling is an essential task for successful projects, and the only question becomes which type of model to create.

Modeling for OLAP databases differs from OLTP databases in the following ways:

- The requirements are different. OLAP database requirements focus on supporting transactions, while OLTP requirements focus on supporting analysis queries.

- OLAP databases usually run on a different platform, which might include a completely different DBMS product that could even be from a different vendor than the DBMS used for the operational OLTP system.

- While some OLTP modeling rules and techniques are the same, others are quite different, including some that are new. Some experts believe that a modeler should forget everything they know about OLTP modeling when they work on an OLAP model. I believe that to be an overstatement and that many of the fundamentals carry over well from one to the other.

- When potentially conflicting data must be consolidated from multiple sources, a commonly used approach is to design a consolidation point know as an *operational data store* (ODS). A complex set of rules are used to resolve conflicting data and to form a data structure containing what can be thought of as "a single version of the truth." The ODS is then used as the single source for data to be loaded into the data warehouse. Thus the ODS is a hybrid that is not exactly an operational database (it is not updated by day-to-day business transactions) nor an analytical database (it holds current data and no history).

Data Warehouse Modeling Guidelines

Here are some guidelines for modeling data warehouse structures:

- Expect to design the data warehouse and the marts separately because they will most likely be deployed on different platforms.

- Flexibility is more important than normalization or limiting redundancy.

- Business users and project sponsors must help determine which operational data is to be included in the data warehouse. As previously stated, the alternative of including everything is clearly not the best use of available computing and human resources.

- Focus on the measures and the data needed to derive them. These measures will vary by industry. For example, typical measures for manufacturing organizations include attributes such as sales volume measured in both units sold and gross sales dollars; however, for health care organizations, typical measures include the number of members and the cost of providing their care. Don't overlook categories that the business users need for their analysis, such as product lines and sales regions for manufacturing organizations, or member ages, diagnosis categories, and procedure categories for health plans.

- Accounting for time is most essential. Nearly every data mart will have a time dimension; therefore, the data warehouse must be able to supply effective dates and times for the transaction results captured from the source operational databases. I present modeling of temporal data in Chapter 10.

- If you do not have existing OLAP models or patterns to use as a starting point, start with the most central and important operational model.

- Expect to grapple with the trade-off between maintaining data close to the form in which it is received from the source systems and consolidating and reformatting it so that data warehouse data is closer to the form required by the data marts. The benefit of consolidating and reformatting is that common transformations have to be done only once instead of in every mart that uses the data. On the other hand, consolidation causes serious and perhaps insurmountable problems when business users require a different summarization or grain. For example, if the data warehouse data is summarized by month and a business user requires weekly data (a smaller grain), there is no way to do so without going back to the source databases, which may no longer carry the required history. There will be pressure to summarize in order to reduce costs, but the best alternative is always the most flexible one.

- When data required in the data warehouse has multiple sources, consider the following when selecting the source to be used:

  - Which sources have the data in the required grain? Data at too large a grain is not useful, and data at a smaller grain than required may be expensive to store and consolidate.

  - Which sources are already being used for other data? Minimizing the total number of sources used for the data warehouse can reduce costs.

  - Will consolidation from multiple sources add to completeness? For example, one source application may include historical data, while the other may include attributes not available in the first one.

  - Which source has more compatible codes? For example, the newest standard for medical diagnosis and procedure codes is ICD-10, which replaced ICD-9. However, adoption of ICD-10 has been slow in the health care industry, largely because the code sets are substantially different. If one source offers ICD-9 and the other ICD-10, you have a choice to make based on which code set is the most compatible with the existing (or planned) data warehouse database.

  - Which source offers the simplest representation that still meets the requirements? In older mainframe systems, developers went to great lengths to compress data because storage was so expensive, yielding complex codes such as bit-mapping where individual bits in a single byte have different meaning. (A *bit* is a binary digit that can hold a value of either 0 or 1. A *byte* in most computer systems is composed of eight bits and is commonly used to represent a single character such as a letter or a numeric digit between 0 and 9. A *bit-mapped data element* uses the eight bits in a byte to represent up to eight different true/false or yes/no code values.) With the exception of DBMS products that support bit data types, we avoid such complex coding in modern systems because storage is now far less expensive and the cost of deciphering complex codes continues to rise.

Data Mart Modeling

The primary goal of modeling data marts is to provide the data required by the business users in a form that they can understand. Data marts are almost always implemented using star schema structures, and end-user analysis tools support them almost exclusively, ranging from spreadsheet pivot tables to complex structures that contain many interrelated star schemas.

Fact tables typically hold transactional data in either the original grain or summarized. Dimensions typically categorize the data in the fact table and assist in interpretation of the summarizations. If the mart contains a time dimension (which most do), and the data is at the original transaction grain, the time dimension provides additional information about the transaction date, such as the fiscal month and quarter into which it falls. On the other hand, if the fact table data is summarized, the time dimension provides information about the time grain such as the month, quarter, and year of the data in the fact table. The grain of the time dimension is an essential decision, including the trade-off between tracking by fiscal periods versus calendar periods should you choose a grain that is larger than one day.

Resolving Snowflake Structures

If you build data mart models directly from normalized structures in the data warehouse, you will likely end up with snowflake structures (dimension tables that have parents and thus form hierarchies). These are not only more difficult for business users to understand and use, many of the end-user analysis tools support only pure star schemas. Thus we need a method of forming star schemas from snowflakes.

Figure 11-5 shows a fact table that holds sales data summarized by month, along with a time dimension (Calendar Month) and a product dimension hierarchy of a Product table that has a Product Line parent table that categorizes the products into product lines. In a real data mart there would likely be additional dimensions, but I have left them out for simplicity.

The most straightforward alternative is to collapse the Product Line table into the Product table as shown in Figure 11-6. Notice that the Product Line ID attribute in the Product table, shown as a foreign key in Figure 11-5, remains in the Product table but is no longer a foreign key. The Product Line Name was moved from the Product Line table to the Product table. This creates a third normal form violation in the Product table because Product Line Name depends on Product Line ID, which is a nonkey attribute, but in data marts this does not matter because there are no update anomalies. Also, if the Product Line ID is not meaningful to business users,

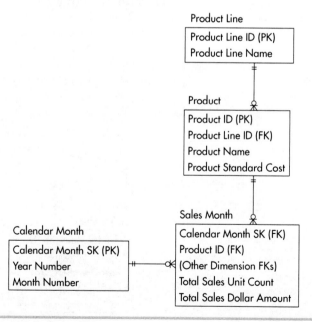

Figure 11-5 Sales snowflake structure

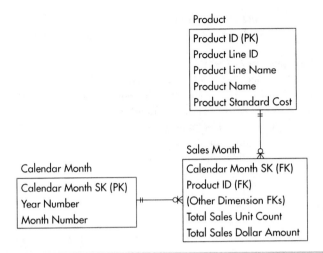

Figure 11-6 Sales structure with flattened product dimension

we can remove it entirely and carry only the Product Line Name to describe the product line to which the product is assigned.

Another alternative comes from examining the grain of the data and asking the business users about the required grain. If monthly sales totals by individual product are not required, we can remove the middle layer entirely, leaving Product Line as the dimension table as shown in Figure 11-7. Note that this changes the grain of the data in the Sales Month fact table because there will now be one row per product line instead of one row per product. The larger grain will be less expensive to implement because there will be fewer (probably considerably fewer) rows in the fact table, but if a requirement for totals by product should surface at a later time, this mart cannot do the job.

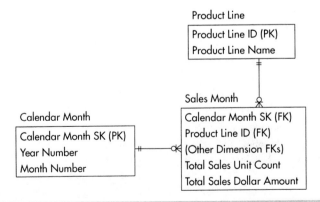

Figure 11-7 Sales structure with product line dimension (larger grain)

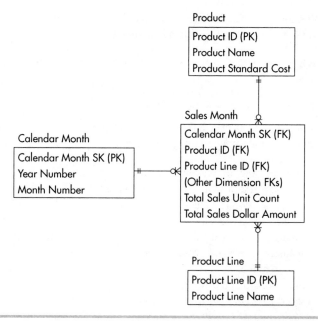

Figure 11-8 Sales structure with product line split to separate dimension

There are likely still other design alternatives, but the final one I present is to split Product and Product Line into separate dimensions as shown in Figure 11-8. The benefit of this approach is that there is no loss of grain. The fact that the product and product line assignments are now separate is a mixed blessing. The bad news is that it is no longer obvious to business users that there is a relationship between products and product lines. However, this arrangement allows us to assign different Product Line dimensions to different rows in the Sales Month table without having to change the Product dimension. For example, if the product line for a given product is changed as of the end of April in a given year, the Sales Month row for April can be assigned to one Product Line while the Sales Month row for May is assigned to the new one, and yet both months can be assigned to the same Product dimension table row. Other alternatives for handling changing dimension data are presented in the next topic.

Handling Slowly Changing Dimensions

Another common problem in designing dimensional data structures is how to handle dimensional data that changes over time. For example, looking back at Figure 11-5, what should we do if the product line to which a given product is assigned changes over time, especially if it changes during a month?

Recall Ralph Kimball's classification of dimension types based on the requirements for maintaining history as the data in the dimension changes over time:

- **Type 1** No history—when an attribute is changed, the new value is simply written over the existing value.

- **Type 2** Complete history—every previous value of the attribute must be retained.

- **Type 3** Limited history—only a finite number of previous values of the attribute must be retained, including the case where only the current and one previous value are required.

The Product/Product Line dimensions used in the structures in Figures 11-5 through 11-8 are all type 1 dimensions. If a product is assigned to a different product line during a given month, the ID of the dimension (Product ID in Figures 11-5 and 11-6, and Product Line ID in Figures 11-7 and 11-8) is overwritten in the Sales Month fact table for that month and sales for the entire month are shown as if they belong to the new value for the dimension. If this is acceptable to the business users and project sponsors, your work is done, but if not, you have a complicated problem to solve.

An obvious solution is to add effective dates to the Product Line dimension as shown in Figure 11-9. However, to do this we need to change the natural key to add the effective date, and thus a surrogate primary key with an arbitrary value becomes an attractive alternative. (In fact, most practitioners prefer the use of surrogate keys in all OLAP data structures.)

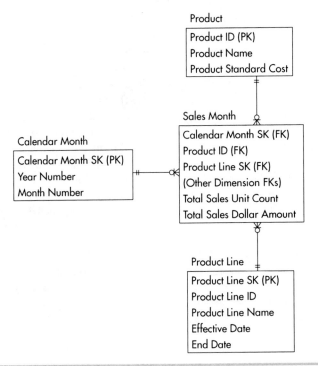

Figure 11-9 Sales structure with effective-dated Product Line dimension

There is a significant problem with this solution: the grain of the Sales Month table changes. Whenever multiple product lines are assigned to the same product during a month, there must be multiple rows in the fact table for that month. This is more complicated for business users, who must remember to summarize the fact tables in order to see complete months of data. Failure to do so yields incomplete results that could have serious consequences if the results are used in making business decisions. On the other hand, end-user analysis tools should be able to handle the consolidation of multiple fact table rows when needed.

As demonstrated by Figure 11-9, sometimes the obvious solution isn't necessarily the best solution. When we introduce changing dimension data within the grain of the fact table, what has really happened is that the relationship between the dimension and fact tables has become many-to-many. Therefore, another possible solution is an intersection table between Product Line and Sales Month. However, in order to maintain a pure star schema, we must treat the intersection table as the fact table, so again the grain of the fact table changes and the result is essentially the same as the structure shown in Figure 11-9. However, nothing stops us from creating two star schemas, one that summarizes by product and a different one that summarizes by product line.

If requirements permit, type 3 dimensions that keep a few of the previous values (foreign keys) for changing dimensions become an attractive alternative. Figure 11-10 shows a snowflake

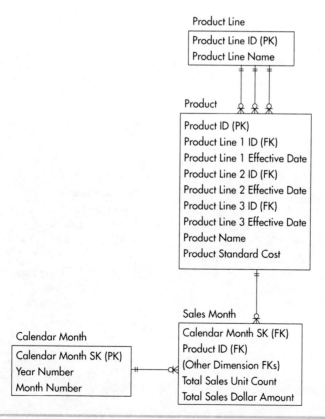

Figure 11-10   Sales structure with history in a dimension table

in which the Product dimension contains up to three values for the product line along with effective dates for each. Essentially we have put history into the Product Line dimension. And of course, we can make this a pure star schema by collapsing Product Line into Product as we did in Figure 11-6. Unfortunately, this gives us no ability to divide the sales totals in the fact table by product line when the product line for a product changes during the course of a month, although it does give us some sense of how much of a given month falls into one product line versus another thanks to the effective dates.

Another alternative is to put history into the fact table. Figure 11-11 shows this alternative with the Sales Month fact table carrying three foreign keys to the Product dimension, one for each of three possible product lines that can be in effect during the month represented in any given fact table row. Note that the Product ID is part of each of the three foreign keys, combined with one of the Product Line ID values. There are numerous alternatives as we vary the number of previous values that we carry in the fact table.

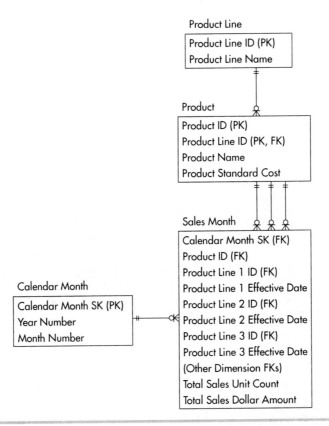

Figure 11-11 Sales structure with history in the fact table

Although I have presented quite a few design alternatives, there really are countless possibilities, as with just about any design effort. And there is far more to designing data marts than I am able to fit into this book. In fact, some modelers specialize in dimensional modeling. There are lots of books and training courses should you want to explore this topic further.

Loading Data into Analytical Databases

No discussion of OLAP databases would be complete without mention of the process of loading them with data. In most organizations, a process known as *extract, transform, and load* (ETL) is used. Figure 11-12 shows a flow diagram of a typical ETL design with two source operational databases feeding data to a common data warehouse.

The ETL processes have little direct bearing on the target OLAP database design, especially because ETL processes are usually built using commercial off-the-shelf software products. However, the data modeler may be required to design data structures to control and report on the ETL processes, and complex designs may include staging tables to hold data that is being prepared for loading into the data warehouse. Moreover, ETL processes can be used to refresh data mart data from the source data warehouse, including the summarizations required in the fact tables. For these reasons, knowing something about how ETL processes work is useful.

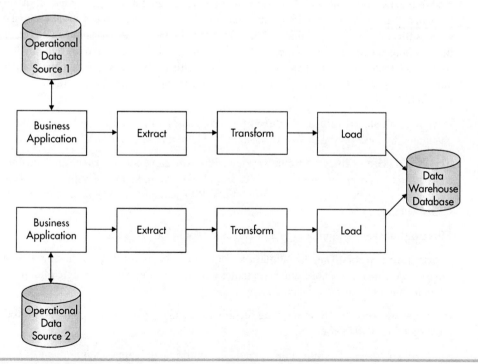

Figure 11-12   Loading a data warehouse using ETL processes

The Extract Process

The extract process is responsible for retrieving the data from the source. The source can be a database, an indexed file, or a flat file extracted from an internal system or acquired from an external source. The extract process may also transform the data into a format suitable to the transform process. In some implementations, the extract process also does rudimentary editing, rejecting records that have missing fields or fields with data that does not match a predefined pattern or format.

The Transform Process

The transform process takes in data from the extract process and derives the data to be loaded by applying a series of predefined rules and/or functions. Here are some of the types of transformations that can be applied:

- **Generating surrogate key values** This is especially important if the target data structure is being reloaded because it is usually essential to assign the same surrogate key values that were assigned when the data was initially loaded. In many environments, this requires support tables that can be used to match the data's natural key to the previously assigned surrogate key.

- **Encoding text data values** For example, a gender code of *M* or *F* is not useful in a fact table because text values cannot be summarized. The transform process should map a code such as this one to attributes that can be summarized—in this case to an attribute for male that contains a value of 0 if the person is not a male and a 1 if the person is a male, along with an attribute for female that likewise contains either a 0 or a 1. The number of males and females can then be determined simply by summing each attribute's column in the fact table.

- **Deriving calculated values** For example, gross sales dollars for a line item can be calculated by multiplying the price per item by the number of items ordered.

- **Translating code values** If source systems have different codes for the same attribute, translation to a common set of codes is essential. For example, inconsistent country codes used in source systems can be transformed into ISO standard country codes in the target OLAP database.

- **Filtering records** Eliminating records that do not meet a set of data selection rules.

- **Consolidating data** Data from multiple sources can be consolidated into single records. For example, hierarchies of dimension tables can be consolidated into single dimensions when the target database is a star schema.

- **Aggregating records** Summarizing records as required to achieve the grain required in the target OLAP database.

- **Splitting columns** Dividing column data into multiple columns, such as parsing addresses into separate attributes for elements such as the city and state.

- **Combining columns**   Combining source column data into a single OLTP attribute, such as combining the individual elements of a phone number (area code, prefix, suffix, extension) into a single column.

- **Pivoting tables**   Converting source table rows into column table columns or source table columns into target table rows. This is an easy way to transform repeating columns in the source table to normalized rows in the target table.

The Load Process

The load process receives data from the transform process and loads it into the target database. Usually this involves inserting new rows to augment those already in the target database. However, in some designs, existing rows can be updated, and in rare circumstances the target database might be cleared of all data and reloaded. The timing of the load process determines how current the data in the target database will be.

Try This 11-1 Design Star Schema Fact and Dimension Tables

In this Try This exercise, you will design a star schema fact table for the BOOK table in the Computer Books Company schema from Try This 6-2, along with its associated dimension tables. For easy reference, here are the normalized OLTP tables that need consideration:

```
BOOK: ISBN (PK), BOOK TITLE, SUBJECT CODE, PUBLISHER ID,
      EDITION CODE, EDITION COST, SELLING PRICE,
      QUANTITY ON HAND, QUANTITY ON ORDER,
      RECOMMENDED QUANTITY, PREVIOUS EDITION ISBN

SUBJECT: SUBJECT CODE (PK), DESCRIPTION

AUTHOR: AUTHOR ID (PK), AUTHOR NAME

BOOK_AUTHOR: AUTHOR ID (PK), ISBN (PK)

PUBLISHER: PUBLISHER ID (PK), PUBLISHER NAME, STREET ADDRESS,
      CITY, STATE, ZIP CODE, AMOUNT PAYABLE
```

Step by Step

1. Design the fact table:

   a. Identify the facts that will go in your fact table. For the BOOK table, the only attributes that can be facts are EDITION COST, SELLING PRICE, QUANTITY ON HAND, QUANTITY ON ORDER, and RECOMMENDED QUANTITY.

(continued)

b. Among the remaining attributes in the BOOK table, identify those that are foreign keys to dimension tables. These are SUBJECT CODE and PUBLISHER ID.

c. The remaining attributes are BOOK TITLE and PREVIOUS EDITION ISBN. What can be done with these? One choice is simply to eliminate them for your star schema. But another is to make a dimension out of them, called something like BOOK TITLE. The fact table can then be joined with the dimension using ISBN when you want to include the title or previous edition ISBN in our query results.

d. List the contents of the fact table.

2. Design the dimension tables:

a. From step 1.c, design a dimension table to hold BOOK TITLE and PREVIOUS EDITION ISBN.

b. SUBJECT becomes a dimension just as it is.

c. AUTHOR and BOOK_AUTHOR pose a small challenge because they form a hierarchy and there is a many-to-many relationship between AUTHOR and BOOK. Star schemas don't support many-to-many relationships or fact tables that have children, so we have a dilemma. One solution is to combine AUTHOR and BOOK_AUTHOR and make the combined BOOK_AUTHOR a dimension. However, this changes the grain of the fact table because one row would be required in the fact table for each author, and therefore we must change the fact table's primary key to a surrogate key. An alternative solution is to put a repeating group of some finite number of authors in the dimension table, and another alternative is to place multiple foreign keys for the AUTHOR dimension in the fact table. If you prefer this solution, allow for up to four authors per book.

d. PUBLISHER looks straightforward enough, but there is a minor issue with AMOUNT PAYABLE. It's a fact, and facts don't belong in dimension tables. So you should eliminate it from this star schema. It may be useful when the fact table is about publisher purchases or something like that, but it has no bearing on our book inventory.

e. List the contents of each dimension table.

Try This Summary

In this Try This exercise, you designed a fact table and several dimension tables. My solution is in Appendix B.

Chapter 11 Self Test

Choose the correct responses to each of the multiple-choice and fill-in-the-blank questions.
Note that there may be more than one correct response to each question.

1. OLTP databases are designed to handle _____ transaction volumes.

2. OLAP queries typically access _____ amounts of data.

3. Compared with OLTP systems, data warehouse systems tend to
have _____-running queries.

4. Data warehousing was pioneered by _____.

5. The process of moving from more summarized data to more detailed data is
known as _____.

6. The snowflake schema allows dimensions to have _____.

7. The starflake schema is a hybrid containing both _____ and _____
dimensions.

8. Redundant data _____ be included in OLAP data structures because update
anomalies _____.

9. A data warehouse is

   A Subject oriented

   B Integrated from multiple data sources

   C Time variant

   D Updated in real time

   E Organized around one department or business function

10. Challenges with the data warehouse approach include

   A Updating operational data from the data warehouse

   B Underestimation of required resources

   C Diminishing user demands

   D Large, complex projects

   E High resource demands

11. The relationship between OLAP databases and business rules is

   A OLAP databases enforce business rules.

   B OLAP databases do not enforce business rules.

    C Business rules influence the design of the data structures required for analysis.

    D Business rules have little influence on the design of the data structures.

    E They have nothing to do with each other.

12. The summary table architecture

    A Was originally developed by Bill Inmon

    B Includes a fact table

    C Includes dimension tables

    D Includes lightly and highly summarized tables

    E Should include metadata

13. The star schema

    A Was developed by Ralph Kimball

    B Includes a dimension table and one or more fact tables

    C Always has fully normalized dimension tables

    D Was a key feature of the Red Brick DBMS

    E Involves multiple levels of dimension tables

14. Factors to consider in designing the fact table include

    A Adding columns to the fact table

    B Reducing column sizes between the source and fact tables

    C Partitioning the fact table

    D How often it must be updated

    E How long history must remain in it

15. Multidimensional databases

    A Use a fully normalized fact table

    B Are best visualized as cubes

    C Have fully normalized dimension tables

    D Are sometimes called MOLAP databases

    E Accommodate dimensions beyond the third by repeating cubes for each additional dimension

16. A data mart

   A Is a subset of a data warehouse

   B Is a shop that sells data to individuals and businesses

   C Supports the requirements of a particular department or business function

   D Can be a good starting point for organizations with no data warehouse experience

   E Can be a good starting point when requirements are sketchy

17. Reasons to create a data mart include

   A It is more comprehensive than a data warehouse.

   B It is a potentially lower-risk project.

   C Data may be tailored to a particular department or business function.

   D It contains more data than a data warehouse.

   E The project has a lower overall cost than a data warehouse project.

18. Building a data warehouse first, followed by data marts

   A Will delay data mart deployment if the data warehouse project drags on

   B Has lower risk than trying to build them all together

   C Has the lowest risk of the three possible strategies

   D Has the highest risk of the three possible strategies

   E May require a great deal of rework

19. Building one or more data marts first, followed by the data warehouse

   A May delay data warehouse delivery if the data mart projects drag on

   B Has the potential to deliver some OLAP functions more quickly

   C Has the lowest risk of the three possible strategies

   D Has the highest risk of the three possible strategies

   E May require a great deal of rework

20. Building the data warehouse and data marts simultaneously

   A Creates the largest single project of all the possible strategies

   B Has the potential to take the longest to deliver any OLAP functions

   C Has the lowest risk of the three possible strategies

   D Has the highest risk of the three possible strategies

   E May require a great deal of rework

21. Modeling OLAP databases differs from OLTP databases in which of the following ways?

    A Some modeling rules and techniques are different.

    B The modeling rules and techniques are completely different.

    C There is no significant difference between the two.

    D The requirements are different.

    E The databases will run on different platforms.

22. Properties of data warehouse systems include

    A Holding historical rather than current information

    B Long-running queries that process many rows of data

    C Support for day-to-day operations

    D Process orientation

    E Medium to low transaction volume

Chapter 12

Enterprise Data Modeling

Key Skills & Concepts

- Enterprise Data Management

- The Enterprise Data Model

U p to this point we have explored data models that support individual projects and databases. This chapter explores higher-level models that describe and document the data for an entire organization.

Enterprise Data Management

Data management is a broad discipline that encompasses all aspects of the management of data, including data modeling, database management, and data quality. Among organizations that excel at managing data across their entire enterprise, one of the common success factors is a centralized organization dedicated to data management. These organizations recognize data as an essential shared resource. In fact, some experts argue that data is the second most important resource in an organization, with only employees and the knowledge they hold being more important.

Effective data management also requires a comprehensive and current metadata repository, but few organizations have one. None of the leading data modeling tools contains a metadata repository, although all of them have provisions for integrating with one. The most common reason that organizations have not implemented such a tool is cost. The tools are expensive, and the organization must dedicate one or more employees (at additional cost) to maintaining the repository and handling discrepancies and gaps as they are uncovered. In this age of leaner organizations that are routinely expected to do more with less, it is unlikely that this situation will improve in the near term. However, much can be done through the creative use of reports that are generated using data modeling tools in concert with simple comparison tools to uncover discrepancies between data models that require further analysis.

The Case for Data Management

The following common problems can be found in organizations that have not adopted an enterprise-wide approach to data management:

- Databases are designed for individual applications and thus end up as silos (or worse yet, so-called "data jails") that cannot be easily shared for other purposes. Such databases are often seen as "owned" by the application they serve.

- Redundant and often inconsistent data abounds. Variations in data models and database designs can make these redundancies difficult to identify.

- Operating costs are typically higher because of the one-to-one correspondence of databases and applications. Managing fewer databases is simply less expensive.

- It is difficult to evaluate the effect of changes or the opportunities for consolidation as new applications, including packaged software applications, are proposed and implemented.

- Standard codes that can be shared across applications are very difficult to identify and implement.

- Data modelers and database designers may not represent common data in the same way.

- Application-focused databases designed by software vendors and application development teams (without guidance from a data modeler) often lack the balance between generalization and specialization required for integration with other applications.

Ask the Expert

Q: If centralized data management is such a superior approach, why haven't most organizations implemented one comprehensive shared database or a set of integrated subject area databases for use by all of their OLTP systems?

A: While there are probably as many reasons as there are organizations, some of the most common factors that work against single, enterprise-wide databases are

- The use of packaged software products instead of in-house-developed applications. Most packaged software applications come with their own database design, and while many of them allow for extensions, you cannot get too far away from the basic structures that come with the product.

- Unless the organization is very young, there will be existing applications, and most organizations cannot afford to replace or rewrite all of them to accommodate a new enterprise-wide database.

Alternatives to Centralized Data Management

If centralized data management cannot be implemented within the enterprise in the near term, there are a number of steps the organization can take to move in the right direction:

- Data architects within the organization can work together and focus on common definitions, standards, and an architectural plan for the organization.

- *Enterprise Application Integration* (EAI), a method of integrating application systems using asynchronous messaging technology that automatically sends changes from source applications to one or more target applications, can be used to loosely integrate common data across disparate applications. For example, a newly deployed Customer Relationship

Management (CRM) system can use messaging technology to send customer address changes to a legacy shipping system. If the CRM application does not provide an outbound messaging interface, then change-capture software tools or database triggers in the database layer can be used to detect the changes as they occur.

- Incremental improvements can be achieved through projects focused on particular areas of interest. Many organizations that have had poor success with large "big bang" projects have turned to smaller, more focused projects that are less risky and easier to manage.

The Enterprise Data Model

Within the data management function, the primary tool used to document and understand the enterprise's data is the enterprise data model.

What Is an Enterprise Data Model?

An *enterprise data model* is a comprehensive yet integrated view of an organization's data. An enterprise data model has the following characteristics:

- It integrates with the overall enterprise model, providing the data-related context for the overall model.

- It contains not only data produced by the organization, but also data consumed by it.

- It incorporates the appropriate perspective of the industry in which the organization operates.

- It provides a single definition of the data without the bias of any particular application or system.

- It is independent of physical implementation details such as how the data is physically stored, accessed, or processed.

- It represents the things that are most important to the organization along with the applicable business rules.

- It is often divided into subject areas.

- It is less detailed compared with application data models; the level of detail depends on the intended use of the model.

- It has a higher level of generalization compared with application project data models, containing no more than a few hundred entities.

- It is usually built in layers as described later in this chapter.

- It evolves progressively over time (application project models are usually time-boxed to fit the project schedule).

- It often requires a team effort, while most application project models are created by a single modeler.

Common uses of enterprise data models include the following:

- An organization-wide overview of the data, including context (data usage vis-à-vis the business rules)

- A collection mechanism for common definitions and other metadata

- A blueprint for enterprise-wide planning and for development of application databases, including data warehouses and data marts

- A context for evaluating how well proposed new application databases, particularly those for packaged software, will fit

- A starting point for new application and analytical database designs, including definitions, naming standards, code sets, and abbreviations

- A standard against which proposed database changes are measured

- A context for integration showing potential data integration points

- A standard of measure for data quality assessments

- Identification of shared data that crosses organizational boundaries and thus may be subject to data ownership issues

- Documentation of a desired future state with which the current state of applications and databases can be compared

The main factors that have worked against implementation of enterprise data models include the following:

- The cost associated with building and maintaining an enterprise data model, particularly if management is not convinced of the expected benefits

- Lack of understanding as to the usefulness of the enterprise data model

The Anatomy of an Enterprise Data Model

Enterprise data models are seldom developed without other models. For example, John Zachman developed his Framework for Information Systems Architecture in the 1980s and has updated it several times since. In practice it is used as a taxonomy for organizing an enterprise architecture. It is essentially a matrix of rows and columns with each cell representing a particular model to be included in the architecture. The rows of the framework represent the functional purpose of the models (contextual, conceptual, logical, physical, and detailed). The columns represent the mission (why), processes (how), data (what), people (who), location (where), and timing (when) of the models. Data models fit in the data (what) column, with enterprise models appearing in the second row (conceptual).

While the Zachman Framework establishes the role that enterprise data models play in the overall enterprise architecture, it only describes the contents and scope of the model in summary form. To look deeper into the organization of an enterprise data model, we need to

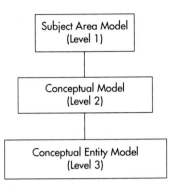

Figure 12-1 Enterprise data model levels

use a more detailed framework. You will find any number of frameworks in published books and articles, many of which combine process models and data models. Among the purely data-centric frameworks, I like the one presented by Kathy Long in an article published in *The Data Administration Newsletter (TDAN)*, ("The Enterprise Data Model: A Key Ingredient for Successful Data Warehousing", Kathy Long, *The Data Administration Newsletter*, June 1, 1998, www.tdan.com/view-articles/4252). Figure 12-1 shows the framework in the form of three levels.

Level 1 contains subject area models. A *subject area* is a high-level classification of data representing a group of concepts pertaining to a major topic of interest to an organization. Without such a subdivision, we would be faced with including all the data that is important to an organization in a single diagram, which would be nothing short of overwhelming. The subject area model contains only subject area names in rectangles with lines showing points where data overlaps multiple subject areas. Figure 12-2 shows a subset of a subject area model.

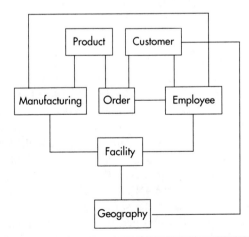

Figure 12-2 Partial subject area model for a manufacturing organization

Notice that cardinality is not shown in a subject area model. The rectangles represent subject areas rather than entities, and the lines show overlap points rather than relationships, so cardinality doesn't make sense in this model. Expect a typical organization to have 10 to 12 subject areas. If you have significantly fewer, your subject areas are too generalized, and if you have significantly more, your subject areas are too specialized.

The second level of the enterprise data model contains the enterprise conceptual model. Although the name suggests this is a conceptual data model like the ones introduced in Chapter 5, the enterprise conceptual model is at a somewhat higher level of abstraction. Instead of entities, the rectangles in enterprise conceptual models represent data concepts. A *data concept* describes information produced or consumed by an organization. While some data concepts may be at the same level as an entity, others will be more on the order of a group of entities. For example, the Product subject area shown in Figure 12-2 might have a data concept called Price that represents all the entities required to establish and track a product price. (You may be tempted to use a name such as Pricing here, but pricing is the name of a process and we must have entity names in this diagram, which will always be nouns.) In other words, concepts within an enterprise conceptual model are at varying levels of granularity.

Figure 12-3 shows an enterprise conceptual model for the Geography subject area that was included in the subject area model shown in Figure 12-2. Note that the lines represent relationships, but cardinality is not shown. It is important to represent the concepts of concern to the business users. You can think of a concept as the things business users talk about. In this example, I included both Region and County as subdivisions of a Country even though I know I will end up representing counties as a subtype of region in the entity model (the next layer down). If users in one country discuss regions and in another they discuss counties, you need to represent both of them in order to define concepts that are important to each group of users. I also know that I will likely need a recursive relationship to link regions to containing regions for countries such as Japan that have hierarchies of regions, but recursive relationships don't add any real value in a level 2 model, so I chose not to show it. A typical subject area will have 10 to 12 concepts in the enterprise conceptual model.

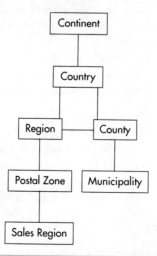

Figure 12-3   Enterprise conceptual model for the Geography subject area

The third level contains the enterprise conceptual entity model. This model is very much like conceptual data models that I introduced in Chapter 5. Like conceptual data models, this model shows the most important entities and they are not necessarily normalized, which means that many-to-many relationships are perfectly acceptable. Unlike the level 1 and 2 models, it shows cardinality (both minimum and maximum) for each relationship. Enterprise conceptual models usually show primary keys and the most important attributes, although some practitioners take a more minimalistic approach. At this level, getting the primary keys and relationships right is the most important key to success down the road.

Building an Enterprise Data Model

There has been considerable debate regarding the best approach for building an enterprise data model. Proponents of the top-down approach argue that processes and the plan for executing them are best controlled and managed by starting with overall objectives and breaking them down into progressively smaller component tasks. They conclude that the process of creating the model is therefore best managed in a top-down manner. On the other hand, proponents of the bottom-up approach argue that the details of the existing data elements must be examined in order to determine how best to organize the data into subject areas and eventually into the overall model.

In my experience, both approaches are necessary. The key is to achieve the proper balance. If too much emphasis is placed on top-down, the process of building the model becomes the goal rather than the means. However, if too much emphasis is placed on bottom-up, you can end up with a model that is heavily biased toward existing implementations instead of capturing definition and context without physical characteristics.

The Planning Window

If the enterprise model is to reflect a desired future state it is essential to establish the window of time to be covered. A good rule of thumb is 3 to 5 years. If you choose something shorter, you are likely to end up with a tactically positioned enterprise data model rather than a strategic planning blueprint. Conversely, if you choose something longer, you will probably find that it is difficult to visualize and predict where things will be at a point that is far into the future.

It's best if the executive sponsor for the enterprise model project establishes the planning window. However, as with all requirements, input from the project team can help guide the decision maker regarding what is reasonable and the risks of overreaching.

Common Dilemmas

Here are some common dilemmas related to enterprise data modeling projects:

Should new applications be designed to use existing data structures (sharing existing databases as much as practical), or should new databases that comply with the enterprise data model be built for the new applications? In an ideal world, everything new would be built to the most current standard (the enterprise data model), but the cost of storing all the common data redundantly in a newly designed structure and of keeping the old and new structures synchronized may be prohibitive.

Should software proposed for purchase be required to conform to the enterprise model? If the software has a sound model, perhaps the enterprise model should be modified to incorporate it. Alternatively, if the software has an inferior model (or no apparent model), you can show its proponents the downside of their proposal by comparing or mapping the application model to your enterprise model. Another possibility is an application model that is so highly generalized that it could hold just about anything and thus is difficult to compare with an industry-specific enterprise model.

Should the new model be divided by subject area, by functional area, or by application? Most people immediately rule out division by application because the goal is to establish a model that transcends all the existing applications. While most data modelers prefer a subject area orientation, the business users who will be providing you with their valuable input think best within the confines of their functional areas. If you do organize the model by subject area, I recommend that you make an attempt to present workshop audiences with a merged view that covers all the main entities within their functional area (if you show them any model at all). For example, if you have separate subject areas for Product and Customer and you present the Customer subject area to a group of sales representatives, you can expect one of them to ask you where the product data is. They sell products to customers, so both entities are essential to their functional area regardless of how you plan to subdivide the model.

What will be the scope of the modeling project? While the ultimate goal is to build a comprehensive enterprise model, tackling all of it at once is seldom successful due to the overwhelming scope. It's far better to satisfy the goal using smaller, more manageable projects that can be completed with shorter, more focused efforts. The team must decide which subject areas to include/exclude with each pass and what level of detail is to be achieved.

Inputs to the Enterprise Model

A comprehensive modeling effort will include the following inputs:

- The business strategy and objectives of the organization

- Measures (key performance indicators, or KPIs) needed to support current and future business objectives

- The IT strategic plan (assuming one exists)

- Existing data models

- Existing process documentation

- Subject matter experts, including outside industry experts, if available

- Business knowledge (modelers should be familiar with the area being modeled)

- Internal and external standards

- An open mind

Try This 12-1 Enterprise Conceptual Model Development

In this Try This exercise, you will expand one of the subject areas in a subject area model to create an enterprise conceptual model for that subject area. You won't have business users to offer their input on which concepts are the most important, so you will have to make assumptions based on your own knowledge and experience, and perhaps some searches on the Internet. Understand that for a real project, your input would come almost exclusively from business users, augmented with patterns used in other models (particularly those used within the organization) and just a dash of your own knowledge and experience.

Step by Step

1. Study the subject area model shown in Figure 12-2 to establish context.

2. List the Product subject area concepts that should be included in the enterprise conceptual model. Keep in mind that concepts can be as granular as individual entities, but more often they represent major groupings of entities. Also recall that Price (representing all the entities required to establish and maintain product prices) was mentioned in the chapter as an example. You should have no more than 10 to 12 concepts in the model.

3. Draw each concept as a rectangle.

4. Draw lines to show relationships between the concepts, but do not show cardinality (either minimum or maximum) on any of the relationships.

Try This Summary

In this Try This exercise, you examined an existing subject area model and created an enterprise conceptual model for one of the subject areas. There are endless possibilities for a solution to this exercise, depending on the modeler's experience and perspective as well as the assumptions made regarding which concepts are most important to the business. My solution appears in Appendix B.

Chapter 12 Self Test

1. Organizations that have not adopted enterprise-wide data management experience which of the following issues?

    A Opportunities to share standard codes across applications are more difficult to identify.

    B It is difficult to evaluate the effects of proposed changes such as new application databases.

    C Operating costs are lower because the organization saves money by not employing data modelers and data quality analysts.

    D Common data may not be represented in the same way.

    E Redundant and inconsistent data abounds.

2. Characteristics of an enterprise data model include which of the following?

    A It is often divided into subject areas.

    B It is independent of physical implementation details.

    C It integrates with an overall enterprise model.

    D It includes only entities and relationships.

    E It is usually built in layers.

3. Common uses of enterprise data models include which of the following?

    A Standard of measure for data quality assessments

    B Documentation of where the organization should be 15 or 20 years into the future

    C Blueprint for enterprise-wide planning

    D Starting point for new application and analytical database designs

    E Collection mechanism for common definitions and other metadata

4. Inputs to the enterprise data model should include which of the following?

    A Physical storage characteristics for existing databases

    B Internal and external standards

    C Existing process documentation

    D The IT strategic plan (if one exists)

    E Business knowledge

5. Data management encompasses all aspects of the management of data, including _____, _____, and _____.

6. Effective data management requires a comprehensive and current metadata _____.

7. Two common factors that work against implementation of a single, enterprise-wide database are _____ and _____.

8. _____ is a method of integrating application systems using asynchronous message technology.

9. An enterprise data model is a _____.

10. Two factors that work against implementation of enterprise models are _____ and _____.

11. A level 1 enterprise data model contains the _____ model.

12. The second level of an enterprise data model contains the _____ model.

13. The third level of an enterprise data model contains the _____ model.

14. A good rule of thumb for a planning window is _____ years.

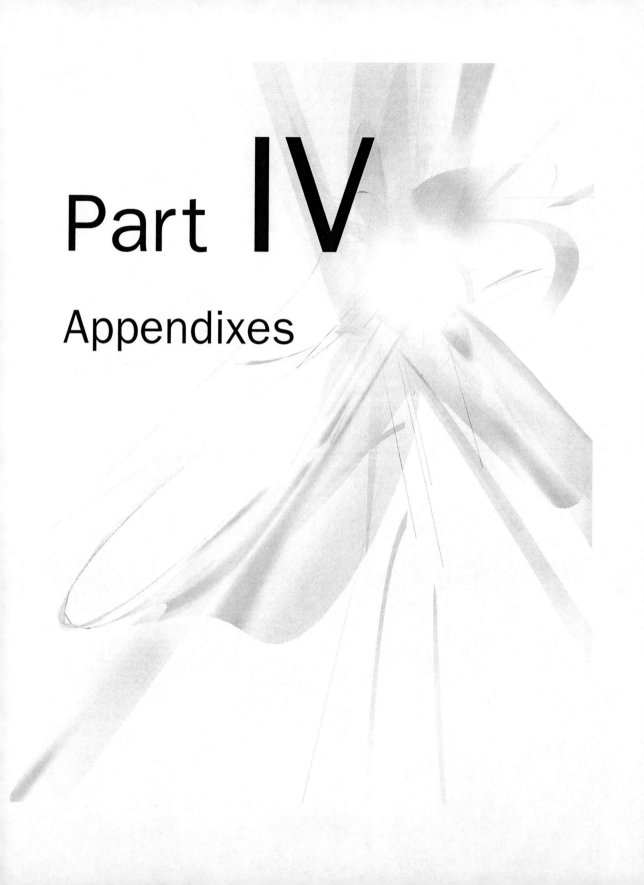

Part IV

Appendixes

Appendix A

Answers to Self Tests

Chapter 1: Introduction to Data Modeling

1. A _____ describes how the data in an information system is represented and accessed.

   data model

2. The physical layer of the ANSI/SPARC model contains _____.

   data files

3. An entity that represents a specialization of another entity is called a _____.

   subtype

4. A _____ model is a data model tailored to a particular type of database management system such as relational, object-relational, object-oriented, hierarchical, or network.

   logical

5. A _____ model is a high-level model that captures data and relationship concepts in a technology-independent manner.

   conceptual

6. A _____ model is a data model that is tailored to the features and constraints of a particular database management system (DBMS).

   physical

7. Data

   A. Exists before automated systems are developed

   B. Is destroyed when application systems are retired

   C. Still exists after automated systems are retired

   D. Is usually converted from old systems to the new ones that replace them

   A, C, and **D** are correct responses.

8. The logical layer of the ANSI/SPARC model

   A. Is also known as the internal layer

   B. Is sometimes called the schema

   C. Contains the data files that implement the database

   D. Always represents the data as 2-D tables

   A and **B** are correct responses.

9. The external layer of the ANSI/SPARC model

    A. Is sometimes called the schema

    B. Is derived directly from the physical layer

    C. Presents data to the database users

    D. Contains user views

   C and **D** are correct responses.

10. Data modeling is important because it

    A. Documents required application processes

    B. Provides a means of visualization of the data

    C. Provides standards for future development

    D. Provides a foundation for future expansion

   B and **D** are correct responses.

11. Measures of good data models include

    A. Enforcement of business rules

    B. Providing a balanced perspective

    C. Meeting processing requirements

    D. Provisions for data integration

   A, **B**, and **D** are correct responses.

12. Participants in data modeling efforts include

    A. Application programmers

    B. Quality assurance (QA) testers

    C. Process modelers

    D. Database administrators

   C and **D** are correct responses.

Chapter 2: Relational Database Components

1. Examples of an entity are

    A. A customer

    B. A customer order

C. An employee's paycheck

D. A customer's name

A, B, and **C** are correct responses.

2. Examples of an attribute are

A. An employee

B. An employee's name

C. An employee's paycheck

D. An alphabetical listing of employees

B is the correct response.

3. On a relationship line, the cardinality of "zero, one, or more" is denoted with which of the following:

A. A perpendicular tick mark near the end of the line and a crow's foot at the line end

B. A circle near the end of the line and a crow's foot at the end of the line

C. Two perpendicular tick marks near the end of the line

D. A circle and a perpendicular tick mark near the end of the line

B is the correct response.

4. Valid types of relationships in a relational database are

A. One-to-many

B. None-to-many

C. Many-to-many

D. One-to-one

A, C, and **D** are correct responses.

5. If a product can be manufactured in many plants, and a plant can manufacture many products, this is an example of which type of relationship?

A. One-to-one

B. One-to-many

C. Many-to-many

D. Recursive

C is the correct response.

6. Which of the following are examples of recursive relationships?

    A. An organizational unit made up of departments

    B. An employee who manages other employees

    C. An employee who manages a department

    D. An employee who has many dependents

  B is the correct response.

7. Examples of a business rule are

    A. A referential constraint must refer to the primary key of the parent table

    B. An employee must be at least 18 years old

    C. A database query eliminates columns an employee should not see

    D. Employees below pay grade 6 are not permitted to modify orders

  B and **D** are correct responses.

8. A relational table

    A. Is composed of rows and columns

    B. Must be assigned a data type

    C. Must be assigned a unique name

    D. Is the primary unit of storage in the relational model

  A, **C**, and **D** are correct responses.

9. A column in a relational table

    A. Must be assigned a data type

    B. Must be assigned a unique name within the table

    C. Is derived from an entity in the conceptual design

    D. Is the smallest named unit of storage in a relational database

  A and **B** are correct responses.

10. A data type

    A. Assists the DBMS in storing data efficiently

    B. Provides a set of behaviors for a column that assists the database user

    C. May be selected based on business rules for an attribute

    D. Restricts characters allowed in a database column

  A, **B**, **C**, and **D** are correct responses.

11. A primary key constraint

   A. Must reference one or more columns in a single table

   B. Must be defined for every database table

   C. Is usually implemented by using an index

   D. Guarantees that no two rows in a table have duplicate primary key values

   A, C, and **D** are correct responses.

12. A referential constraint

   A. Must have primary key and foreign key columns that have identical names

   B. Ensures that a primary key does not have duplicate values in a table

   C. Defines a many-to-many relationship between two tables

   D. Ensures that a foreign key value always refers to an existing primary key value in the parent table

   D is the correct response.

13. A logical data model

   A. May contain many-to-many relationships

   B. Is used as the basis for the physical data model

   C. Contains implementation details such as tablespace names

   D. Usually contains view definitions

   B is the correct response.

14. Major types of integrity constraints are

   A. CHECK constraints

   B. One-to-one relationships

   C. NOT NULL constraints

   D. Constraints enforced with triggers

   A, C, and **D** are correct responses.

15. _____ tables are used to resolve many-to-many relationships.

   Intersection

16. An entity in the conceptual model becomes a(n) _____ in the logical model.

   entity

17. An attribute in the logical model becomes a(n) _____ in the physical model.

   table column

18. Items in the external level of the ANSI/SPARC model become _____ in the physical model.

views

19. A relationship in the logical design becomes a(n) _____ in the physical design.

referential constraint

20. A unique identifier becomes a(n) _____ in the logical model.

primary key

Chapter 3: Data and Process Modeling

1. Why is it important for a database designer to understand process modeling?

   A. Process design is a primary responsibility of the DBA.

   B. The process model must be completed before the data model.

   C. The data model must be completed before the process model.

   D. The database designer must work closely with the process designer.

   E. The database design must support the intended process model.

  D and **E** are correct answers.

2. The IDEF1X ERD format

   A. Was first released in 1983

   B. Follows a standard developed by the National Institute of Standards and Technology

   C. Has many variants

   D. Has been adopted as a standard by many U.S. government agencies

   E. Covers both data and process models

  B and **D** are correct answers.

3. The IDEF1X ERD format shows

   A. Identifying relationships with a solid line

   B. Minimal cardinality using a combination of small circles and vertical lines shown on the relationship line

   C. Maximum cardinality using a combination of small vertical lines and crow's feet drawn on the relationship line

   D. Dependent entities with squared corners on the rectangle

   E. Independent entities with rounded corners on the rectangle

  A is the correct answer.

4. A subtype

    A. Is a subset of the supertype

    B. Has a one-to-many relationship with the supertype

    C. Has a conditional one-to-one relationship with the supertype

    D. Shows various states of the supertype

    E. Is a superset of the supertype

    A and **C** are correct answers.

5. Examples of possible subtypes for an Order entity supertype include

    A. Order line items

    B. Shipped order, unshipped order, invoiced order

    C. Office supplies order, professional services order

    D. Approved order, pending order, canceled order

    E. Auto parts order, aircraft parts order, truck parts order

    C and **E** are correct answers.

6. In IE notation, subtypes

    A. May be shown with a type discriminator attribute name

    B. May be connected to the supertype via a symbol composed of a circle with a line under it

    C. Have the primary key of the subtype shown as a foreign key in the supertype

    D. Usually have the same primary key as the supertype

    E. May be shown using a crow's foot

    A, **B**, and **D** are correct answers.

7. The strengths of flowcharts are

    A. They are natural and easy to use for procedural language programmers

    B. They are useful for spotting reusable components

    C. They are specific to application programming only

    D. They are equally useful for nonprocedural and object-oriented languages

    E. They can be easily modified as requirements change

    A, **B**, and **E** are correct answers.

8. The basic components of a function hierarchy diagram are

    A. Ellipses to show attributes

    B. Rectangles to show process functions

    C. Lines connecting the processes in order of execution

    D. A hierarchy to show which functions are subordinate to others

    E. Diamonds to show decision points

  B and **D** are correct answers.

9. The strengths of the function hierarchy diagram are

    A. Checking quality is easy and straightforward

    B. Complex interactions between functions are easily modeled

    C. It is quick and easy to learn and use

    D. It clearly shows the sequence of process steps

    E. It provides a good overview at high and medium levels of detail

  C and **E** are correct answers.

10. The basic components of a swim lane diagram are

    A. Lines with arrows to show the sequence of process steps

    B. Diamonds to show decision points

    C. Vertical lanes to show the organization units that carry out process steps

    D. Ellipses to show process steps

    E. Open-ended rectangles to show data stores

  A, C, and **D** are correct answers.

11. The data flow diagram (DFD)

    A. Is the most data-centric of all process models

    B. Was first developed in the 1980s

    C. Combines diagram pages together hierarchically

    D. Was first developed by E. F. Codd

    E. Combines the best of the flowchart and the function diagram

  A, C, and **E** are correct answers.

12. The strengths of the DFD are

    A. It's good for top-down design work

    B. It's quick and easy to develop, even for complex systems

    C. It shows overall structure without sacrificing detail

    D. It shows complex logic easily

    E. It's great for presentation to management

    A, C, and **E** are correct answers.

13. The components of the CRUD matrix are

    A. Ellipses to show attributes

    B. Major processes shown on one axis

    C. Major entities shown on the other axis

    D. Reference numbers to show the hierarchy of processes

    E. Letters to show the operations that processes carry out on entities

    B, C, and **E** are correct answers.

14. The CRUD matrix helps find the following problems:

    A. Entities that are never read

    B. Processes that are never deleted

    C. Processes that only read

    D. Entities that are never updated

    E. Processes that have no create entity

    A, C, and **D** are correct answers.

15. Peter Chen's ERD format represents "many" with _____.

    the symbol *M* placed near the end of the relationship line

16. The diamond in Chen's ERD format represents a(n) _____.

    relationship

17. The relational ERD format represents "many" with _____.

    no symbol on the line end (an arrow goes on the other end of the line, pointing to the parent entity)

18. When subtypes are being considered in a database design, a trade-off exists between _____ and _____.

    generalization, specialization

19. In a flowchart, process steps are shown as _____, and decision points are shown as _____.

rectangles, **diamonds**

20. In a DFD, data stores are shown as _____, and processes are shown as _____.

open-ended rectangles, **rounded rectangles**

Chapter 4: Organizing Database Project Work

1. The phases of a systems development life cycle (SDLC) methodology include which of the following?

A. Physical design

B. Logical design

C. Prototyping

D. Requirements gathering

E. Ongoing support

A, **B**, **D**, and **E** are correct responses.

2. During the requirements phase of an SDLC project,

A. User views are discovered

B. The quality assurance (QA) environment is used

C. Surveys may be conducted

D. Interviews are often conducted

E. Observation may be used

A, **C**, **D**, and **E** are correct responses.

3. The advantages of conducting interviews are

A. Interviews take less time than other methods

B. Answers may be obtained for unasked questions

C. A lot can be learned from nonverbal responses

D. Questions are presented more objectively than with survey techniques

E. Entities are more easily discovered

B and **C** are correct responses.

4. The advantages of conducting surveys include

    A. A lot of ground can be covered quickly

    B. Nonverbal responses are not included

    C. Most survey recipients respond

    D. Surveys are simple to develop

    E. Prototyping of requirements is unnecessary

    A is the correct response.

5. The advantages of observation are

    A. You always see people acting normally

    B. You are likely to see lots of situations where exceptions are handled

    C. You may see the way things really are instead of the way management and/or documentation presents them

    D. The Hawthorne effect enhances your results

    E. You may observe events that would not be described to you by anyone

    C and **E** are correct responses.

6. The advantages of document reviews are

    A. Pictures and diagrams are valuable tools for understanding systems

    B. Document reviews can be done relatively quickly

    C. Documents will always be up to date

    D. Documents will always reflect current practices

    E. Documents often present overviews better than other techniques can

    A, **B**, and **E** are correct responses.

7. During implementation and rollout,

    A. Users are placed on the live system

    B. Enhancements are designed

    C. The old and new applications may be run in parallel

    D. Quality assurance testing takes place

    E. User training takes place

    A, **C**, and **E** are correct responses.

8. During ongoing support:

   A. Enhancements are immediately implemented

   B. Storage for the database may require expansion

   C. The staging environment is no longer required

   D. Bug fixes may take place

   E. Patches may be applied if needed

  B, **D**, and **E** are correct responses.

9. Application program modules are specified during the SDLC _____ phase.

  conceptual design

10. A feasibility study is often conducted during the _____ phase of an SDLC project.

  planning

11. Normalization takes place during the _____ phase of an SDLC project.

  logical design

12. DDL is written to define database objects during the _____ phase of an SDLC project.

  physical design

13. Program specifications are written during the _____ phase of an SDLC project.

  logical design

14. When requirements are sketchy, _____ can work well.

  prototyping

15. Rapid Application Development develops systems rapidly by skipping _____.

  20 percent of the requirements

16. The three objectives depicted in the application triangle are _____, _____, and _____.

  good, fast, cheap

17. The database is initially constructed in the _____ environment.

  development

18. Database conversion is tested during the _____ phase of an SDLC project.

  implementation and rollout

19. User views are analyzed during the _____ phase of an SDLC project.

requirements gathering

20. The relational database was invented by _____.

E. F. (Ted) Codd

Chapter 5: Conceptual Data Modeling

1. The essential steps that must take place during conceptual data modeling are

    A. Evaluation of solutions

    B. Normalization

    C. Preparation

    D. Solution design

    E. Bottom up modeling

    A, C, and **D** are correct responses.

2. Inputs to the conceptual modeling phase may include

    A. Existing physical models

    B. Programming specifications

    C. Requirements from the Requirements Gathering phase

    D. Existing logical models

    E. A CRUD matrix

    A, C, and **D** are correct responses.

3. Guidelines for conceptual modeling should include

    A. Normalization rules

    B. Naming conventions

    C. Inclusion of attributes

    D. Subject area selection

    E. Generalization versus specialization

    B, C, D, and **E** are correct responses.

4. Individuals who should have input to conceptual modeling include

    A. Subject matter experts (SMEs)

    B. Project team members

C. The project sponsor

D. Other data modelers

E. Others who may offer useful perspectives

A, **B**, **C**, **D**, and **E** are correct responses.

5. Criteria for first cut models are

A. Attributes are always included

B. The most important entities are included

C. The more specialized, the better

D. Relationships are included with maximum cardinalities

E. Details such as transaction logs and audit data are included

B and **D** are correct responses.

6. The modeling approach most commonly used in conceptual modeling is

A. Normalization

B. Bottom up

C. Structured design

D. Top down

E. Specialization

D is the correct answer.

7. Measures of a good conceptual model include

A. Balance between generalization and specialization

B. Completeness

C. Independence from processes

D. Conciseness

E. Precision

A, **B**, **D**, and **E** are correct responses.

8. An advantage of using supertypes is that they _____ unimportant implementation details.

hide

9. Application program modules are specified during the SDLC _____ phase.

    conceptual design

10. Attributes are _____ in conceptual models.

    optional

11. Generalized data structures are _____ in conceptual models.

    common

12. Conceptual models are _____ normalized.

    seldom

13. The guiding principles for subtypes are that they do not _____, and every occurrence of the supertype must fit into _____ subtype.

    overlap, exactly one

14. In hierarchies, each entity has _____ parent entity/entities.

    no more than one

15. Generalized structures can be _____ for literal thinkers to understand.

    more difficult

16. In network structures, each entity has _____ parent entity/entities.

    any number of

17. In linked lists, each entity instance has _____ related instance in each direction.

    no more than one

18. Large and/or complex models can be broken up using _____.

    subject areas

Chapter 6: Logical Database Design Using Normalization

1. Normalization

    A. Was developed by E.F. Codd

    B. Was first introduced with five normal forms

    C. First appeared in 1972

    D. Provides a set of rules for each normal form

    E. Provides a procedure for converting relations to each normal form

    A, C, D, and **E** are correct answers.

2. The purpose of normalization is

    A. To eliminate redundant data

    B. To remove certain anomalies from the relations

    C. To provide a reason to denormalize the database

    D. To optimize data-retrieval performance

    E. To optimize data for inserts, updates, and deletes

  B and **E** are correct answers.

3. When implemented, a third normal form relation becomes a(n) _____.

  table

4. The insert anomaly refers to a situation in which

    A. Data must be inserted before it can be deleted

    B. Too many inserts cause the table to fill up

    C. Data must be deleted before it can be inserted

    D. A required insert cannot be done due to an artificial dependency

    E. A required insert cannot be done due to duplicate data

  D is the correct answer.

5. The delete anomaly refers to a situation in which

    A. Data must be deleted before it can be inserted

    B. Data must be inserted before it can be deleted

    C. Data deletion causes unintentional loss of another entity's data

    D. A required delete cannot be done due to referential constraints

    E. A required delete cannot be done due to lack of privileges

  C is the correct answer.

6. The update anomaly refers to a situation in which

    A. A simple update requires updates to multiple rows of data

    B. Data cannot be updated because it does not exist in the database

    C. Data cannot be updated due to lack of privileges

    D. Data cannot be updated due to an existing unique constraint

    E. Data cannot be updated due to an existing referential constraint

  A is the correct answer.

7. The roles of unique identifiers in normalization are

   A. They are unnecessary

   B. They are required once you reach third normal form

   C. All normalized forms require designation of a primary key

   D. You cannot normalize relations without first choosing a primary key

   E. You cannot choose a primary key until relations are normalized

   C and **D** are correct answers.

8. Writing sample user views with representative data in them is

   A. The only way to successfully normalize the user views

   B. A tedious and time-consuming process

   C. An effective way to understand the data being normalized

   D. Only as good as the examples shown in the sample data

   E. A widely used normalization technique

   B, C, and **D** are correct responses.

9. Criteria useful in selecting a primary key from among several candidate keys are

   A. Choose the simplest candidate

   B. Choose the shortest candidate

   C. Choose the candidate most likely to have its value change

   D. Choose concatenated keys over single attribute keys

   E. Invent a surrogate key if that is the best possible key

   A, B, and **E** are correct responses.

10. First normal form resolves anomalies caused by _____.

    multivalued attributes

11. Second normal form resolves anomalies caused by _____.

    partial dependencies

12. Third normal form resolves anomalies caused by _____.

    transitive dependencies

13. In general, violations of a normalization rule are resolved by:

    A. Combining relations

    B. Moving attributes or groups of attributes to a new relation

C. Combining attributes

D. Creating summary tables

E. Denormalization

B is the correct answer.

14. A foreign key in a normalized relation may be

    A. The entire primary key of the relation

    B. Part of the primary key of the relation

    C. A repeating group

    D. A nonkey attribute in the relation

    E. A multivalued attribute

    A, **B**, and **D** are correct answers.

15. Proper handling of multivalued attributes when converting relations to first normal form usually prevents subsequent problems with _____.

    fourth normal form

Chapter 7: Beyond Third Normal Form

1. For a relation to be in Boyce-Codd normal form, it must

    A. Be in domain key normal form

    B. Be in third normal form

    C. Be in fourth normal form

    D. Be in fifth normal form

    E. Have no determinants that are not either the primary key or a candidate key

    B and **E** are the correct answers.

2. Fourth normal form problems can be avoided during resolution of first normal form problems by

    A. Placing all candidate keys in separate entities

    B. Placing all multivalued attributes in common reference table structures

    C. Placing all multivalued attributes in separate entities

    D. Removing constraints that are not a result of the definitions of domains and keys

    E. Using roles to resolve all multivalued attributes

    C is the correct answer.

3. When choosing the level of generalization versus specialization in a model, you should

   A. Find the one correct solution

   B. Find the solution that is in the highest normal form

   C. Select the alternative with the most subtypes

   D. Strive for the best fit with known and expected requirements

   E. Select the simplest alternative

   D is the correct answer.

4. Advantages of generalized reference data structures include which of the following?

   A. They are easier for business users to understand

   B. They help to simplify data models by consolidating many small reference tables into a single structure

   C. Database constraints can be used to prevent values from other code sets from being accidentally selected

   D. They provide support for additional functions such as language translation

   E. They are more normalized than specialized reference tables

   B and **D** are correct answers.

5. Advantages of specialized reference data structures include which of the following?

   A. They are easier for business users to understand

   B. They require more joins than generalized reference data structures

   C. Database constraints can be used to prevent values from other code sets from being accidentally selected

   D. They provide support for additional functions such as language translation

   E. They are more normalized than generalized reference tables

   A and **C** are correct answers.

6. Intersection tables involving more than two parent tables

   A. Should be carefully scrutinized by the data modeler

   B. Are perfectly okay in all cases

   C. Are always considered to be modeling errors

   D. Can be an indication of an anomaly addressed by one of the advanced forms of normalization

   E. Are highly recommended because they simplify data models

   A and **D** are correct answers.

7. Boyce-Codd normal form deals with anomalies caused by _____.

   determinants that are not primary or candidate keys

8. Fourth normal form deals with anomalies caused by _____.

   multivalued attributes

9. Instead of dealing with a specific type of anomaly, fifth normal form specifies _____.

   a desired end state

10. Domain key normal form deals with anomalies caused by _____.

    constraints that are not the result of the definitions of domains and keys

11. Most business systems require that you normalize only as far as _____.

    third normal form

12. In IE notation, the type or category symbol looks like _____.

    a circle with a line under it

13. An attribute used to indicate which subtype a particular occurrence of an entity falls into is known as a(n) _____.

    type discriminator

14. A table used to translate code values from one system to another is known as a(n) _____ table.

    crosswalk

Chapter 8: Physical Database Design

1. When you're designing tables,

   A. Each normalized relation becomes a table

   B. Each attribute in the relation becomes a table column

   C. Relationships become check constraints

   D. Unique identifiers become triggers

   E. Primary key columns must be defined as NOT NULL

   A, B, and E are correct answers.

2. Supertypes and subtypes

   A. Must be implemented exactly as specified in the logical design

   B. May be collapsed in the physical database design

   C. May have the supertype columns folded into each subtype in the physical design

    D. Usually have the same primary key in the physical tables

    E. Apply only to the logical design

    B, **C**, and **D** are correct answers.

3. Table names

    A. Should be based on the attribute names in the logical design

    B. Should always include the word "table"

    C. Should use only uppercase letters

    D. Should include organization or location names

    E. May contain abbreviations when necessary

    C and **E** are correct answers.

4. Column names

    A. Must be unique within the database

    B. Should be based on the corresponding attribute names in the logical design

    C. Must be prefixed with the table name

    D. Must be unique within the table

    E. Should use abbreviations whenever possible

    B and **D** are correct answers.

5. Referential constraints

    A. Define relationships identified in the logical model

    B. Are always defined on the parent table

    C. Require that foreign keys be defined as NOT NULL

    D. Should have descriptive names

    E. Name the parent and child tables and the foreign key column

    A and **D** are correct answers.

6. Check constraints

    A. May be used to force a column to match a list of values

    B. May be used to force a column to match a range of values

    C. May be used to force a column to match another column in the same row

    D. May be used to force a column to match a column in another table

    E. May be used to enforce a foreign key constraint

  A, **B**, and **C** are correct answers.

7. Data types

    A. Prevent incorrect data from being inserted into a table

    B. Can be used to prevent alphabetic characters from being stored in numeric columns

    C. Can be used to prevent numeric characters from being stored in character format columns

    D. Require that precision and scale be specified also

    E. Can be used to prevent invalid dates from being stored in date columns

  B and **E** are correct answers.

8. View restrictions include which of the following?

    A. Views containing joins can never be updated

    B. Updates to calculated columns in views are prohibited

    C. Privileges are required in order to update data using views

    D. If a view omits a mandatory column, inserts to the view are not possible

    E. Any update involving a view may reference columns only from one table

  B, **C**, **D**, and **E** are correct answers.

9. Some advantages of views are

    A. Views may provide performance advantages

    B. Views may insulate database users from table and column name changes

    C. Views may be used to hide joins and complex calculations

    D. Views may filter columns or rows that users should not see

    E. Views may be tailored to the needs of individual departments

  A, **B**, **C**, **D**, and **E** are correct answers.

10. Indexes

    A. May be used to assist with primary key constraints

    B. May be used to improve query performance

    C. May be used to improve insert, update, and delete performance

D. Are usually smaller than the tables they reference

E. Are slower to sequentially scan than corresponding tables

A, B, and **D** are correct answers.

11. General rules to follow regarding indexes include which of the following?

A. The larger the table, the more important indexes become.

B. Indexing foreign key columns often helps join performance.

C. Columns that are frequently updated should always be indexed.

D. The more a table is updated, the more indexes will help performance.

E. Indexes on very small tables tend not to be very useful.

A, B, and **E** are correct answers.

12. Business rules are implemented in the database using _____.

constraints

13. Two key differences between unique constraints and primary key constraints are _____ and _____.

a table may have many unique constraints but only one primary key constraint, columns referenced by primary key constraints must be defined as NOT NULL

14. Relationships in the logical model become _____ in the physical model.

referential constraints

15. Constraint names are important because _____.

they appear in error messages

Chapter 9: Alternatives for Incorporating Business Rules

1. A _____ is a word or phrase that has a single definition.

term

2. A _____ is a statement that relates terms to each other.

fact

3. A _____ is an attribute that is derived from other attributes.

derivation

4. A _____ is a condition that prescribes the values a relationship or attribute must have.

constraint

5. _____ shows the maximum number of occurrences that are possible for a given entity.

Cardinality

6. A _____ is a specification of the values that a particular attribute may have.

domain

7. _____ rules determine how many of one entity or attribute can be associated with some other entity or attribute.

Cardinality

8. _____ rules require that foreign key values always have a matching key value in the parent entity.

Referential integrity

9. _____ rules determine what processing the system must do in particular circumstances.

Process

10. _____ rules determine the definition of entities and attributes.

Definitional

11. _____ rules determine the required characteristics of data that is to be stored.

Data validation

12. The Business Rules Group defines which of the following categories of business rules?

   A. Term

   B. Entity

   C. Fact

   D. Derivation

   E. Constraint

A, C, D, and **E** are correct answers.

13. Origins of business rules include which of the following?

   A. Laws and regulations

   B. Business policies

   C. Certification rules and guidelines

   D. Process models

   E. User views

A, B, C, and **D** are correct answers.

14. A term can fall into which of these categories?

 A. Attribute name

 B. Relationship

 C. Entity name

 D. Supertype/subtype

 E. Other business term

 A, **C**, and **E** are correct answers.

15. A fact can fall into which of these categories?

 A. Attribute name

 B. Attribute

 C. Relationship

 D. Supertype/subtype

 E. Entity name

 B, **C**, and **D** are correct answers.

16. An entity relationship model supports which of the following forms of constraints?

 A. Unique identifiers

 B. Domains

 C. Exclusive subtypes

 D. Cardinality

 E. Optionality

 A, **B**, **C**, **D** and **E** are correct answers.

Chapter 10: Alternatives for Handling Temporal Data

1. Methods for adding temporal data to a data model include

 A. Changing all relationships to many-to-many

 B. Adding history tables

 C. Adding an effective date to the primary key

 D. Adding a data structure to log changes

 E. Adding an effective date to the natural key

 B, **C**, **D**, and **E** are correct answers.

2. Commonly used audit attributes include

   A. A code for the reason a change was made

   B. The end date of the currently effective transaction

   C. The date and time (timestamp) when the change occurred

   D. The identifier of the database user who made the change

   E. The begin date of the currently effective transaction

  A, C, and **D** are correct answers.

3. Advantages of generalized logging structures include

   A. They can handle past, present, and future data values

   B. They seldom require changes when the database structure is changed

   C. Current data values can be included

   D. Data can be obtained using DBMS logging facilities or third-party auditing software

   E. Data models are simpler than those using effective-dated entities and history tables

  B, C, D, and **E** are correct answers.

4. Recording the net change amount instead of old and new data values is applicable for which of the following?

   A. Numeric data

   B. Nonnumeric data

   C. Data elements where null values are permitted

   D. All of the above

   E. None of the above

  A is the correct answer.

5. Methods for handling deletion of effective-dated data include which of the following?

   A. Adding a new record with a new effective date and a status of "deleted"

   B. End-dating the existing record

   C. Setting a status code in the existing record with a status of "deleted"

   D. Physically deleting the current record and logging the deletion

   E. All of the above

  B, C, and **D** are correct answers.

6. Business rules for temporal data should address

   A. Whether consecutive rows for the same logical data combination should be permitted

   B. Whether overlapping time periods should be permitted

   C. How to handle end dates that are earlier than the effective date in the same record

   D. Whether gaps in time are acceptable

   E. Whether the begin date should be after some logical starting point

   A, B, C, D, and **E** are correct answers.

7. Adding temporal structures to everything in the model will _____.

   needlessly overcomplicate the model

8. In _____ models, time-related components should appear only in entities where time is of direct interest to the business.

   conceptual

9. A requirement for standard audit attributes can be easily handled in the _____ model by mechanically adding the attributes to every applicable data structure.

   physical

10. Adding temporal data to an existing data model often changes the _____ of the relationships.

    cardinality

11. Generally, only _____ relationships change when temporal data is added to an existing model.

    transferable

12. A distinct advantage of effective-dated keys as opposed to history tables or generic audit structures is the ability to handle _____.

    future data values

Chapter 11: Modeling for Analytical Databases

1. OLTP databases are designed to handle _____ transaction volumes.

   high

2. OLAP queries typically access _____ amounts of data.

   large

3. Compared with OLTP systems, data warehouse systems tend to have _____- running queries.

   longer

4. Data warehousing was pioneered by _____.

Bill Inmon

5. The process of moving from more summarized data to more detailed data is known as _____.

drilling down

6. The snowflake schema allows dimensions to have _____.

dimensions of their own

7. The starflake schema is a hybrid containing both _____ and _____ dimensions.

normalized, denormalized

8. Redundant data _____ be included in OLAP data structures because update anomalies _____.

can, do not exist

9. A data warehouse is

 A. Subject oriented

 B. Integrated from multiple data sources

 C. Time variant

 D. Updated in real time

 E. Organized around one department or business function

 A, B, and **C** are correct answers.

10. Challenges with the data warehouse approach include

 A. Updating operational data from the data warehouse

 B. Underestimation of required resources

 C. Diminishing user demands

 D. Large, complex projects

 E. High resource demands

 B, D, and **E** are correct answers.

11. The relationship between OLAP databases and business rules is

 A. OLAP databases enforce business rules

 B. OLAP databases do not enforce business rules

 C. Business rules influence the design of the data structures required for analysis

D. Business rule have little influence on the design of the data structures

E. They have nothing to do with each other

B and **C** are correct answers.

12. The summary table architecture

    A. Was originally developed by Bill Inmon

    B. Includes a fact table

    C. Includes dimension tables

    D. Includes lightly and highly summarized tables

    E. Should include metadata

    A, **D**, and **E** are correct answers.

13. The star schema

    A. Was developed by Ralph Kimball

    B. Includes a dimension table and one or more fact tables

    C. Always has fully normalized dimension tables

    D. Was a key feature of the Red Brick DBMS

    E. Involves multiple levels of dimension tables

    A, **B** and **D** are correct answers.

14. Factors to consider in designing the fact table include

    A. Adding columns to the fact table

    B. Reducing column sizes between the source and fact tables

    C. Partitioning the fact table

    D. How often it must be updated

    E. How long history must remain in it

    B, **C**, **D**, and **E** are correct answers.

15. Multidimensional databases

    A. Use a fully normalized fact table

    B. Are best visualized as cubes

    C. Have fully normalized dimension tables

D. Are sometimes called MOLAP databases

E. Accommodate dimensions beyond the third by repeating cubes for each additional dimension

B, **D**, and **E** are correct answers.

16. A data mart

   A. Is a subset of a data warehouse

   B. Is a shop that sells data to individuals and businesses

   C. Supports the requirements of a particular department or business function

   D. Can be a good starting point for organizations with no data warehouse experience

   E. Can be a good starting point when requirements are sketchy

   A, **C**, **D**, and **E** are correct answers.

17. Reasons to create a data mart include

   A. It is more comprehensive than a data warehouse

   B. It is a potentially lower-risk project

   C. Data may be tailored to a particular department or business function

   D. It contains more data than a data warehouse

   E. The project has a lower overall cost than a data warehouse project

   B, **C**, and **E** are correct answers.

18. Building a data warehouse first, followed by data marts

   A. Will delay data mart deployment if the data warehouse project drags on

   B. Has lower risk than trying to build them all together

   C. Has the lowest risk of the three possible strategies

   D. Has the highest risk of the three possible strategies

   E. May require a great deal of rework

   A and **B** are correct answers.

19. Building one or more data marts first, followed by the data warehouse

   A. May delay data warehouse delivery if the data mart projects drag on

   B. Has the potential to deliver some OLAP functions more quickly

   C. Has the lowest risk of the three possible strategies

    D. Has the highest risk of the three possible strategies

    E. May require a great deal of rework

    B, C, and **E** are correct answers.

20. Building the data warehouse and data marts simultaneously

    A. Creates the largest single project of all the possible strategies

    B. Has the potential to take the longest to deliver any OLAP functions

    C. Has the lowest risk of the three possible strategies

    D. Has the highest risk of the three possible strategies

    E. May require a great deal of rework

    A, B, and **D** are correct answers

21. Modeling OLAP databases differs from OLTP databases in which of the following ways?

    A. Some modeling rules and techniques are different.

    B. The modeling rules and techniques are completely different.

    C. There is no significant difference between the two.

    D. The requirements are different.

    E. The databases will run on different platforms.

    A, D, and **E** are correct answers.

22. Properties of data warehouse systems include

    A. Holding historical rather than current information

    B. Long-running queries that process many rows of data

    C. Support for day-to-day operations

    D. Process orientation

    E. Medium to low transaction volume

    A, B, and **E** are correct answers.

Chapter 12: Enterprise Data Modeling

1. Organizations that have not adopted enterprise-wide data management experience which of the following issues?

    A. Opportunities to share standard codes across applications are more difficult to identify.

    B. It is difficult to evaluate the effects of proposed changes such as new application databases.

C. Operating costs are lower because the organization saves money by not employing data modelers and data quality analysts.

D. Common data may not be represented in the same way.

E. Redundant and inconsistent data abounds.

A, B, D, and **E** are correct answers.

2. Characteristics of an enterprise data model include which of the following?

A. It is often divided into subject areas.

B. It is independent of physical implementation details.

C. It integrates with an overall enterprise model.

D. It includes only entities and relationships.

E. It is usually built in layers.

A, B, C, and **E** are correct answers.

3. Common uses of enterprise data models include which of the following?

A. Standard of measure for data quality assessments

B. Documentation of where the organization should be 15 or 20 years into the future

C. Blueprint for enterprise-wide planning

D. Starting point for new application and analytical database designs

E. Collection mechanism for common definitions and other metadata

A, C, D, and **E** are correct answers.

4. Inputs to the enterprise data model should include which of the following?

A. Physical storage characteristics for existing databases

B. Internal and external standards

C. Existing process documentation

D. The IT strategic plan (if one exists)

E. Business knowledge

B, C, D, and **E** are correct answers.

5. Data management encompasses all aspects of the management of data, including _____, _____, and _____.

data modeling, database management, data quality

6. Effective data management requires a comprehensive and current metadata _____.

repository

7. Two common factors that work against implementation of a single enterprise-wide database are _____ and _____.

software packages with their own data models, existing applications

8. _____ is a method of integrating application systems using asynchronous message technology.

Enterprise Application Integration (EAI)

9. An enterprise data model is a _____.

comprehensive yet integrated view of an organization's data

10. Two factors that work against implementation of enterprise models are _____ and _____.

cost, lack of understanding of their usefulness

11. A level 1 enterprise data model contains the _____ model.

subject area

12. The second level of an enterprise data model contains the _____ model.

enterprise conceptual

13. The third level of an enterprise data model contains the _____ model.

enterprise conceptual entity

14. A good rule of thumb for a planning window is _____ years.

3 to 5

Appendix B

Solutions to Try This Exercises

Refining a Conceptual Model

Here is the revised conceptual model for Try This 1-1:

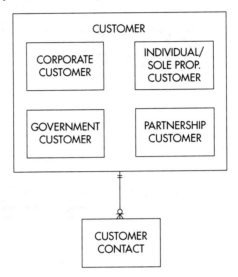

Try This 2-1 Conceptual Model Modification

Here is the revised conceptual model for Try This 2-1:

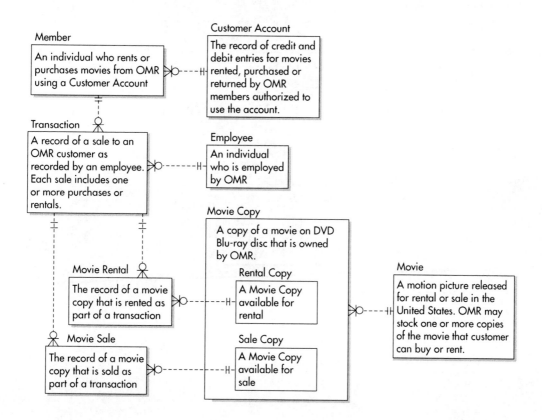

Member
An individual who rents or purchases movies from OMR using a Customer Account

Customer Account
The record of credit and debit entries for movies rented, purchased or returned by OMR members authorized to use the account.

Transaction
A record of a sale to an OMR customer as recorded by an employee. Each sale includes one or more purchases or rentals.

Employee
An individual who is employed by OMR

Movie Copy
A copy of a movie on DVD Blu-ray disc that is owned by OMR.

Movie Rental
The record of a movie copy that is rented as part of a transaction

Rental Copy
A Movie Copy available for rental

Movie
A motion picture released for rental or sale in the United States. OMR may stock one or more copies of the movie that customer can buy or rent.

Movie Sale
The record of a movie copy that is sold as part of a transaction

Sale Copy
A Movie Copy available for sale

Try This 3-1 Drawing a Conceptual Model with Nested Subtypes

Here is the completed conceptual model for Try This 3-1:

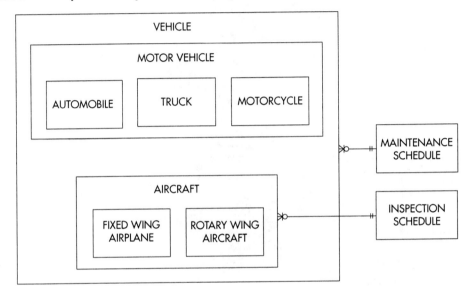

Try This 4-1 The Database Life Cycle

Project Phase	Task
Planning	w. Evaluate available DBMS options.
Requirements Gathering	f. Determine the views required by the business users.
	r. Identify the attributes required by the business users.
	t. Identify and document business data requirements.
Conceptual Design	l. Specify a logical name for each entity and attribute.
	q. Document business rules that cannot be represented in the data model.
	s. Identify the relationships between the entities.
Logical Design	a. Normalization.
	b. Add foreign keys to the database.
	d. Specify the unique identifier for each relation.
	g. Remove data that is easily derived.
	h. Resolve many-to-many relationships.
	l. Specify a logical name for each entity and attribute.
	p. Translate the conceptual data model into a logical model.
	q. Document business rules that cannot be represented in the data model.
	s. Identify the relationships between the entities.
Physical Design	c. Specify the physical placement of database objects on storage media.
	e. Specify the primary key for each table.
	j. Modify the database to meet business requirements.
	m. Specify a physical name for each table and column.
	o. Specify database indexes.
Construction	i. Define views in the database.
	u. Ensure that user data requirements are met.
Implementation and Rollout	k. Denormalize the database for performance.
	n. Add redundant data to improve performance.
	v. Tune the database to improve performance.
Ongoing Support	j. Modify the database to meet business requirements.
	k. Denormalize the database for performance.
	n. Add redundant data to improve performance.
	u. Ensure that user data requirements are met.
	v. Tune the database to improve performance.

Try This 5-1 Conceptual Model for International Addresses

Here is the completed conceptual model for Try This 5-1:

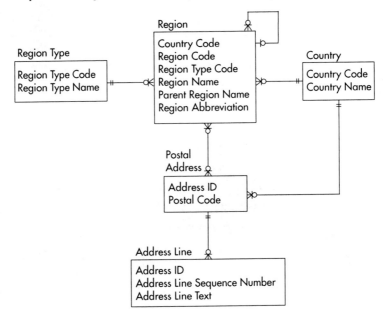

Try This 6-1   UTLA Academic Tracking

Here are the normalized relations for Try This 6-1, with (PK) denoting primary key attributes:

```
COURSE: COURSE ID (PK), TITLE, DESCRIPTION, NUMBER OF CREDITS

INSTRUCTOR: INSTRUCTOR ID (PK), GIVEN NAME,
            MIDDLE NAME, FAMILY NAME, HOME ADDRESS STREET,
            HOME ADDRESS CITY, HOME ADDRESS STATE,
            HOME ADDRESS ZIP CODE, HOME PHONE, OFFICE PHONE

COURSE SECTION: SECTION ID (PK), CALENDAR_YEAR, SEMESTER, COURSE ID,
            BUILDING, ROOM, MEETING DAY, MEETING TIME,
            INSTRUCTOR ID

STUDENT: STUDENT ID (PK), GIVEN NAME,
            MIDDLE NAME, FAMILY NAME, HOME ADDRESS,
            HOME ADDRESS CITY, HOME ADDRESS STATE,
            HOME ADDRESS ZIP CODE, HOME PHONE

STUDENT SECTION: STUDENT ID (PK), SECTION ID (PK), GRADE

COURSE PREREQUISITE: COURSE ID (PK), PREREQUISITE COURSE ID (PK)

COURSE INSTRUCTOR QUALIFIED: INSTRUCTOR ID (PK), COURSE ID (PK)
```

A few notes on this particular solution are in order:

- There was no simple natural key for the Course Section relation, so a surrogate key was added.

- The Course Prerequisite relation can be quite confusing. This is the intersection relation for a many-to-many recursive relationship. A course can have many prerequisites, which may be found by joining COURSE ID in the COURSE relation with COURSE ID in the COURSE PREREQUISITE relation. At the same time, any course may be a prerequisite for many other courses. These may be found by joining COURSE ID in the COURSE relation with PREREQUISITE COURSE ID in the COURSE PREREQUISITE relation. This means that there are *two* relationships between the COURSE and COURSE PREREQUISITE: one where COURSE ID is the foreign key and another where PREREQUISITE COURSE ID is the foreign key. Comparing the upcoming illustrations for the COURSE and COURSE_PREREQUISITE tables should help make this point clear.

- If it were common for instructors to also be students, then combining the STUDENT and INSTRUCTOR tables into a more general PERSON entity would be a good idea. A PERSON ROLE entity could then be used to assign roles (Student, Instructor, etc.) to the individuals.

To assist you in visualizing how all this works, the following illustration shows the ERD for the solution, using the Microsoft Relationships panel as the presentation media, followed by illustrations that show each of the tables as implemented in a Microsoft Access database, each loaded with the data from the original user view (report) examples.

Entity Relationship Diagram (ERD) for Try This 6-1 Solution (TLA University):

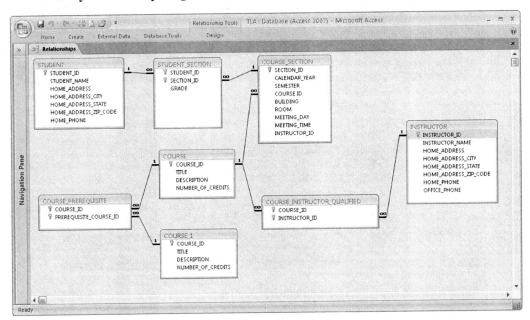

NOTE

You may have noticed the Course_1 table in the preceding illustration. This is not a real table, but rather just another copy of the Course table on the diagram. There are two foreign keys to the Course table in the Course Prerequisite table, and the only way that Microsoft Access can illustrate this situation is to place the Course table on the diagram twice and draw one relationship to each copy.

COURSE table:

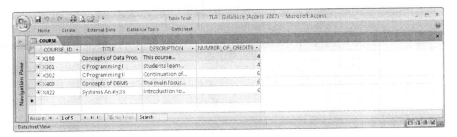

INSTRUCTOR table:

INSTRUCTOR_ID	INSTRUCTOR_NAME	HOME_ADDRESS	HOME_ADDRESS_CITY	HOME_ADDRESS_STATE	HOME_ADDRESS_ZIP_CODE	HOME_PHONE	OFFICE_PHONE
756	Werdna Leppo	12 Main St.	Alameda	CA	94501	510-555-1234	x-7463
795	Cora Coder	32767 Binary Way	Abend	CA	21304	510-555-1010	x-5328
901	Tillie Talker	123 Forms Rd.	Paperwork	CA	95634	510-555-2629	408-555-2047

COURSE_SECTION table:

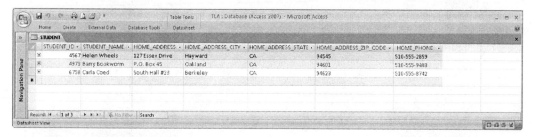

SECTION_ID	CALENDAR_YEAR	SEMESTER	COURSE_ID	BUILDING	ROOM	MEETING_DAY	MEETING_TIME	INSTRUCTOR_ID
1	2008	Spr	X409	Evans	70	Tu	7-10	756
2	2008	Spr	X409	SFO	7	We	7-10	756
3	2008	Spr	X100	Evans	70	M,Fr	7-9	901

STUDENT table:

STUDENT_ID	STUDENT_NAME	HOME_ADDRESS	HOME_ADDRESS_CITY	HOME_ADDRESS_STATE	HOME_ADDRESS_ZIP_CODE	HOME_PHONE
4567	Helen Wheels	127 Essex Drive	Hayward	CA	94545	510-555-2859
4973	Barry Bookworm	P.O. Box 45	Oakland	CA	94601	510-555-9403
6758	Carla Coed	South Hall #23	Berkeley	CA	94623	510-555-8742

STUDENT_SECTION table:

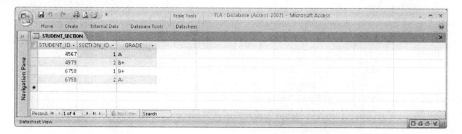

STUDENT_ID	SECTION_ID	GRADE
4567	1	A
4973	2	B+
6758	1	B+
6758	2	A-

COURSE_PREREQUISITE table:

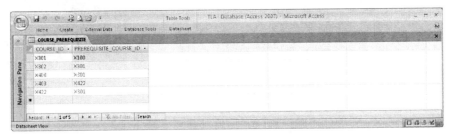

COURSE_INSTRUCTOR_QUALIFIED table:

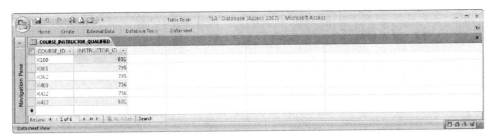

Try This 6-2   Computer Books Company

Here are the normalized relations for Try This 6-2, with primary keys noted with (PK):

```
BOOK: ISBN (PK), BOOK TITLE, SUBJECT CODE, PUBLISHER ID,
      EDITION CODE, EDITION COST, SELLING PRICE,
      QUANTITY ON HAND, QUANTITY ON ORDER,
      RECOMMENDED QUANTITY, PREVIOUS EDITION ISBN

CUSTOMER ORDER: CUSTOMER ORDER NUMBER (PK), CUSTOMER ID,
      ORDER DATE

CUSTOMER ORDER BOOK: CUSTOMER ORDER NUMBER (PK), ISBN (PK),
      QUANTITY, BOOK PRICE

SUBJECT: SUBJECT CODE (PK), DESCRIPTION

AUTHOR: AUTHOR ID (PK), AUTHOR NAME

BOOK-AUTHOR: AUTHOR ID (PK), ISBN (PK)

CUSTOMER: CUSTOMER ID (PK), CUSTOMER_NAME, STREET ADDRESS, CITY,
      STATE, ZIP CODE, PHONE NUMBER, BALANCE DUE
```

PUBLISHER: PUBLISHER ID (PK), PUBLISHER NAME, STREET ADDRESS,
        CITY, STATE, ZIP CODE, AMOUNT PAYABLE

SHIPPED ORDER (RECEIVABLE): SALES INVOICE NUMBER (PK),
        CUSTOMER ORDER NUMBER, SALES TAX, SHIPPING CHARGES

SHIPPED ORDER BOOK: SALES INVOICE NUMBER (PK), ISBN (PK),
        PRICE_AT_SALE, QUANTITY

PURCHASE (PAYABLE): PURCHASE INVOICE NUMBER (PK), PUBLISHER_ID,
        INVOICE DATE, INVOICE AMOUNT

PURCHASE BOOK: PURCHASE INVOICE NUMBER (PK), ISBN (PK), QUANTITY,
        COST EACH

Here is an entity relationship diagram that shows the complete design, implemented in
Microsoft Access:

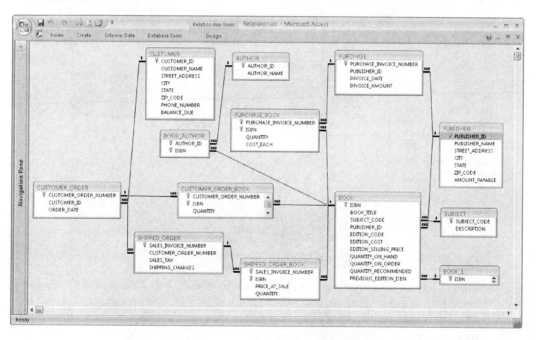

Try This 7-1 Complex Logical Data Model

Here is the completed logical model for Try This 7-1:

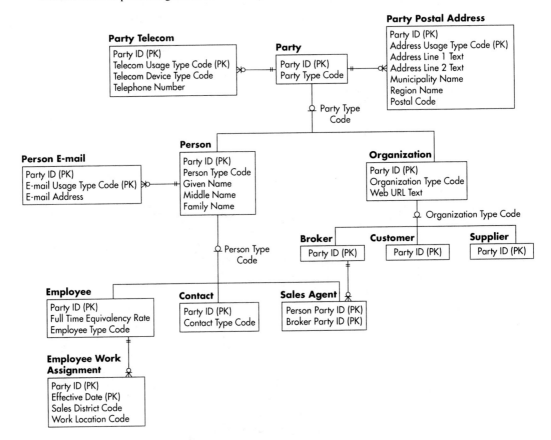

Here are a few things worth noting in this solution:

● The primary key of the subtypes is identical to the primary key of the supertype. However, in the case of Sales Agent, the Party ID is inherited from the Person supertype as well as from the Broker parent entity. Therefore, I gave each inherited foreign key a single-word role name prefix to differentiate between them.

● In the Employee entity, the potential subtypes of permanent versus contract and full time versus part time overlap. Rather than create a subclass for each possible permutation (permanent full time, permanent part time, contract full time, and contract part time), I separated them into two classification attributes, since I thought there was an appreciable risk of additional classes being added later (at the whim of management). For added flexibility, I represented full time versus part time as a full-time equivalency rate, where 1.0 represents a full-time employee and 0.5 represents a half-time employee. This is a typical attribute in human resources systems. The Employee Type Code denotes permanent versus contract (or any other similar classification that might come up later).

- The subtypes Broker, Customer, and Supplier are good candidates for a role instead of subtypes. In particular, it might be possible for a Customer to also be a Supplier. With the added chance that management will come up with an additional role later on, there are several good arguments in favor of using a role here.

Try This 8-1 Drawing a Physical Data Model

Here is the completed logical model for Try This 8-1:

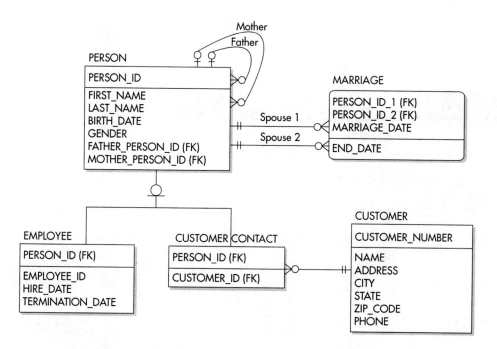

Try This 8-2 Mapping a Logical Model to a Physical Database Design

Here is the completed logical model for Try This 8-2:

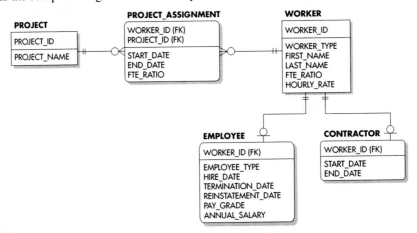

Try This 9-1 Modeling Business Rules

Here is my solution for Try This 9-1. Keep in mind that data modeling is a design effort which means that there are endless possible solutions.

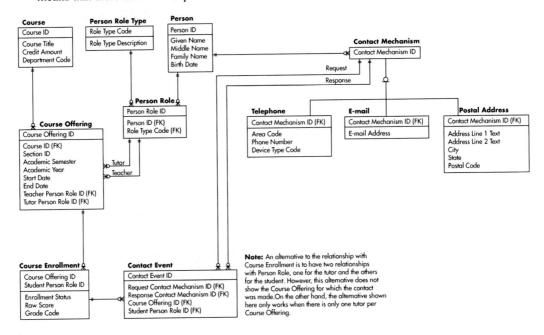

Try This 10-1 Adding History to Data Structures

Here is my solution for Try This 10-1. Keep in mind that this exercise has countless possible solutions that meet the requirements.

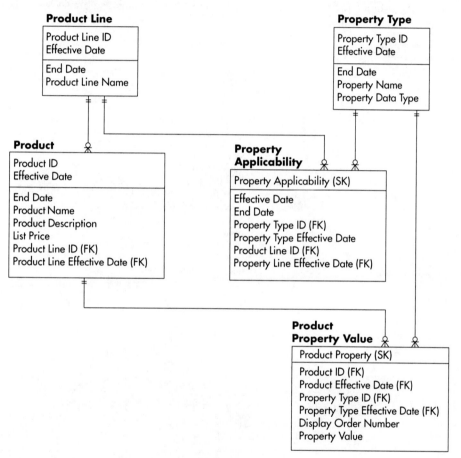

Try This 11-1 Design Star Schema Fact and Dimension Tables

Here is my solution to Try This 11-1 in the form of a star schema diagram showing the entities (tables) and relationships.

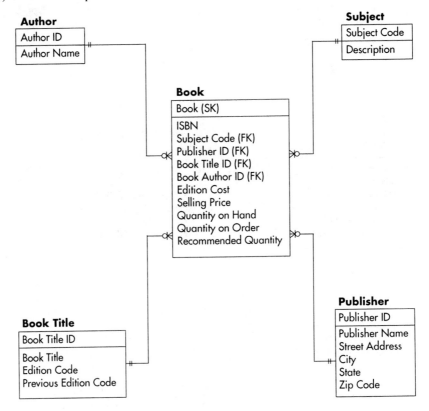

Try This 12-1 Enterprise Conceptual Model Development

Here is my solution to Try This 12-1.

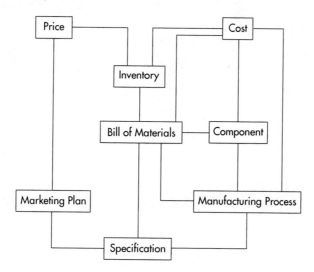

Index

A

ad hoc queries, 8
adaptability, 15
aggregation, 71
Agile methodologies, 18
alternatives for data structure design, 13
analysis paralysis, 85
anchors, 117
anomalies, 130–131
applications, 6
artificial identifiers, 133
attributes, 10, 30
    definition, 32
    derivable attributes, 32
    generalizing, 162–166
    inclusion of, 104
    multivalued, 131–132, 136
    naming, 31
    notation, 30–31
    type discriminators, 159
automation, provisions for, 13–14

B

backend, 4
balanced perspective, 15
BCNF. *See* Boyce-Codd Normal Form (BCNF)
bi-directional linked lists, 117
bill of materials, 116
bitmap indexes, 196
bit-mapped data elements, 250
bits, 250
block size, 178
bottom up modeling, 118–120
    vs. top down modeling, 122
Boyce-Codd Normal Form (BCNF), 152–155
bugs, 91
business analysts, 18
business operations, observing, 87
business rules, 39, 248
    cardinality rules, 215
    categories, 206
    data derivation rules, 215
    data validation rules, 214–215

business rules (*continued*)
    definitional rules, 214
    derivations, 210–211
    documentation of, 12
    enforcement of, 14
    facts, 209–210
    implementing in data models, 207–210,
      211–214
    integrating with data integrity, 189–194
    origin of, 207
    process rules, 215
    referential integrity rules, 215
    for temporal data, 231–233
    terms, 207–208
Business Rules Group, 206
business users, 18
bytes, 250

C

calendar data structures, 230–231
candidate key, 134
cardinality, 211
    rules, 215
centralized data management. *See* data
    management
change log structures, adding, 227–228
CHECK constraints, 47, 193
Chen, Peter, 54
chicken method, 91
class words, 31
clustering, 178–179
Codd, E.F. (Ted), 128, 238
code structures, 166–167
cold turkey, 90–91
columns, 41–42
Communication Channel data
    structure, 108–109
conceptual data model, 8–9
    alternative conceptual model diagram
      notation, 29–30
      components, 24–25

conceptual design, 88–89
conceptual layer, 8
conceptual modeling process, 102, *103*
    bottom up vs. top down modeling,
      118–122
    collecting and evaluating inputs, 103
    Communication Channel data structure,
      108–109
    establishing guidelines, 103–105
    establishing objectives, 103
    evaluating the model, 123
    first cut diagrams, 109
    generic models and patterns, 106–109
    hierarchies, 113–116
    linked lists, 117–118
    vs. logical modeling process, 105–106
    measures of a good conceptual model,
      123
    networks, 116
    Party data structure, 107–108
    preparation, 102–105
    roles vs. subtypes, 109–112
    solution design, 105
    subject areas, 122–123
conformed dimensions, 243
constraints, 39, 43
    implementing, 211–212
    intersection tables, 45–46
    primary key constraints, 43–44
    referential constraints, 44–45
    that cannot be shown in entity
      relationship models, 212–214
    See also integrity constraints
construction, 90
crosswalk tables, 167–168
CRUD matrix, 73–75, 175

D

Darwen, Hugh, 157
data availability, 248
data compression, 178

data concepts, 271
data derivation rules, 215
data flow diagrams, 68–70
data integration, 16
data integrity, 189
    integrating business rules with, 189–194
data management, 266
    alternatives to centralized data
        management, 267–268
    reasons for enterprise-wide approach,
        266–267
    reasons why enterprise-wide databases
        aren't used, 267
data mart modeling, 250–257
data marts, 245–247
data modelers, 18
data modeling
    importance of, 12–14
    participants, 18–19
data models
    and application development, 16–18
    defined, 4
    measures of a good data model, 14–16
    as a product of data-oriented design, 5
    types of, 8–11
data redundancy, 247
data requirements, 175
data reusability, promotion of, 16
data reuse, 248
data stores, 68
data types, 41–42, 193–194
    equivalent data types in major DBMS
        products, 43
data validation rules, 214–215
data warehouse modeling, 248–250
data warehouses, 239
    multidimensional databases, 244–245
    vs. OLTP systems, 240
    star schema architecture, 242–244
    summary table architecture, 240–242
data warehousing, 238
database administrators, 7, 18
database constraints, 189

database specialists, 84
databases, layers of abstraction, 6–8
data-driven approach, 84
data-oriented design, 5
data-oriented methodologies, 17
Date, C.J. (Chris), 157
DBAs, 7, 18
definitional rules, 214
delete anomaly, 130–131
deletions, 228–230
denormalization, 142
        See also normalization
dependent entities, 27
designing tables, 176–181
designing views, 196–197
determinants, 152
development schedule, 175
dimension tables, 242–243
disk space constraints, 175
DKNF. *See* domain-key normal form (DKNF)
documentation, reviewing, 87–88
domain-key normal form (DKNF), 158
domains, 212

E

effective dates, adding, 223–224
80/20 rule, 93
Enterprise Application Integration (EAI),
    267–268
enterprise architects, 19
enterprise data management. *See* data
    management
enterprise data models, 268–269
    anatomy of, 269–272
    building, 272–273
    common dilemmas, 272–273
    inputs, 273
    planning window, 272
entities, 9, 25–30
    definition, 27, *29*
    naming, 27

entities (*continued*)
  nested entities, 60–61
  notation, 27, *29*
entity classes. *See* entities
entity relationship diagrams (ERDs), 54
  Chen's format, 55–56
  ERD formats, 54–60
  guidelines for drawing, 63
  IDEF1X format, 59–60
  information engineering (IE), 57–59
  relational format, 56–57
ERDs. *See* entity relationship
  diagrams (ERDs)
ETL. *See* extract, transform, and load (ETL)
executive sponsors, 18
exercises. *See* Try This exercises
existence dependency, 192
expansion, foundation for, 13
extension tables, 11
external design, 88
external entities, 26, 68
external layer, 8
external model. *See* external layer
extract, transform, and load (ETL), 257–259

F

fact tables, 242–243
Fagin, Ron, 158
feasibility studies, 84
fifth normal form, 157–158
file groups, 178
files, 41
Finkelstein, Clive, 17, 57
first cut diagrams, 109
first normal form, 135–137
flexibility, 15, 247
flowcharts, 64–65
foreign key constraints, 191–192
foreign keys, 31, 136
fourth normal form, 155–157
free space, 178

function hierarchy diagrams, 66–67
functional dependence, 137–138

G

generalization, vs. specialization, 104
generic models and patterns, 106–109

H

hashing, 179
Hawthorne effect, 87
hierarchies, 113–116
history tables, 225–227
horizontal splitting, 179
hybrid methodologies, 17

I

IDEF1X format, 59–60
identifying relationships, 46
implementation, 90–91
independent entities, 27
Index Organized Tables (IOT), 178, 196
index selectivity, 196
indexes, adding for performance, 194–196
information engineering (IE), 17, 57–59
Inmon, William H. (Bill), 238
insert anomaly, 130
instances, 26
integrity constraints, 46
  CHECK constraints, 47
  constraint enforcement using
    triggers, 47–48
  NOT NULL constraints, 46–47
  See also constraints
internal design, 89
internal layer. *See* logical layer
intersection data, 36
intersection tables, 36, 45–46
interviews, conducting, 85–86
ISO 639-1 standard, 16

J

Joint Application Design (JAD), 92

K

Kimball, Ralph, 220, 242

L

language translation tables, 168–169
layers of abstraction, 6–8
life cycles
    prototyping, 92
    system development life cycle
      (SDLC), 82–92
linked lists, 117–118
logical data model, 9–10
    components, 24–25, *26*
logical database design, 175
logical design, 89
logical layer, 8
logical model. *See* logical layer
logical modeling process, vs. conceptual
    modeling process, 105–106
logical terms, 128–129
Long, Kathy, 270
Lorentzos, Nikos, 157

M

many-to-many relationships, 36, 37
Martin, James, 17, 18, 57
maximum cardinality, 32
McClure, Carma, 57
minimum cardinality, 32
modules, 89
multivalued attributes,
    131–132, 136

N

naming conventions, 104
    for columns, 187
    for constraints, 188
    for indexes, 188
    for tables, 186–187
    for views, 189
natural identifiers, 133
natural key, 45, 137
nested entities, 60–61
networks, 116
non-identifying relationships, 46
nonprocedural languages, 65
normalization, 16, 39, 89, 128, *129*
    advanced, 152–158
    applying the normalization process,
      131–142
    need for, 130–131
    See also denormalization
NOT NULL constraints, 46–47, 191

O

object-oriented methodologies, 17
OLAP. *See* online analytical processing
    (OLAP)
OLTP. *See* online transaction processing
    (OLTP)
one-to-many relationships, 34–35
one-to-one relationships, 33–34
ongoing support, 91–92
online analytical processing (OLAP), 221, 238
    database requirements, 247–248
    loading data into analytical
      databases, 257–259
online transaction processing
    (OLTP), 221, 238
    vs. data warehousing, 240
operations specialists, 19
optionality, 211

P

partitioning, 40, 179
partitioning column, 179
Party data structure, 107–108
performance, 248
performance requirements, 175
physical data model, 10–11, 12, 39
    columns, 41–42
    constraints, 43–46
    data types, 41–43
    integrity constraints, 46–48
    tables, 39–41
    views, 48
physical design, 89
physical design process, 174–175
physical layer, 6–7
physical terms, 129
planning, 84–85
precision, 193–194
primary key, 128
    choosing, 133–135
primary key constraints, 43–44, 191
procedural languages, 65
process modelers, 18
process models, 63–64, 175
    data flow diagrams, 68–70
    flowcharts, 64–65
    function hierarchy diagrams, 66–67
    swim lane diagrams, 67–68
process rules, 215
process-driven approach, 84
process-oriented design, 5
process-oriented methodologies, 16–17
project managers, 84
project triangle, 93–94
prototyping, 17, 92

Q

quality assurance, 90

R

RAD. *See* Rapid Application Development (RAD)
Rapid Application Development (RAD), 18, 93
Rational Unified Process (RUP), 17, 70, 91
recursive processes, 65
recursive relationships, 33, 36–37
redundant relationships, 37–38
reference data, alternatives for, 166–169
reference tables, 166
referential constraints, 44–45, 191–192
referential integrity constraints. *See* referential constraints
referential integrity rules, 215
relational databases, 129
relational format, 56–57
relational tables, 12
relations, 128, 129
relationships, 32–33
    conditional, 34
    degrees, 38
    many-to-many, 36, 37
    naming, 37
    one-to-many, 34–35
    one-to-one, 33–34
    optional, 34
    recursive, 33, 36–37
    redundant, 37–38
    transferability, 34
repeating group, 135
requirements gathering, 85–88
roles, vs. subtypes, 109–112
rollout, 90–91
RUP. *See* Rational Unified Process (RUP)

S

scale, 193–194
schema, 8
SDLC. *See* system development life cycle (SDLC)

second normal form, 137–139
self test answers
    Chapter 1, 280–281
    Chapter 2, 281–285
    Chapter 3, 285–289
    Chapter 4, 289–292
    Chapter 5, 292–294
    Chapter 6, 294–297
    Chapter 7, 297–299
    Chapter 8, 299–302
    Chapter 9, 302–304
    Chapter 10, 304–306
    Chapter 11, 306–310
    Chapter 12, 310–312
self tests
    Chapter 1, 20–21
    Chapter 2, 50–52
    Chapter 3, 76–79
    Chapter 4, 96–98
    Chapter 5, 125–126
    Chapter 6, 148–150
    Chapter 7, 171–172
    Chapter 8, 199–202
    Chapter 9, 217–218
    Chapter 10, 235–236
    Chapter 11, 261–264
    Chapter 12, 274–276
slowly changing dimensions, 244, 253–257
snowflake schemas, 244
snowflake structures, resolving, 251–253
Social Security numbers, as identifiers, 134
solution design, 105
specialization, vs. generalization, 104
stability, 248
standard structures, promotion of, 13
star schema architecture, 242–244
starflake schemas, 244
stored procedures, 197
strong entities, 27
subject areas, 105, 122–123, 270
subject matter experts (SMEs), 18, 86
subschema, 8

subtypes, 9
    collapsing into the supertype table, 185–186
    converting to UML notation, 72
    exclusive, 212
    implementing as a discrete table, 184–185
    implementing as is, 183–184
    representing in data model diagrams, 60–62
    resolving, 158–162
    vs. roles, 109–112
summary table architecture, 240–242
supertypes, 9
    converting to UML notation, 72
    representing in data model diagrams, 60–62
    resolving, 158–162
surrogate identifiers, 133
surrogate key, 45
surveys, conducting, 86–87
swim lane diagrams, 67–68
system development life cycle (SDLC)
    conceptual design, 88–89
    construction, 90
    implementation and rollout, 90–91
    logical design, 89
    ongoing support, 91–92
    overview, 82–84
    physical design, 89
    planning, 84–85
    requirements gathering, 85–88

T

table replication, 179
table splitting, 179
tables, designing, 176–181
tablespaces, 40, 41, 178
target DBMS, 175
temporal data structures, 220
    adding a change log structure, 227–228
    adding effective dates, 223–224
    adding history tables, 225–227
    adding history to data structures, 221–223
    business rules, 231–233

temporal data structures (*continued*)
deletions, 228–230
processing rules for history, 228
temporal data requirements, 220–221
third normal form, 139–140
top down modeling, 120–121
vs. bottom up modeling, 122
transferability, 34
transitive dependence, 139–141
triggers, 47–48, 194
trivial splits, 157
Try This exercises
adding history to data structures, 233–235
complex logical data model, 169–170
Computer Books Company, 146–148
conceptual model for international
addresses, 124
conceptual model modification, 48–49
design star schema fact and dimension
tables, 259–260
drawing a conceptual model with nested
subtypes, 75–76
drawing a physical data model, 182
enterprise conceptual model
development, 274
mapping a logical model to a physical
database design, 198–199
modeling business rules, 216
project database management tasks,
94–95
refining a conceptual model, 19
solutions, 314–329
UTLA academic tracking, 143–146
type discriminators, 159

U

UML. *See* Unified Modeling Language (UML)
understandability of data models, 15
unification, 38

Unified Modeling Language (UML), 17, 70
behavior diagrams, 72–73
class diagrams, 70–71
structure diagrams, 72–73
unique constraints, 192–193
unique identifiers, 30, 128, 133, 212
update anomaly, 131
usability, 248
user views, 6, 85
users, 6

V

vertical splitting, 179
views, 48
designing, 196–197
visualization, 12–13

W

waterfall effect, 16
weak entities, 27
web-based information systems, 4
diagram, 5

Z

Zachman, John, 269
Zachman Framework for Information Systems
Architecture, 269

Stop Hackers in Their Tracks

**Hacking Exposed,
6th Edition**

**Hacking Exposed
Malware & Rootkits**

**Hacking Exposed Computer
Forensics, 2nd Edition**

**24 Deadly Sins of
Software Security**

**Hacking Exposed
Linux, 3rd Edition**

**Hacking Exposed
Windows, 3rd Edition**

**Hacking Exposed
Web 2.0**

**Hacking Exposed:
Web Applications, 2nd Edit**

**Gray Hat Hacking,
2nd Edition**

**Hacking Exposed
Wireless**

**Hacking Exposed
VoIP**

**IT Auditing: Using Controls
Protect Information Asse**

Expert Microsoft® SQL Server® 2008
RESOURCES

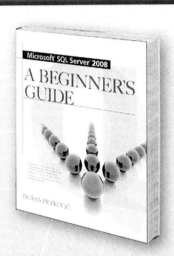

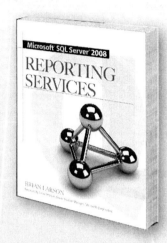

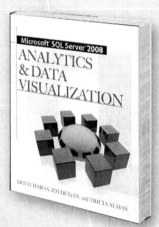

COMING SOON
Microsoft SQL Server 2008 Administration for Oracle DBAs
Practical MDX Queries

CPSIA information can be obtained
at www.ICGtesting.com
Printed in the USA
FFOW01n1451090816
26612FF